I0792976

IMAGES
of America

TUBAC

On the Cover: From left to right, Fr. Pat Callanan, William Morrow, Sid Cedargreen, and Ross Stefan stand in front of the Tubac Art Center in 1959. (Tubac Presidio State Historic Park.)

IMAGES
of America

TUBAC

Shaw Kinsley

ARCADIA
PUBLISHING

ISBN 978-0-7385-7864-4

Published by Arcadia Publishing
Charleston, South Carolina

Printed in the United States of America

Library of Congress Control Number: 2009929237

For all general information contact Arcadia Publishing at:
Telephone 843-853-2070
Fax 843-853-0044
E-mail sales@arcadiapublishing.com
For customer service and orders:
Toll-Free 1-888-313-2665

Visit us on the Internet at www.arcadiapublishing.com

This book is dedicated to everyone who helped create Tubac's rich history and to all who work so tirelessly to treasure and preserve it.

Contents

ACKNOWLEDGMENTS

I am indebted to the great institutions in our area that make it their business to acquire, preserve, and make available photographs of our past. I wish particularly to thank Michael Friesinger at Tubac Presidio State Historic Park; Rebecca Donnely, photographic curator of the Arizona State Museum; Posey Piper at the Cowbelles Museum and Ranchers' Heritage Center; Teresa Leal at the Pimería Alta Historical Society; Dan Brocious at the Fred Lawrence Whipple Observatory; Marty Schuyler at the Santa Cruz Valley Art Association; Regina Ford at the *Green Valley News*; Genaro Rivera at the Tubac Fire District; and Irene Deaton at the Tubac Historical Society. I was blessed to be given access to a number of private photograph collections, and I express my gratitude to Lorraine Mitchell Halvorsen, Alex Megariz, Nancy Lilly, Barbara Ruppman, Hattie Wilson, Jean England Neubauer, Isabelle Norstad, Silke Schneider, Nancy Bohman, Jean and Dave Allen, Gillian Brooks, Jennifer Tougas, Frank Bertolino, Diana and Bob Warren, Jarvis Harriman, Randy Williams, Olivia Cabot, Jeff and Wendy Williams, Jean Burke, Tom Shultz, and Trudi Fletcher. For invaluable assistance in editing, I am grateful for the help and friendship of Amy Rule, Jeffery Dean, and Emilio Falco, and for help in research, I record my thanks to Randy Babb, Pixie Geren, George Proctor, Allen Dart, Nancy Valentine, James Gastelum, Pinau Merlin, Joe Solares, Jean Reid, Walter and Patty Wilson, Alan Ferg, Leila Pearsall, Ceva Ciruli, Jan Munger, John Duncklee, Pete Alegria, Annie Wyer, and Tom Hoffman. For all the help and assistance I have been given, the mistakes, errors, and infelicities of style are mine alone. Any photographs without a courtesy line came from the Tubac Historical Society.

INTRODUCTION

Tubac had an incredibly rich history before the invention of photography. Unwitnessed by humankind, the land that Fr. Eusebio Kino called the Pimería Alta, the land of the Upper Pimas (stretching roughly from the Sonoran Rio Magdalena in the south to Phoenix in the north and from the Sea of Cortez in the west to the San Pedro River in the east), was formed in a geologic period of faulting and folding, then populated by the exotic flora and fauna of the Pleistocene. From those mist-shrouded times to the millennia of habitation by indigenous people, to the arrival of the Europeans as miners and missionaries, to the establishment of colonial New Spain, to an independent Mexico, and to the American purchase of the lands south of the Gila River, all of these signal events went unrecorded by photography.

What would we give for images of giant mastodons snuffling along the antediluvian banks of what would one day become the Santa Cruz River? Two Tubac boys, Nathan Fancher and Jason Hinshaw, found a petrified mammoth tooth in 1985, but even that photograph of them with their discovery is lost. Snapshots of the aboriginal way of life would reveal more to us than the much later documentary images of the archaeological excavations shown putting our ancestors' history back together piece by piece. We think we know the progression from Anasazi to Hohokam to Mogollon, but time before the arrival of the Spanish remains a confusing puzzle. We know the Native American people in the Pimería Alta were Pima-speaking when Kino arrived and that they raised corn, beans, squash, and cotton. But we also know that they did not have ball courts, platform mounds, or large canals and are left wondering whether they descended from the Hohokam who vanished 200 years before Kino or not.

Archaeological work in the Santa Cruz Valley has never been approached systematically, but four sites in the Tubac area were examined in the early and mid-1970s as part of the Arizona statewide highway salvage program. Paul Frick recorded a total of 216 sites ranging in age from 500 to 1400 AD within 20 miles between Tubac and Sahuarita in 1954. So much evidence gives the impression of solid occupation, but most scholars agree that only a portion of our valley was inhabited at any one time.

Our understanding of Father Kino's spiritual and ecological missions and the impact on this ancient way of life would be enhanced by photography, as would our knowledge of the establishment of Tubac as a presidio and the growth of a town around it. Juan Bautista de Anza's celebrated journeys of exploration culminating in the founding of San Francisco, the expulsion of the Jesuits by the Spanish and the expulsion of the Spanish by the Mexicans, the Mexican War, and the terms of surrender that awarded vast lands to the United States are all events sadly undocumented by photographs.

For the first chapter of this photographic survey of Tubac, I have employed images of reenactments and of archeological work and photographs of surviving artifacts from the Arizona State Museum, Tubac Presidio State Historic Park, Tubac Historical Society, and several private collections in an attempt to convey some of this history. But for a better understanding of what we think we know, the reader must turn to the written word of past scholars and be on the lookout for new interpretations of Tubac's colorful and pre-photographic past.

Although photography had been invented by the time territorial Tubac came into being (1853–1912), few practitioners of the daguerreotype or wet-plate photography popular at the time were inclined to carry the fragile, heavy cameras and associated paraphernalia into rough terrain and harsh desert conditions so frequently ravaged by Native American attacks. The fact that these photographs required access to a water supply and had to be developed right away meant the photographers also had to carry a massive load of supplies. The eight or more steps necessary to produce these early photographs could easily have interfered with one's flight to safety.

No photograph has surfaced of the December 30, 1853, Gadsden Purchase ceremony that took place under a cottonwood tree to mark the sale of nearly 30,000 square miles of territory south of the Gila River. Word of the treaty, which brought Tubac under American control for the first time, did not even reach the residents here until September 1854. Some photographs taken later in the life of Charles Poston document what he looked like, and surviving reports to stockholders (only rediscovered in the 1960s) give us a fair idea of the goings on at the Sonora Exploring and Mining Company, but for what life was really like under the constant threat of Native American attack, we have mainly words again, those of Raphael Pumpelly, Poston's technical expert, and of J. Ross Browne, who came through the area in 1865 and presciently wrote, "Tubac is now a city of ruins, ruin and desolation wherever the eye rests. Yet I cannot but believe that the spirit of American enterprise will revisit this delightful region and all that has been lost, and as much more as its American founder conceived in his most sanguine anticipations."

The only pictures we have of the American forts that protected the area after the withdrawal of Mexico show them in ruins, and it is easier to show the final resting places of the miners, map-makers, and ranchers (if they were lucky enough to be buried in marked graves) than to find images of them going about their work in and around Tubac. Images of the Overland stage, even of the horse-drawn ambulance that brought Phocion Way and Horace Grosvenor to Tubac, are so far undiscovered, but we do have Way's sketch of the old Santa Gertrudis Church as it looked in the late 1850s.

Only text accounts of the Mowry-Cross duel give us the details we long for, although the original press used to print Arizona's first newspaper does survive. Images of it being returned to the place of its first journalistic use satisfy some of our visual cravings but hardly communicate how that great achievement was accomplished. In our imaginations, we may be able to look at the image of a manuscript letter written in Tubac and imagine the writer at his task, just as the re-enactors distill their research and knowledge into a modern presentation that hints at the real-life dramas of long ago.

The story of Larcena Page Pennington's ordeal is illustrated by photographs taken by Robert H. Forbes, her son-in-law, but 50 years after the event itself. Two houses lived in by Larcena and her family remain—indeed one of them is Tubac's oldest gallery—and residents and visitors to Tubac can search for the genius loci by standing within the thick adobe walls and imagining how it might have been 150 years ago. Henry Glassman's Christmas dinner of 1868 has to rely solely on the mental images conjured up by words describing the roasted goat he served, invariably referred to as "the fowl, the turkey, or the bird" by his guests. Even though photographs of Geronimo exist, I selected a painting by Tubac artist Francis Beaugureau to get at the humanity of a man who saw his way of life overrun by what one side called "progress" and the other saw as "ruination."

The story of territorial Tubac is told with a mix of later photographs, maps, drawings, a painting, manuscript letters, lithographs, and engravings from period books, as well as surviving artifacts and images of reenactments. These have come from four institutional collections (Tubac Presidio State Historic Park, Pimería Alta Historical Society, Tubac Historical Society, and the Cowbelles Museum and Ranchers' Heritage Center) and the private collection of Hattie Wilson.

I have called the period after Geronimo's surrender to the end of the Second World War "Agricultural Tubac." Even though some small-scale mining was still going on in the area, the big mines had shifted north near Twin Buttes. This period was a time when photography had become less awkward, and wonderful images of new two-story houses, vast herds of cattle and horses, and visitors in automobiles and fancy hats abound.

The arrival of new people in the valley homesteading or purchasing land from those who had been here from the Spanish times is straightforward and noble in some cases but convoluted and less than honorable in the case of the decades-long Baca Float No. 3 litigation. The image of a four-year-old boy leaving the house his parents and grandparents had lived in is symbolic of scores of other heartless evictions.

Charles Lindbergh landed his famous *Spirit of St. Louis* in Tucson in September 1927, and other fliers found Tubac soon after. The first aerial photographs of our valley and new airfields showed times were changing as the new mobility permitted people to migrate between ever more distant homes. Guest ranches brought people here from other parts, and the ease of portable photography allowed them to capture images of the West they could take home and share with others.

Agricultural Tubac is illustrated almost exclusively with photographs. These come from the same wonderful institutional sources plus a new one: the Pima Air and Space Museum in Tucson. Half dozen private collections held a wealth of photographic detail for this section. I am sure many ranch and farm families have photograph collections documenting their work, holdings, and amusements. I hope everyone with such collections will consider donating them to their local historical societies, where they can enhance the future's understanding of the past and be available to a much larger group of viewers.

The final chapter, "Artistic Tubac," combines the story of Tubac's growth as an art colony with that of the people who recognized and set out to preserve and share its history. This chapter also documents Tubac's growth as more and more people discovered its beauty and charm and decided to live here. People still run cows and raise horses here, not everyone is an artist, and not everyone shares the same passions for the depth of Tubac's rich history, but it was as an art colony that Tubac found itself again.

Amateur photography was commonplace in the postwar period. We took photographs of everything—people, animals, buildings, ceremonies, and events. Prints, contact sheets, and negatives all survive—sometimes cared for, sometimes by chance—but a huge body of evidence of our past survives because of the ease and availability of cameras and film and of our penchant for snapping photographs. What is going to happen in the digital age? Will we be able to read the laptops, hard drives, CD-ROMs, mobile electronic devices, and memory sticks that hold today's photographs? For people who will want to tell the story of Tubac's next 100 years, we can only hope that digital photography will prove as lasting and accessible as film has been.

For much of the detail in this section, I am most indebted to a collection of recordings and transcripts of oral histories conducted by the Tubac Historical Society in the 1980s. These remarkable documents illuminate the personalities of the people responsible for the creation of modern Tubac. Their memories, insights, and recollections bring a vanished past to life and provide a soundtrack to the wonderful quantity of photographs that survive. I encourage everyone to continue this endeavor: share what you recall and what you think is important. Out of a whole tapestry of memories some approximation of what it was really like comes forth, and people can share an appreciation of Tubac, past, present, and future.

What makes Tubac special? Here is what Lorraine Mitchell Halvorsen said in an interview in 1986: "Living in a beautiful place where you're constantly exposed to beautiful mountains, beautiful skies, beautiful light, beautiful buildings, it can't help but give you ideas and make you want to do something to preserve the feelings that you get. Being surrounded by creative people is exciting. It's fun to live in a place where people are living here just because they want to live here, not because they were sent here. It's a very great joy to live with people who live exactly where they want to live and do what they want to do."

One

Archaeological Tubac

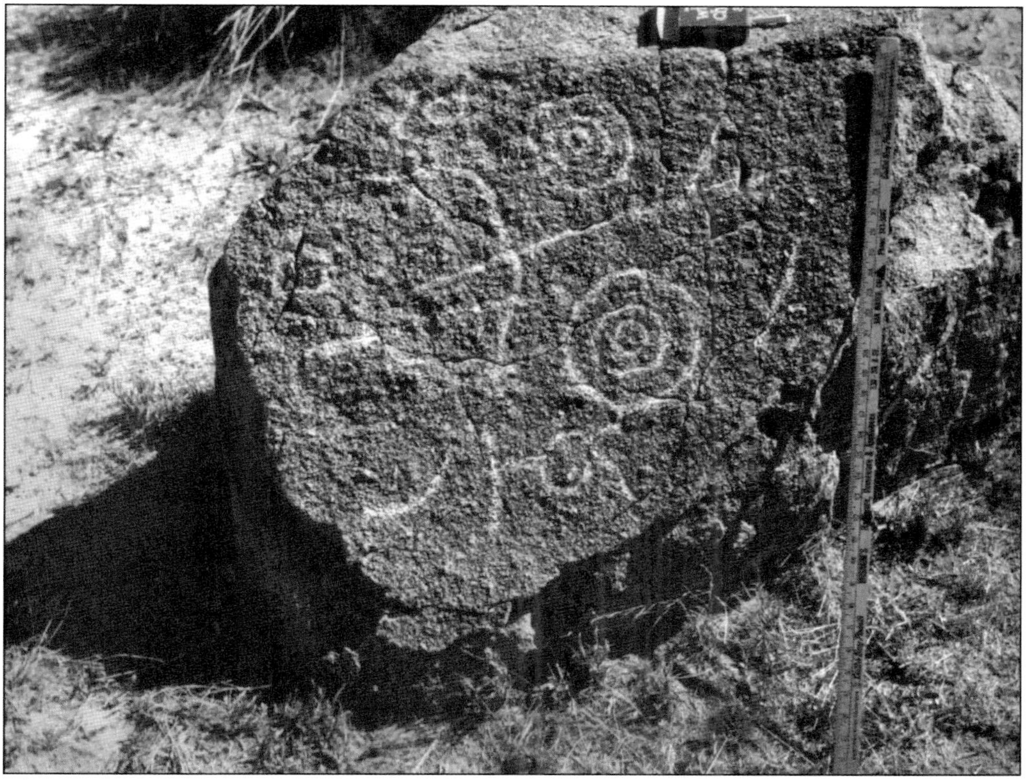

These petroglyphs northwest of Tubac are typical of the spectacular intaglios created by the indigenous population of the Pimería Alta before the arrival of the Spanish. It is unknown what the designs symbolized and the method used to create them. Presumably part of religious endeavors, designs include geometric and stylized natural forms. They can be encountered individually or massed in great density.

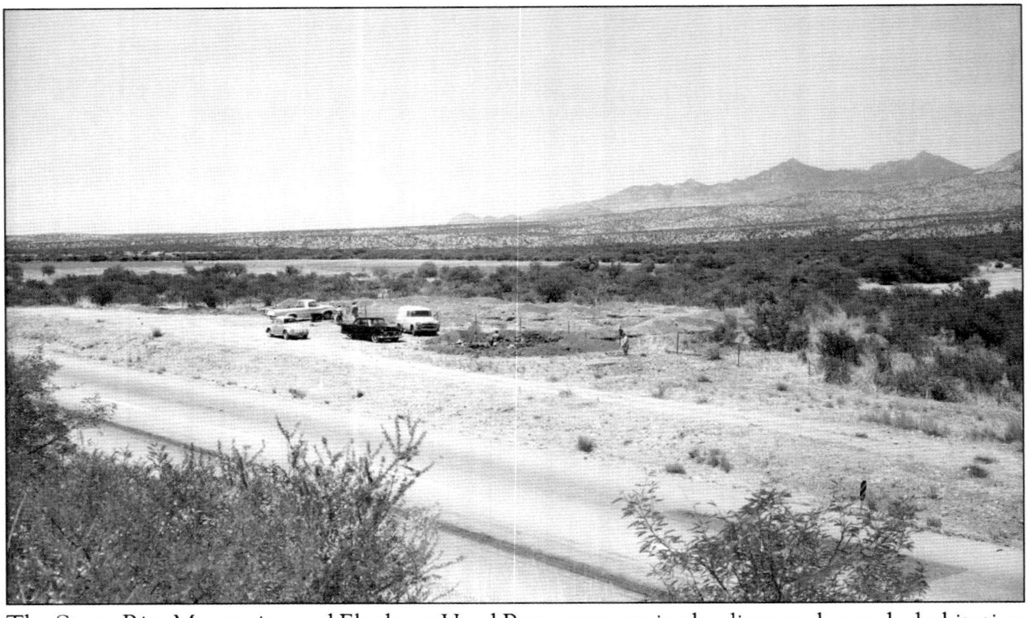

The Santa Rita Mountains and Elephant Head Butte are seen in the distance beyond a habitation site dating back long before the arrival of the Spanish. The excavation revealed that the "England Ranch Ruin" included oval houses made of mud or thatch. The inhabitants made brown-ware pottery and lived by a combination of farming, gathering native plants, and hunting. (Arizona State Museum.)

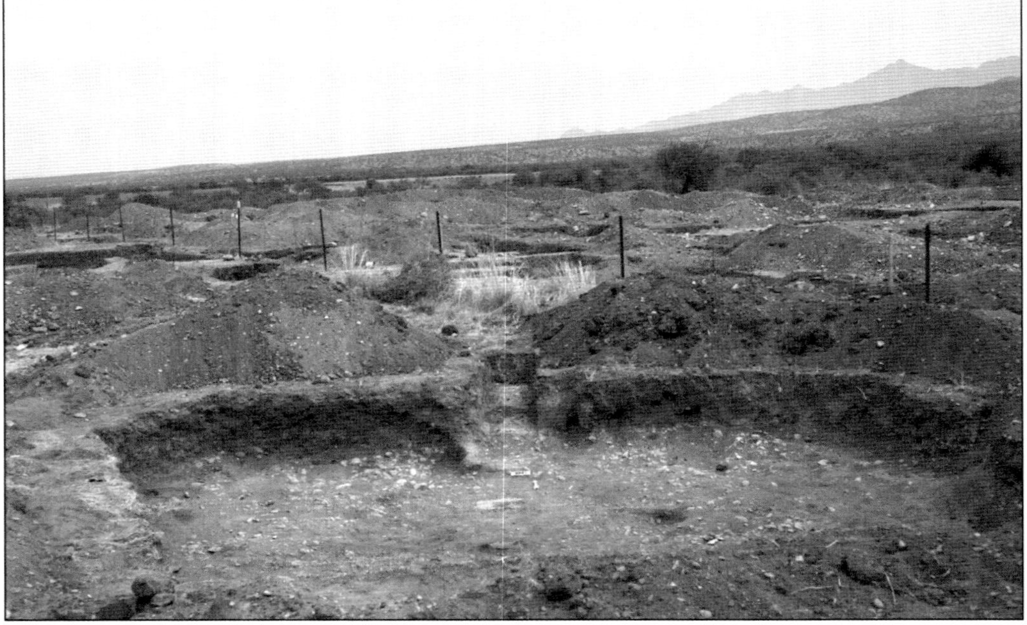

The "England Ranch Ruin" site also included what might be a pre-classic Hohokam pit house, as seen in this 1965 photograph. Archaeologists now believe these structures, made of wooden poles and roofed with grass, had functional uses such as food storage in addition to providing shelter. (Arizona State Museum.)

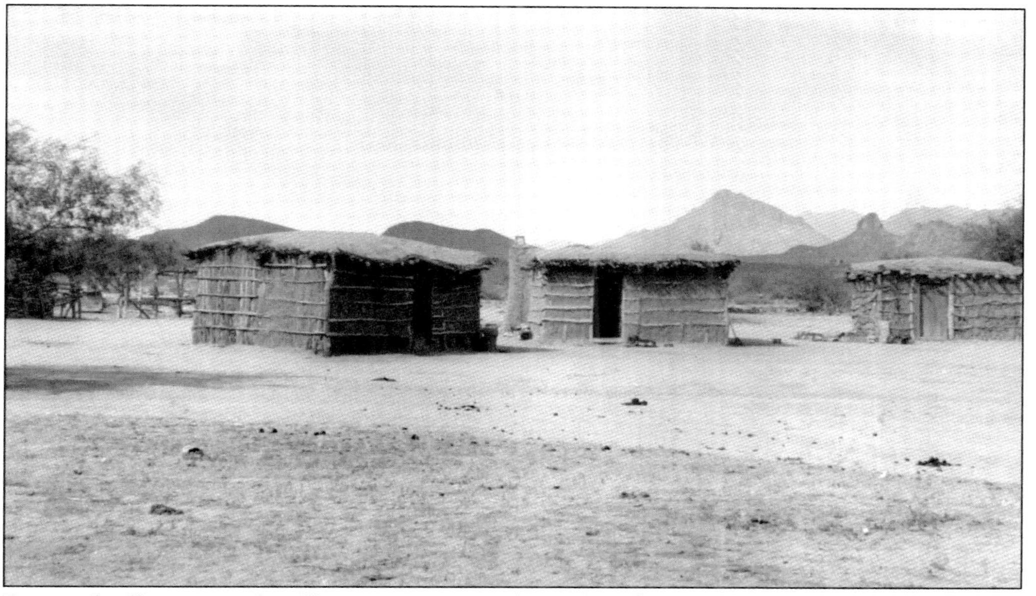

Papago dwellings near San Xavier are seen in this 1930s photograph. The word *Papago* means "bean-eater," a derogatory term used by the Apache to describe the Tohono O'odham, whose own name for themselves means "desert dwellers." Their ancestral lands stretched from the San Pedro River on the east to the Gulf of California on the west and from just north of Phoenix well into Sonora on the south. (Shaw Kinsley.)

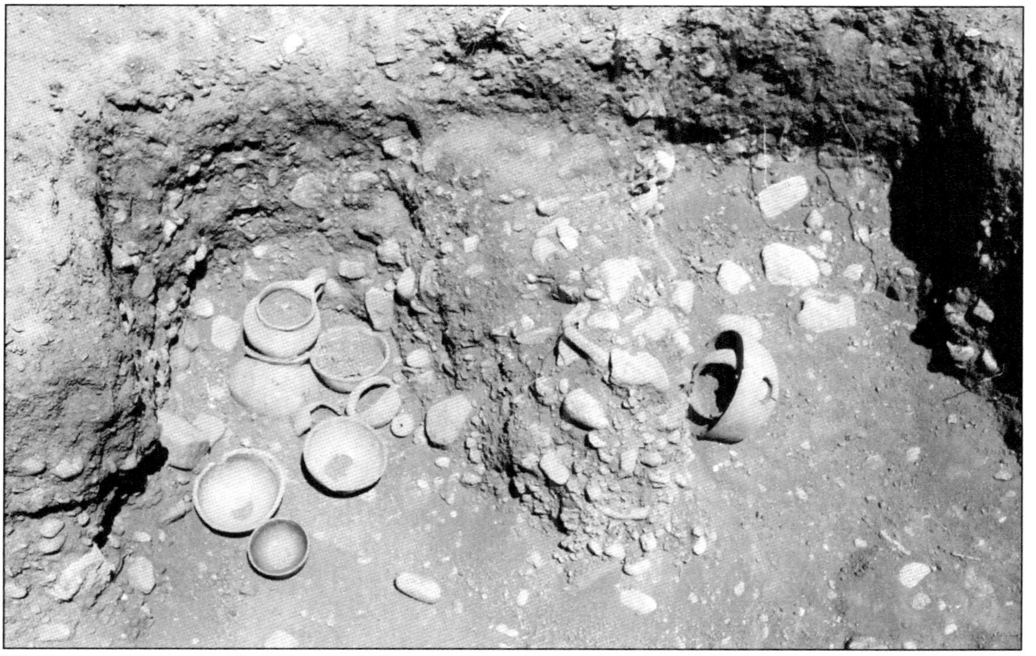

This trove of pottery found near Palo Parado includes Rio Rico polychrome, Trincheras purple-on-red, Nogales polychrome, and Rincon polychrome. The variety indicates the likelihood of trade between the related but not identical cultures of the Sobaipuri, the Pima, and the Tohono O'odham peoples. (Arizona State Museum.)

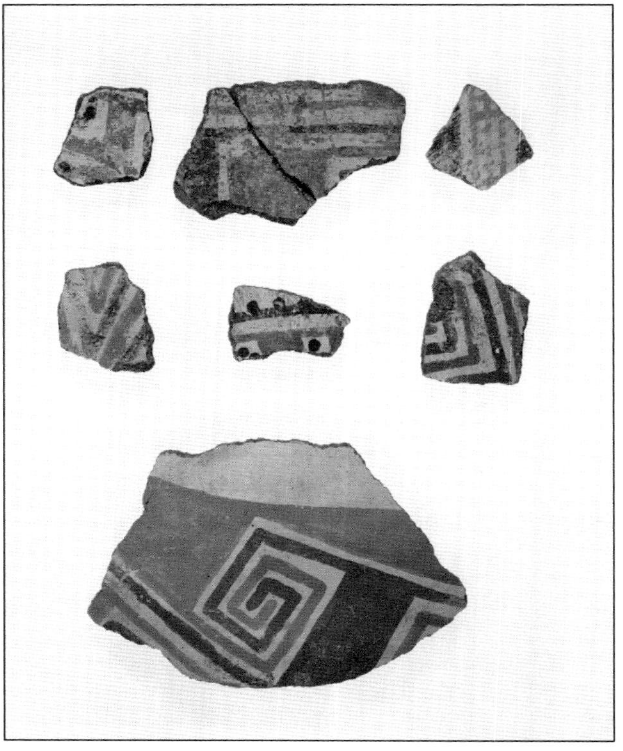

Between 700 AD and 1500 AD, Hohokam red-on-buff pottery dominated Native American ceramics from Flagstaff to as far south as the Santa Cruz Valley. Shown here are examples of Rio Rico polychrome in which the paint is red-on-brown or black. (Arizona State Museum.)

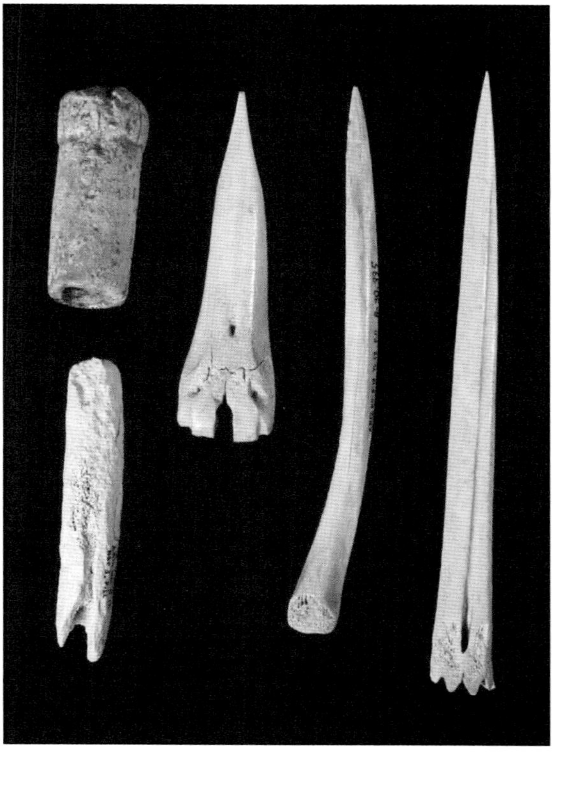

Among the artifacts recovered from the England Ranch Ruin and others during archaeology in the 1970s were these bone awls and needles. They suggest perishable cultural artifacts such as baskets and clothing. Also found were stone manos and metates for grinding seeds into flour, scrapers for hides, and projectile points for hunting. The collective data provides insights on what prehistoric settlements and subsistence systems were like, but our knowledge is really only bits and pieces. (Arizona State Museum.)

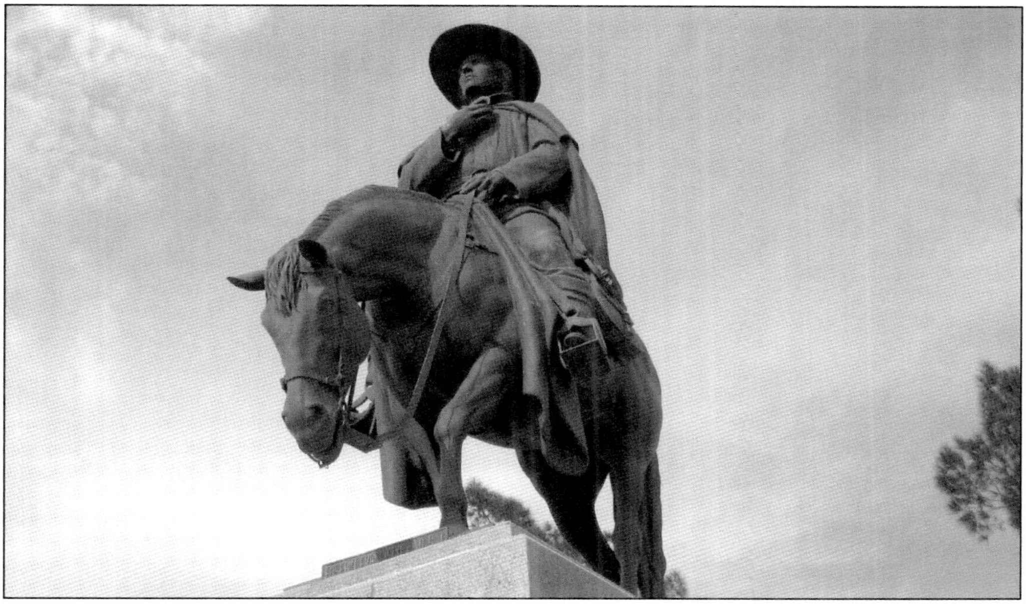

The Italian-born Jesuit Fr. Eusebio Francisco Kino (here honored in a Tucson sculpture), served in the Pimería Alta for 24 years, making more than 50 journeys inland and establishing a chain of missions from Caborca to Tucson. The horses, cattle, fruits, and vegetables brought by Kino were part of his promise to the native population of a more prosperous life within the Spanish fold. (Shaw Kinsley.)

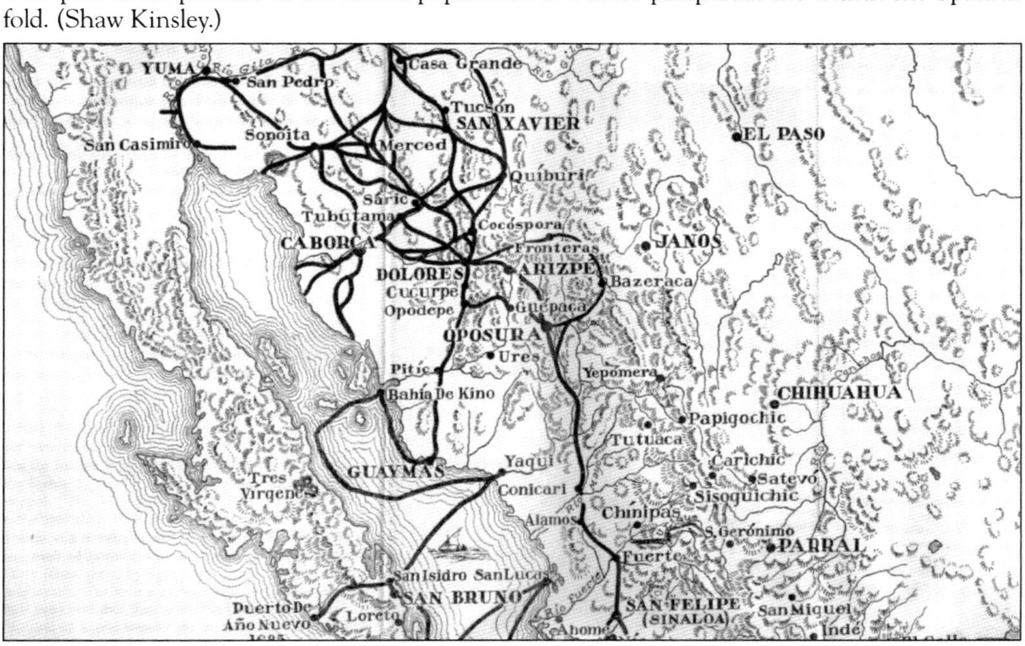

This map shows the amazing breadth of Father Kino's travels in the Pimería Alta and underscores how widely the population was scattered. His writings show that he traveled the Santa Cruz River valley at least nine times and never mentioned Tubac by name once. His travels along the Santa Cruz ceased after 1702 when he devoted himself to determining whether or not California was an island.

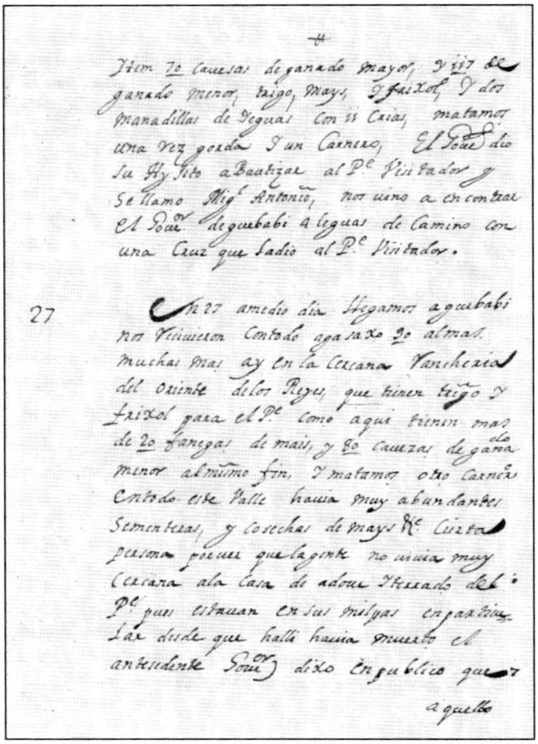

+

Item 70 cauesas de ganado mayor, y 117 de
ganado menor, trigo, mays, y frixol, y dos
manadillas de yeguas con sus crias; matamos
una vez gorda y un carnero, El Gover dio
su hyjito a bautizar al Pe Visitador y
se llamo Migl Antonio; nos vino a encontrar
el Gover de quebabi 4 leguas de camino con
una cruz que salio al Pe Visitador.

27 El 27 a medio dia llegamos a quebabi
nos recivieron con todo agasaxo 90 almas
muchas mas ay en la cercana rancheria
del oriente de los Reyes, que tienen trigo y
frixol para el Pe como aqui tienen mas
de 20 fanegas de mais, y 80 cauezas de ganado
menor al mismo fin, y matamos otro carnero
en todo este valle havia muy abundantes
sementeras, y cosechas de mays Rl. cierta
persona porque que la gente no vivia muy
cercana ala casa de adove y terrado del
Pe. pues estauan en sus milpas enpartic-
lar desde que halli havia muerto el
antecedente Govor) dixo en publico que
aquello

Kino's field diary recounts a 1699 expedition into southwestern Arizona and includes descriptions of the geography, resources, and native peoples in the area. Written and signed in his own hand, it is actually a revised, clean copy made in consultation with his companion on the journey, Fr. Antonio Leal. The diaries, now at the University of Arizona Library, were the source for *Favores Celestiales*, Kino's major work.

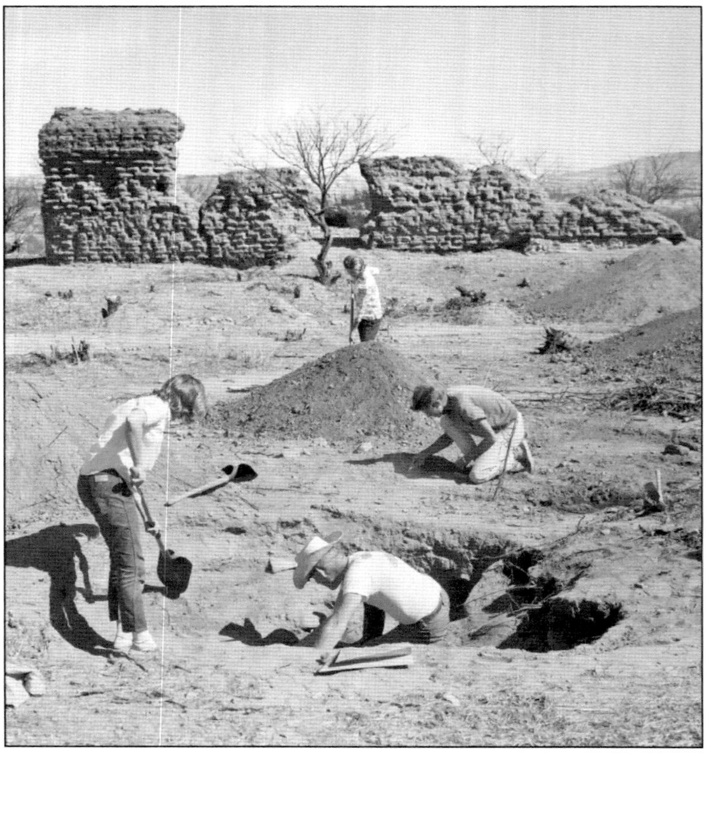

On a hot day in 1966, archaeologists from Arizona State University worked on the Convento at Guevavi, the Kino mission founded in 1701. Guevavi declined in importance as population shifted to the Tubac-Tumacácori area, and the mission was abandoned by 1773. Researchers have recovered Piman pottery, shell beads and ornaments, Mexican-made ceramics, glass trade beads, a crucifix, and portions of a brass candlestick, as well as lead musket balls and iron nails. (Arizona State Museum.)

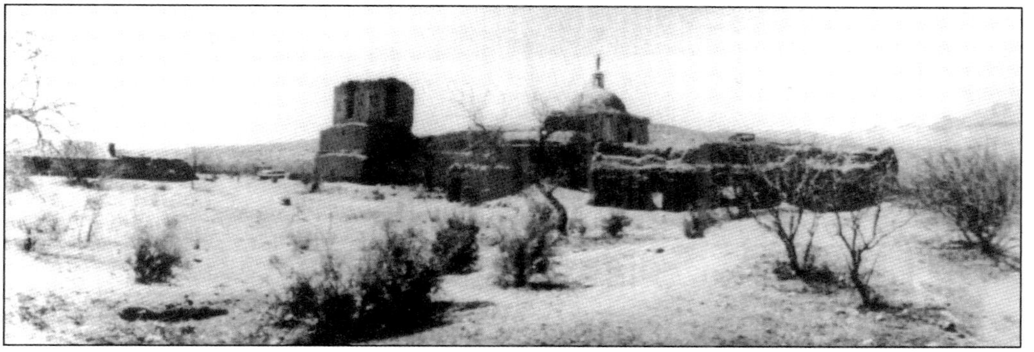

Originally established on the east side of the Santa Cruz River as San Cayetano de Tumacácori, the mission was moved to the west side of the river after the 1751 Pima Rebellion. In one of the earliest photographs of the area, Mission San Jose de Tumacácori is shown as it looked in 1889. Franciscans built their structure on older foundations, but by 1848 it was abandoned. The religious artifacts were transferred to Mission San Xavier del Bac near Tucson.

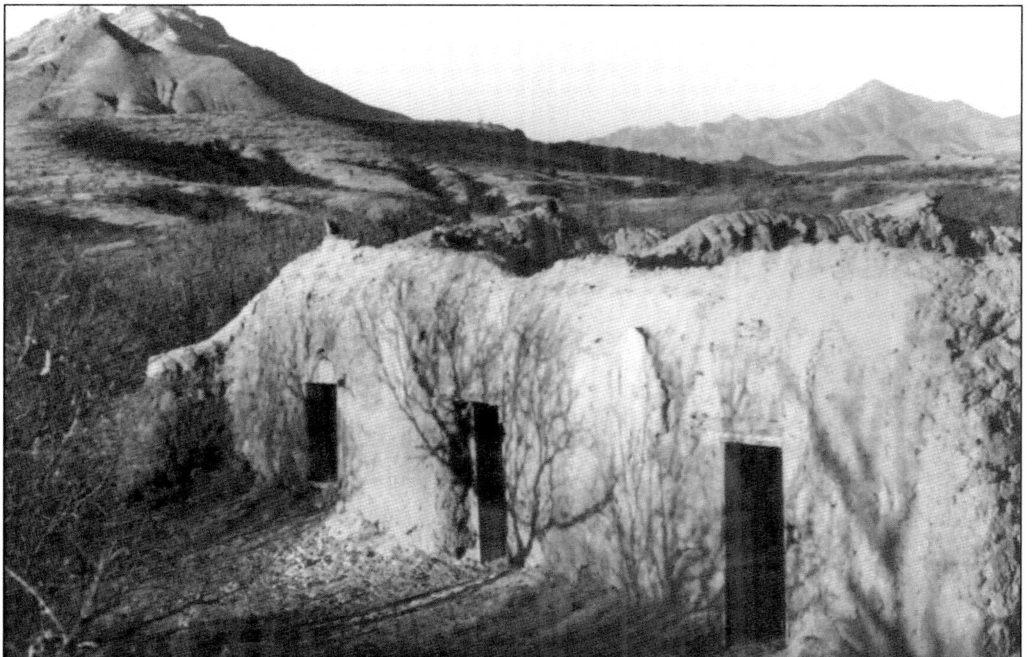

Calabaza means squash, pumpkin, or gourd in Spanish. It first appeared as a local place name in 1756 when Fr. Francisco Pauer baptized 78 Papago (or O'odham) there. The ruins of Father Pauer's 18th-century mission were still recognizable in this photograph from 1929. Today the site is adjacent to the Rio Rico golf course. (Pimería Alta Historical Society.)

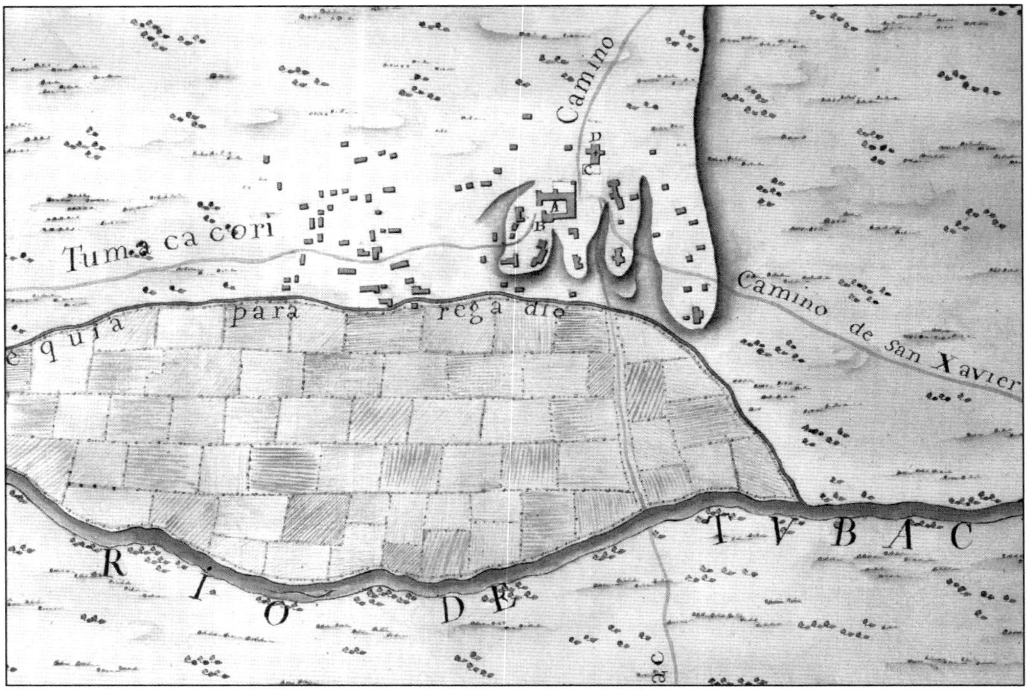

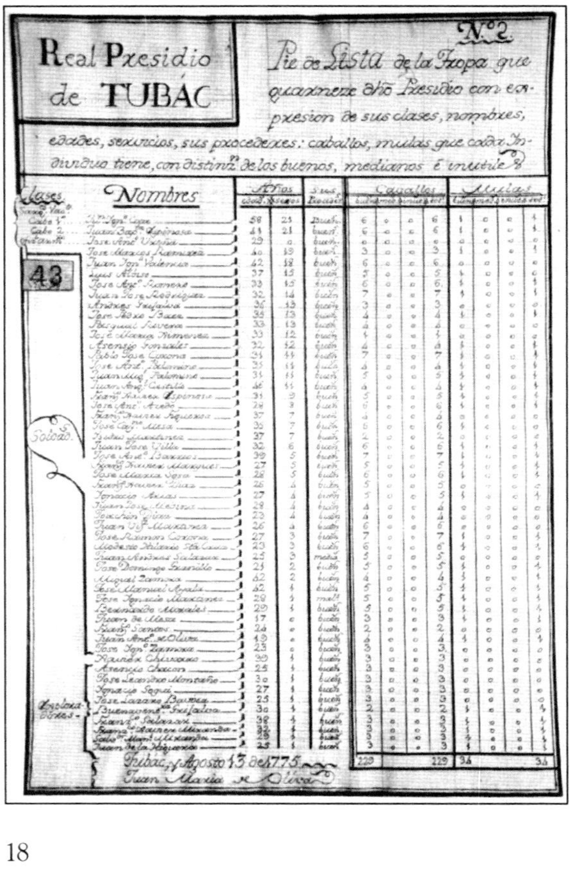

José de Urrutia's 1767 map of the Presidio de San Ignacio de Tubac depicts the topography, river, and settlement 15 years after its founding. Today the Tubac Presidio State Historic Park occupies the areas marked A and B. St. Ann's Church now stands where Santa Gertrudis once did at C and D. Remnants of the cluster of buildings to the left are protected by the Barrio de Tubac Archaeological Preserve.

Housed in the Archivo General de Indias in Seville, manuscript records like these detailed the military inhabitants of 18th-century Tubac by name, rank, age, conduct, and years of service and provided an inventory of horses and mules. This tally was made in August 1775, when Commandant-Inspector Hugo Oconor decided to move the Presidio from Tubac to Tucson, exposing the former fort to constant attacks until it was re-established 12 years later.

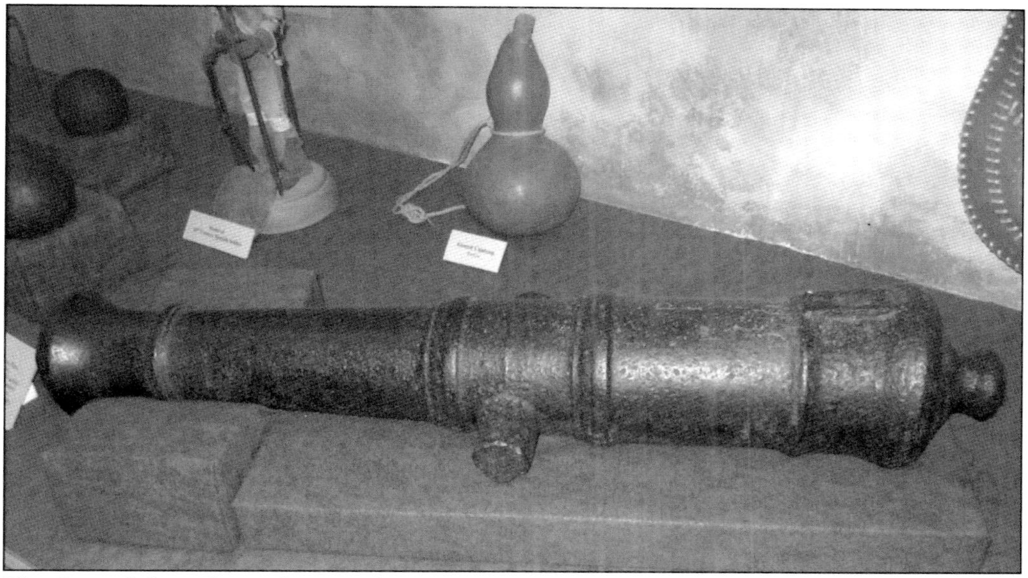

The Spanish brought modern warfare to Pimería Alta. This museum display includes a period Spanish colonial (possibly naval) cannon to represent the four cannon used to protect Tubac in the 18th century. The originals, cast in New Spain, fired 4-pound balls but were unfortunately of inferior craftsmanship—two of them were entirely useless because of cracks in their breeches. Frontier soldiers possessed little skill in the use of cannons, a good thing considering the potentially explosive flaws of manufacture. (Tubac Presidio State Historic Park.)

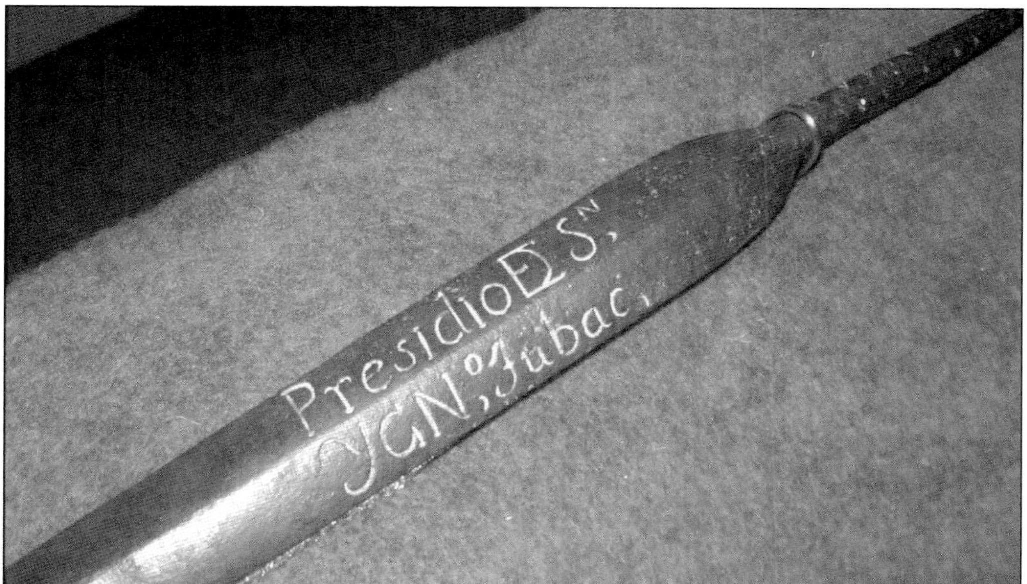

Presidial soldiers were equipped with modern weapons (muskets and pistols) as well as sabers, shields, and a heavy coat of leather armor, which gave them the name *soldados de cuera*. The hand-forged lance blade above dates from 1752 to 1770 and is inscribed, "PRESIDIO De Sn YGNo, TUBAC" abbreviated to mean Presidio de San Ignacio de Tubac. It was found in Tubac in the 20th century. (Tubac Presidio State Historic Park.)

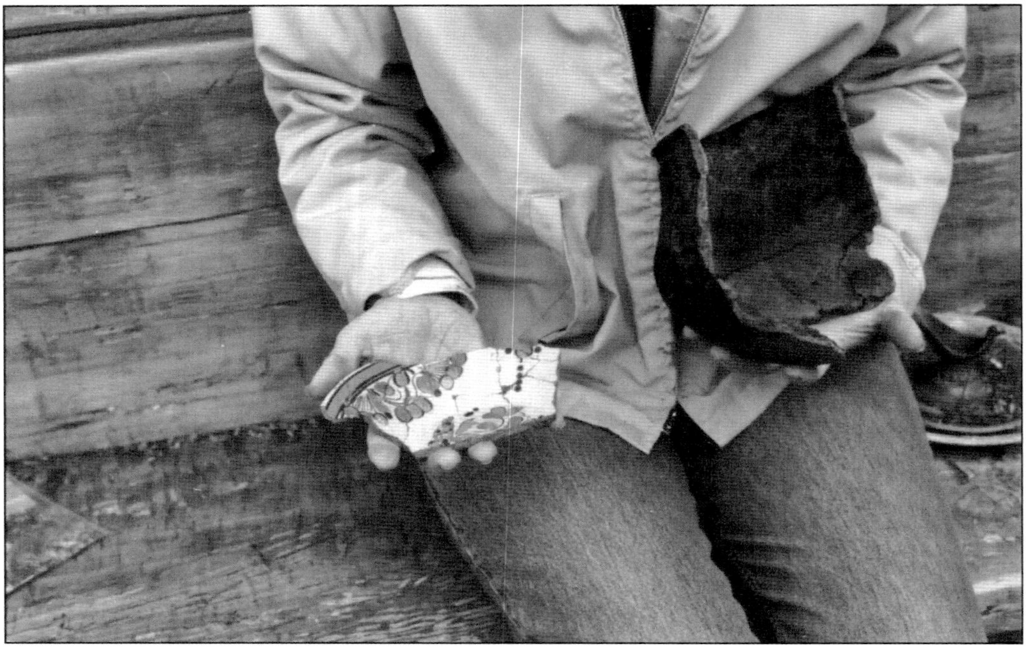

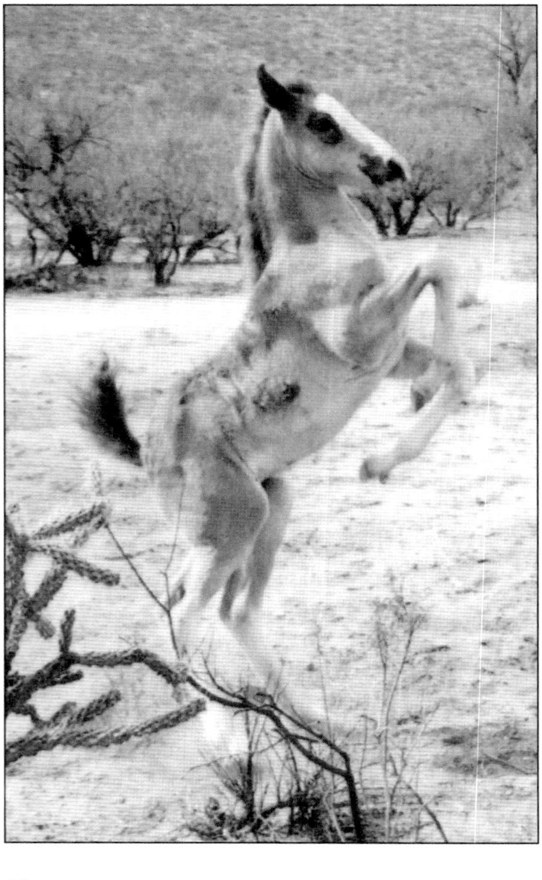

Barbara Ruppman is holding a majolica earthenware fragment in her right hand and a redware pottery fragment in her left, just two items in more than 240 cubic feet of artifact material recovered by the Center for Spanish Colonial Archaeology in its Tubac excavation begun in 1988. Buttons, buckles, religious medallions and crosses, projectile points, and musket decorations were among the items found and will one day be displayed in the Presidio Museum. (Barbara Ruppman.)

The horses Father Kino brought to the Pimería Alta were descended from the Spanish Barb, a breed developed in Spain after the 8th-century Moorish invasion. A rare strain of horses directly related to this Spanish colonial stock has lived on the Wilbur-Cruce Ranch near Arivaca since 1876. This playful nine-week-old colt is shedding out its foal coat and will grow into a handsome roan mare. (Silke Schneider.)

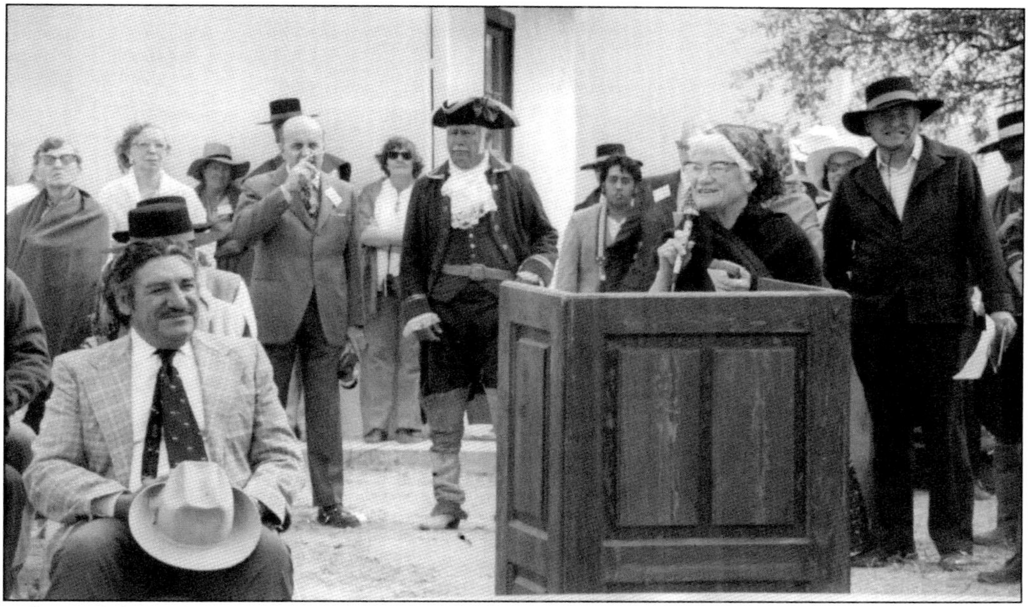

Tubac celebrated twin bicentennials in 1975–1976, marking America's War of Independence and Juan Bautista de Anza's historic expedition to secure Northern California for Spain. The reenactment ride began in Horcasitas, Sonora, on September 25, 1975, and ended nine months later in San Francisco on June 27, 1976. Authentic details overseen by the Arizona Historical Society made the reenactment a historical and cultural triumph.

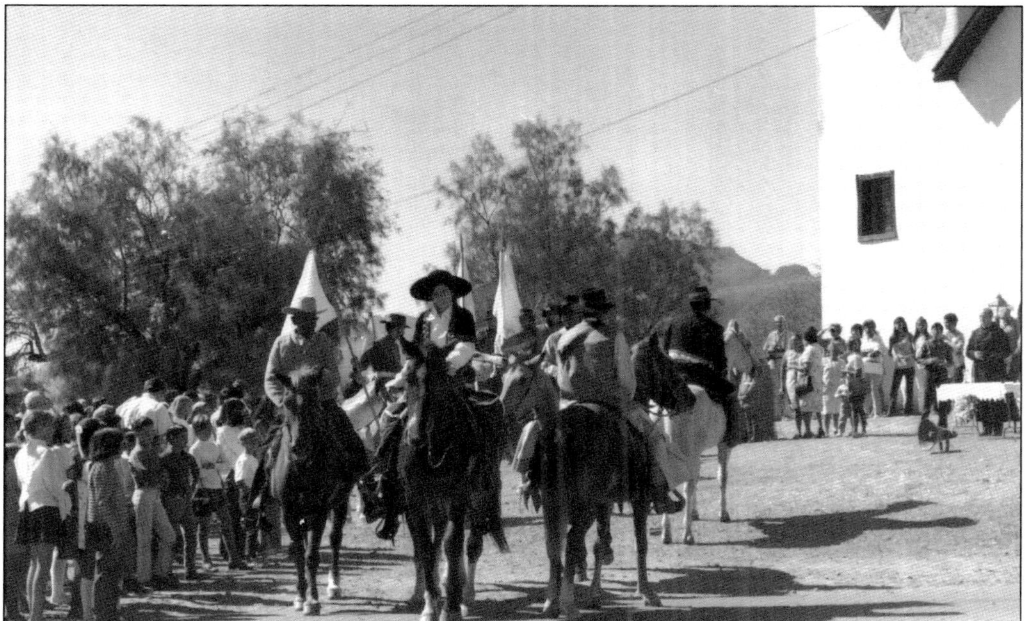

Tubac was selected as the final point of departure before crossing the desert, and the 1975 reenactment send-off was a gala affair. Speakers included Arizona governor Raul Castro, Sen. Barry Goldwater, Yginio Aguirre (in costume), who portrayed Anza in the reenactment, Elizabeth Brownell of the Tubac Historical Society, and Will Rogers Jr.

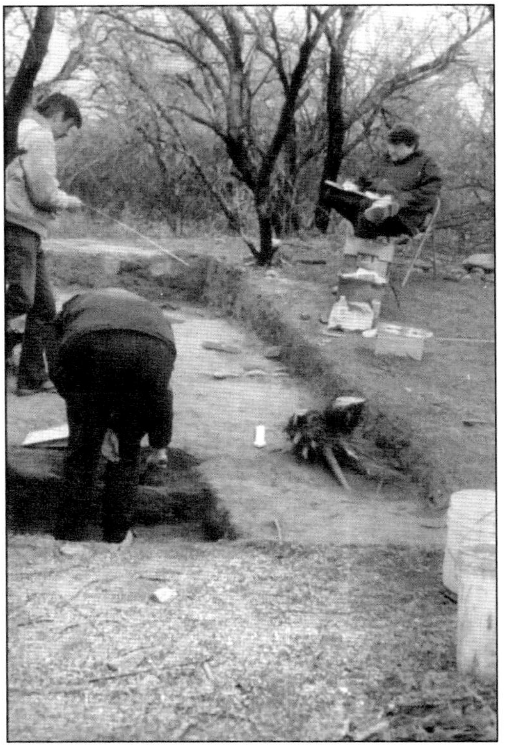

Archaeologist Jack S. Williams (right) of the Center for Spanish Colonial Archaeology conducted excavations and subsurface tests in the Barrio de Tubac Archaeological Preserve in the 1980s. After the artifacts were cleaned and studied by the Arizona State Museum, the many contributions by Native American, missionary, Spanish, Mexican, and American people were illuminated in greater detail. (Barbara Ruppman.)

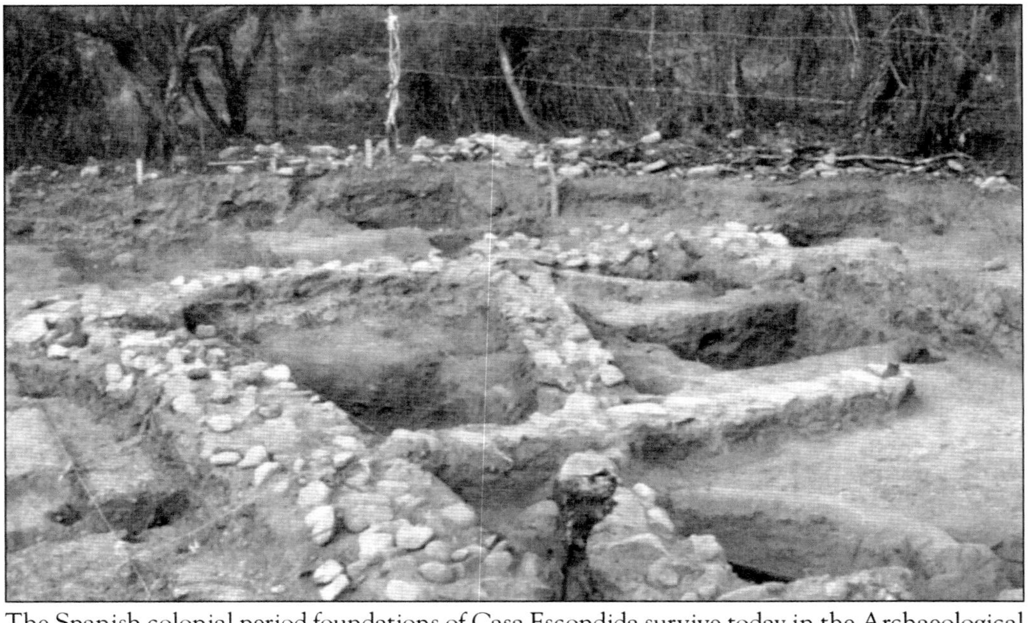

The Spanish colonial period foundations of Casa Escondida survive today in the Archaeological Preserve of Tubac. These stones were reused at least five times to rebuild or modify the structure over time. Artifacts recovered demonstrate Tubac's historical importance as a military, population, and economic center. Authorized tours are available through the Tubac Historical Society or the Tubac Presidio State Historic Park visitors' center. (Barbara Ruppman.)

Two

Territorial Tubac

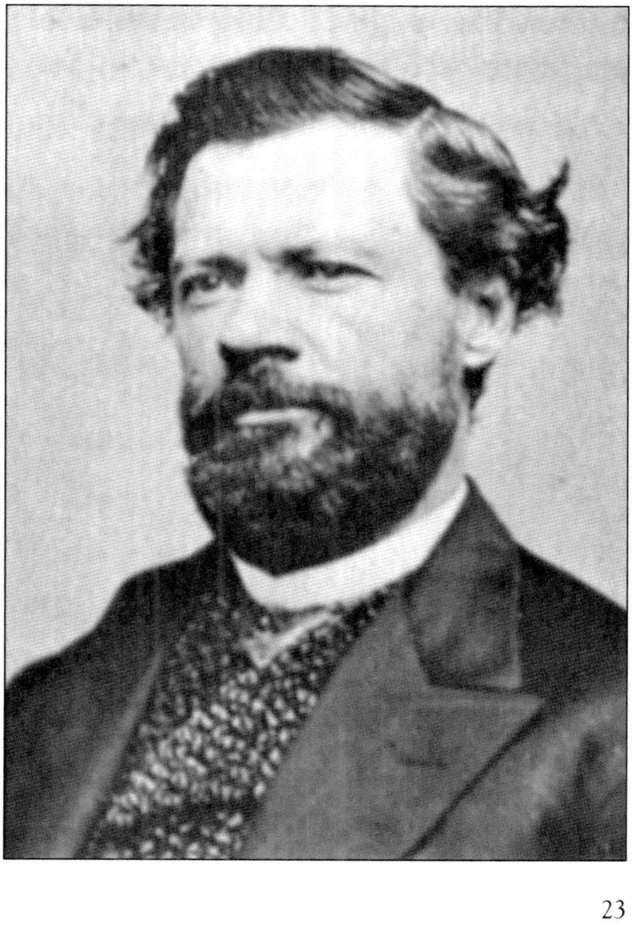

Charles Debrille Poston was 30 when he became manager of the Sonora Exploring and Mining Company. The business was headquartered in Tubac because of its central location between the Salero mines and the Cerro Colorado mines. As alcalde, or mayor, Poston performed marriages, dispensed justice, and even issued paper currency. He also reveled in his role as host, serving visitors meals of local wild game with French wines from Guaymas.

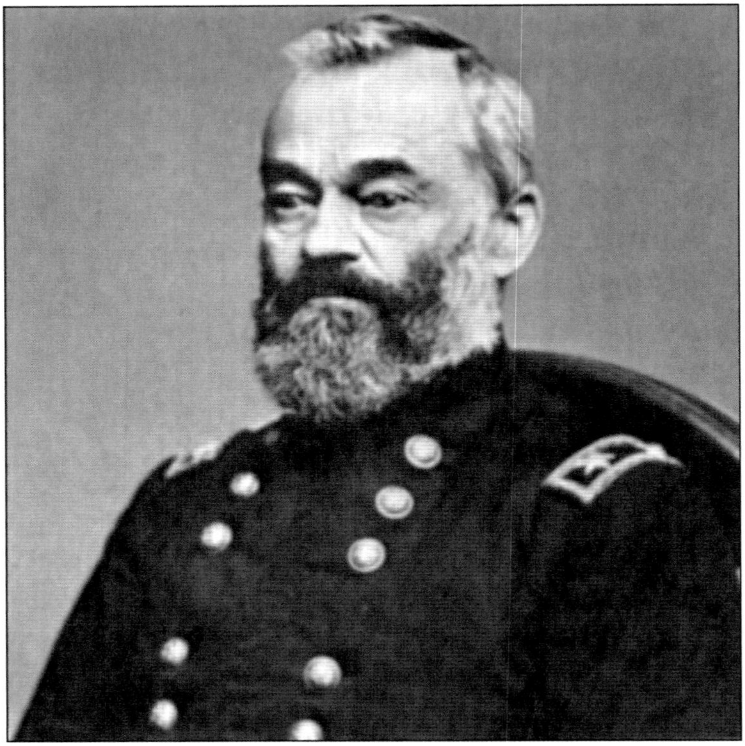

Maj. Gen. Samuel Heintzelman's name became associated with the Cerro Colorado mine west of Tubac after he arranged for a Cincinnati, Ohio, syndicate to fund the Sonora Exploring and Mining Company. Other directors were Samuel Colt, William Coleman, and William Wrightson. By 1861, the mine was producing $1,000 of silver daily. The Civil War brought an end to the bonanza.

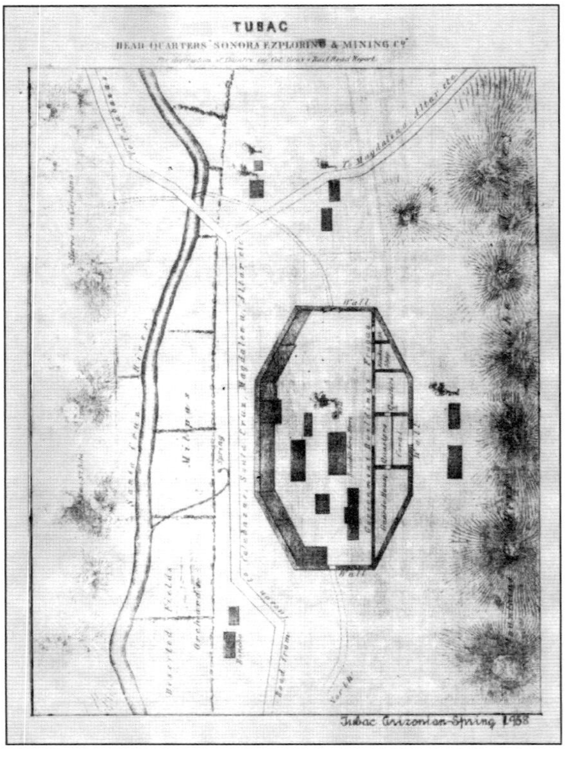

When Poston took possession of the Tubac Presidio in 1856, he wrote, "There was not a soul in the village. The quarters would accommodate about 300 men. The old 'quartel' was still up and made a good storehouse. The tower on the north of which three stories remained was utilized as a lookout." This diagram from a report of the Sonora Exploring and Mining Company shows Poston's plans for the enterprise.

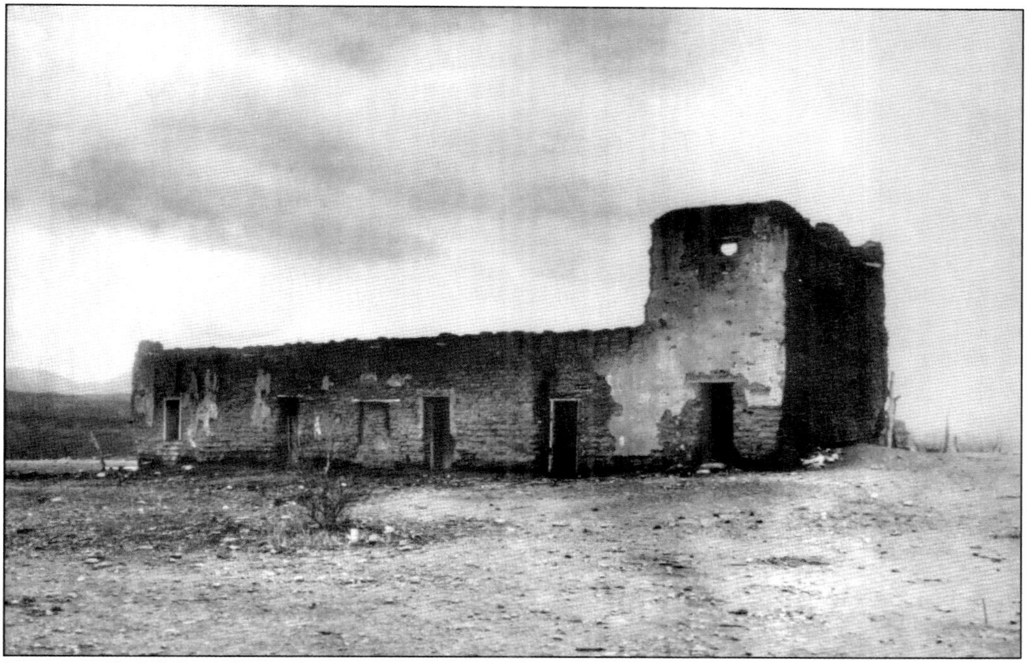

Poston called Tubac the "Athens of Arizona" and described it as a utopia in which there was "no law but love, and no occupation but labor. No government, no taxes, no public debt, no politics." This photograph from the 1880s shows a ruined presidio much as Poston saw it. (Tubac Presidio State Historic Park.)

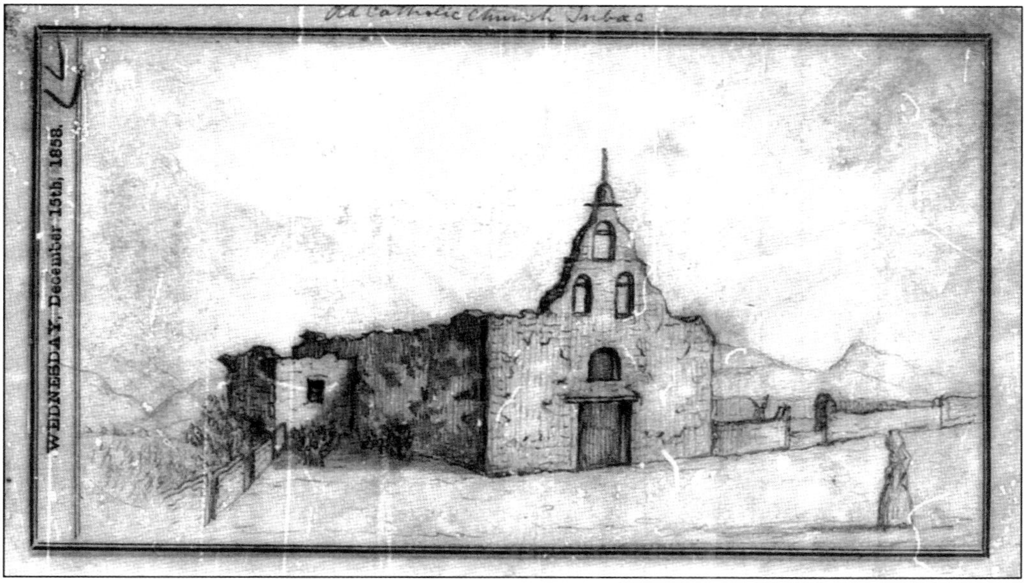

This drawing of Tubac's original church was made in 1858 by Phocion Way, a major stockholder in Poston's mining enterprise. It shows the ruins of the Santa Gertrudis Church built by Juan Bautista de Anza in the 1760s when he commanded the presidio. Today's St. Ann's Church sits on the same site. Way traveled to Tucson by Overland Mail Stage with his friend and fellow stockholder Gilbert Grosvenor. (Tubac Presidio State Historic Park.)

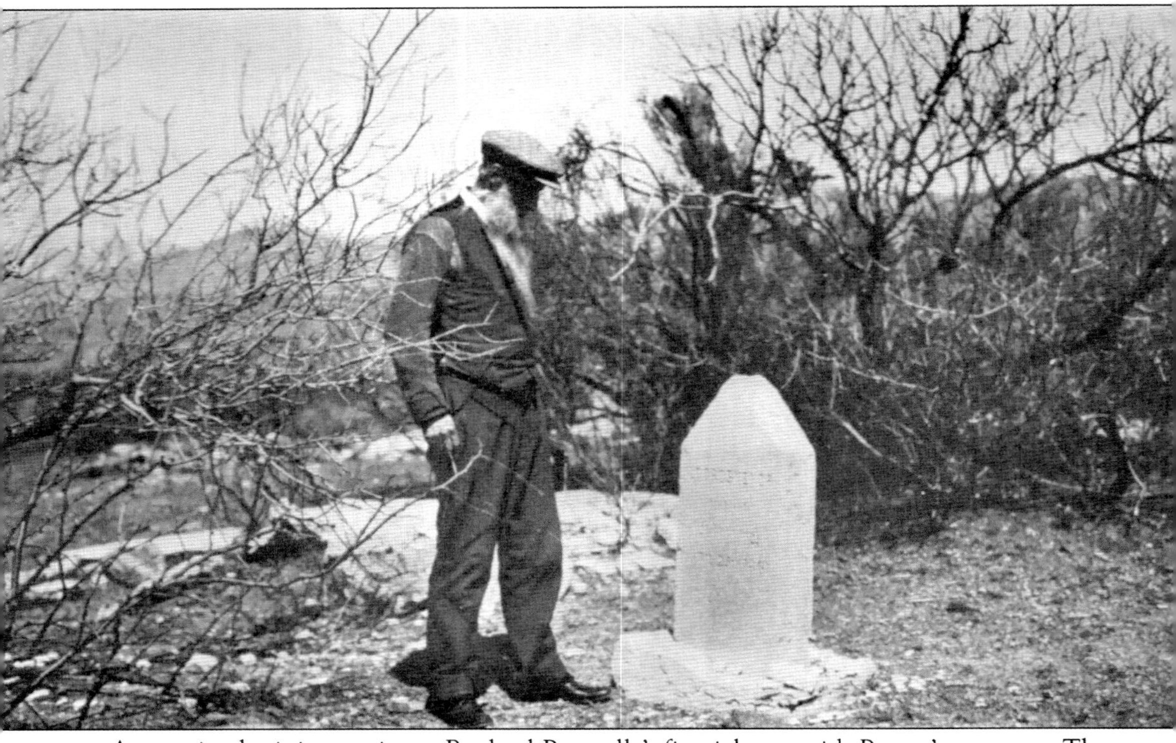

As a trained mining engineer, Raphael Pumpelly's first job was with Poston's company. These mines lost their protection and were closed down when troops from Fort Buchanan were recalled to eastern battlefields during the Civil War. Pumpelly and Horace Grosvenor planned to process a quantity of silver ore to pay off some of the company's debts. Before the ore could be delivered, Apaches killed the wagon drivers, cut loose the mules, and dumped out the ore. Grosvenor was killed in the attack, but according to legend, Pumpelly was able to escape when alerted to danger by his house cat. He managed to process the ore, pay off the hired hands, and escape the area. He returned in 1915 and was photographed at Grosvenor's grave east of Tubac in the Santa Rita Mountains.

This letter by William Wrightson describes his journey to "Tubock" in August 1858 to join Poston's management team. A year later, his brother John was murdered by Mexicans, and in 1865, while William was surveying Baca Float No. 3 for the U.S. Land Office with mineralogist Gilbert Hopkins, both men were killed by Apaches on February 17, 1865. The two highest peaks in the Santa Ritas are named for them.

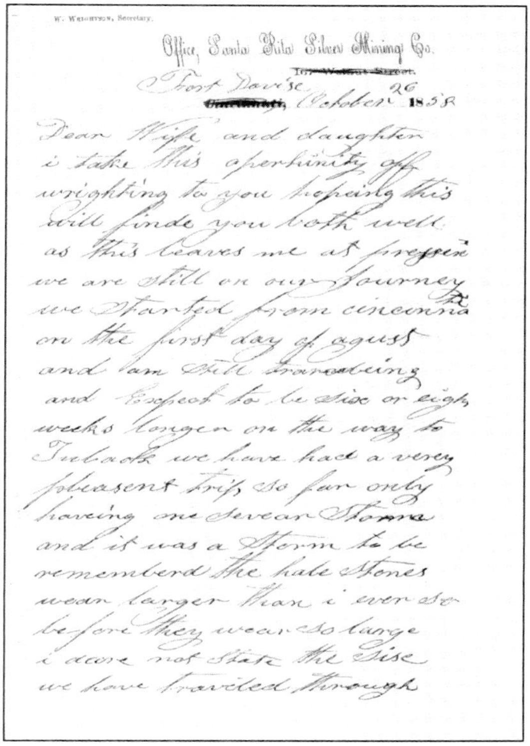

W. Wrightson, Secretary.

Office, Santa Rita Silver Mining Co.

Fort Davise October 26 1858

Dear Wife and daughter
i take this aperhunity off
wrighting to you hoping this
will finde you both well
as this leaves me at presen
we are still on our Journey
we Started from cincinna
on the first day of agust
and am Still traveling
and Expect to be Sixe or eigh
weeks longer on the way to
Tuback we have had a very
pleasent trip so far only
having one Sevear Storme
and it was a Storm to be
rememberd the hale Stones
wear larger than i ever so
before they wear so large
i dare not State the Sise
we have traveled through

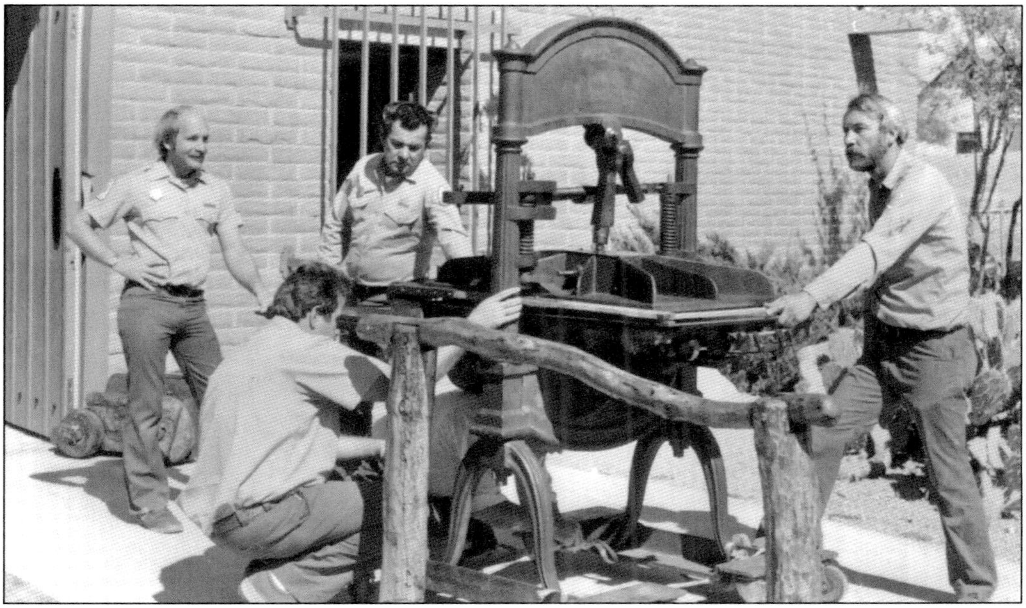

William Wrightson brought the Washington printing press to Tubac where on March 3, 1859, it was used to print the *Arizonian*, the first newspaper in Arizona. Manufactured in Cincinnati in 1858, the press arrived on the "Jackass Mail," as the mule teams were called. Here the press is being moved into the Tubac Presidio State Historic Park museum in 1980 after an absence of 120 years. (Tubac Presidio State Historic Park.)

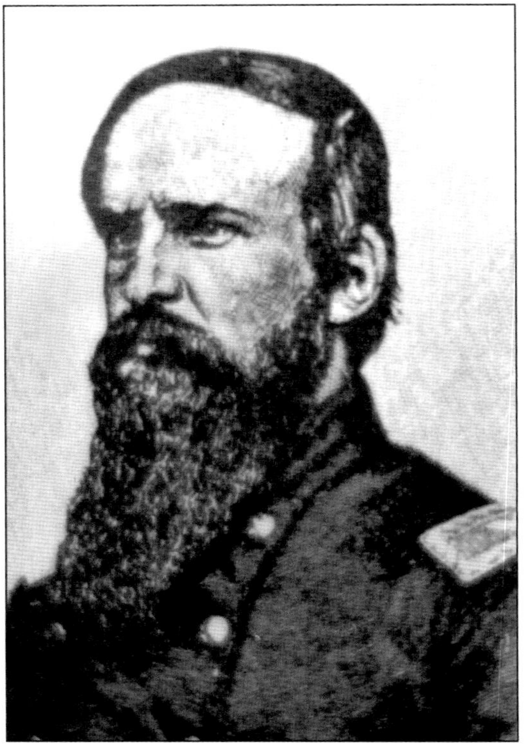

Edward Cross, editor of the *Arizonian*, had strong convictions. He was offended by articles written by Sylvester Mowry of Tucson and published in Eastern newspapers. These articles Cross felt inflated both size of the local population and of mining operations. Ultimately, Mowry challenged Cross to a duel. Cross later attained the rank of colonel in the New Hampshire Infantry and was killed at the Battle of Gettysburg. (Tubac Presidio State Historic Park.)

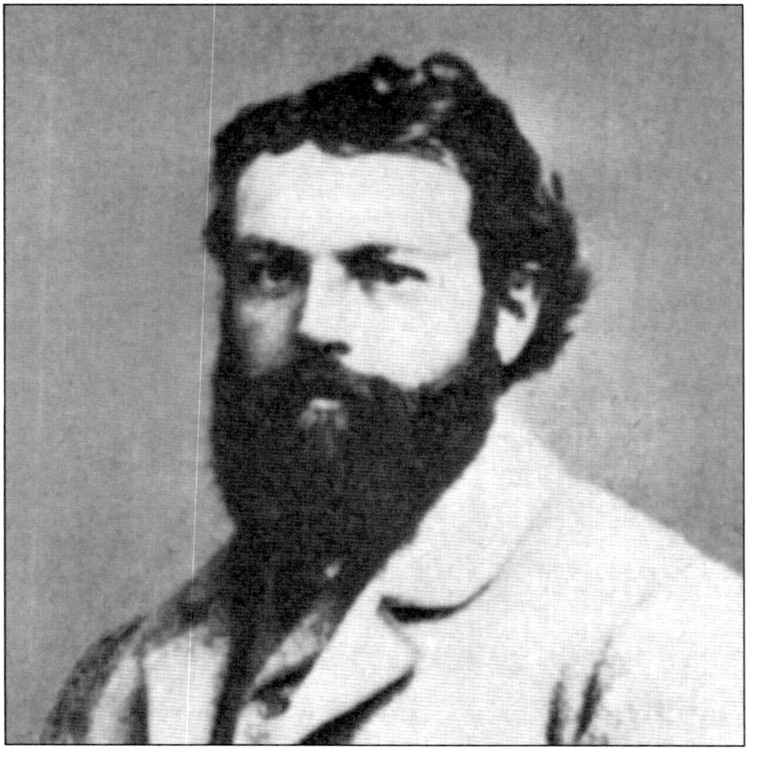

Sylvester Mowry was stationed at Fort Yuma in 1857 where he became impressed with Arizona's mineral wealth. He resigned from the army in 1858 and was part of a group of army officers who purchased an ancient silver mine 9 miles from Patagonia. He was Arizona's most active champion for territorial development and hoped Guaymas would be annexed by the United States as a port.

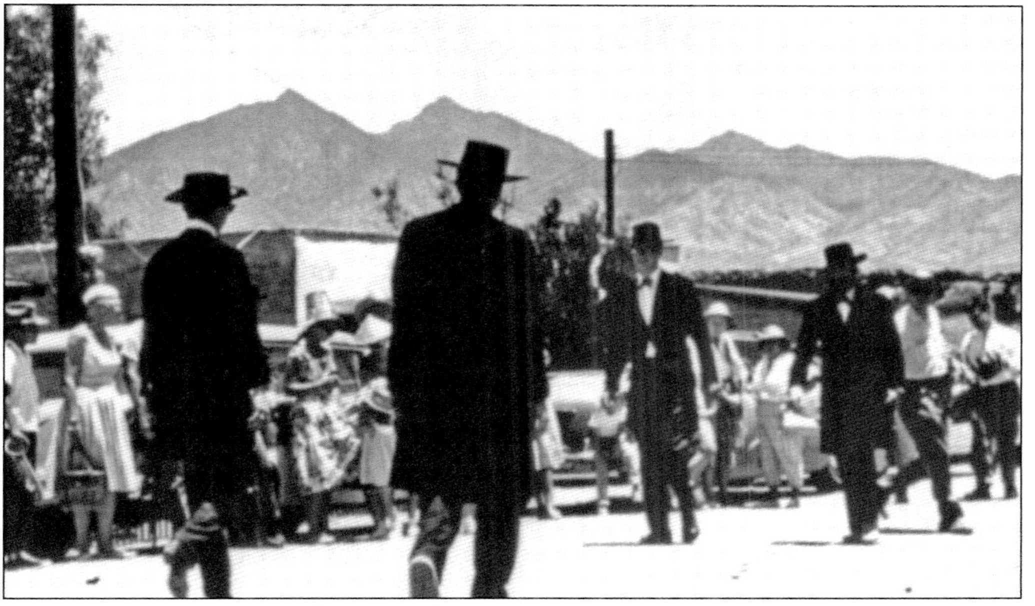

The duel between Mowry and Cross took place on July 8, 1859, using Burnside rifles. Four shots were fired before Mowry's gun failed. It was determined that Mowry was entitled to another shot, and Cross waited unarmed. Mowry refused to fire at an unarmed man, ending the duel. Both men exchanged apologies in person and in the *Arizonian*. This 1961 photograph shows a historically inaccurate reenactment.

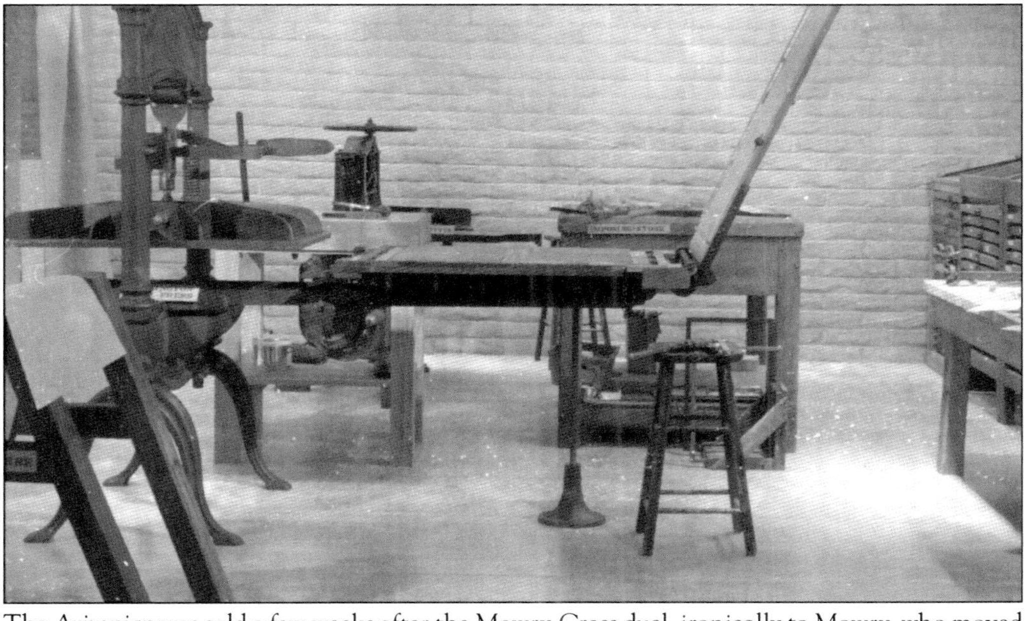

The *Arizonian* was sold a few weeks after the Mowry-Cross duel, ironically to Mowry, who moved it to Tucson where it printed the first issue of the *Citizen* and possibly the *Star*. Later it printed the *Tombstone Nugget*. In 1910, the press was donated to the Arizona Historical Society and not returned to Tubac until 1980, when it was installed in the period print shop shown here. (Tubac Presidio State Historic Park.)

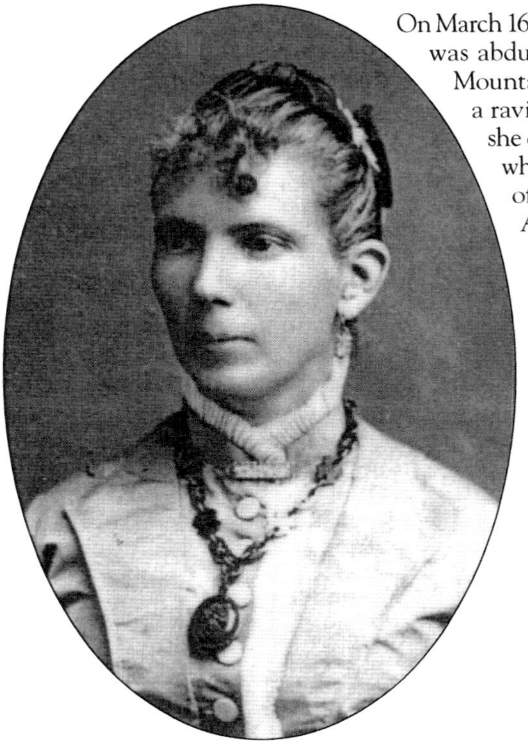

On March 16, 1860, twenty-three-year-old Larcena Pennington was abducted from a lumber camp in the Santa Rita Mountains by Apaches, stripped, beaten, thrown into a ravine, and left for dead. Unconscious three days, she crawled back to camp over the following 10 days, where she was met by her astonished family. One of Arizona's greatest pioneers, she lived to see Arizona's statehood and died in 1913.

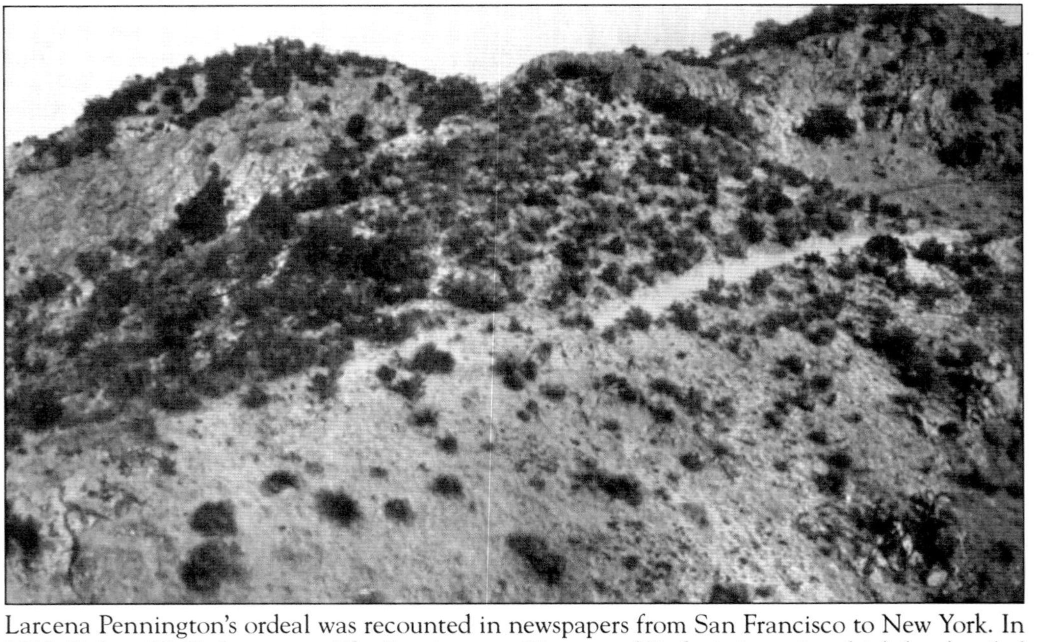

Larcena Pennington's ordeal was recounted in newspapers from San Francisco to New York. In 1915, Robert H. Forbes wrote *The Penningtons, Pioneers of Early Arizona* in which he detailed the whole story and included this photograph of "the old Apache Trail east of Helvetia" where she was left for dead. Virginia Cullin Roberts told the story again in 1991 in her book *In Their Own Blood*.

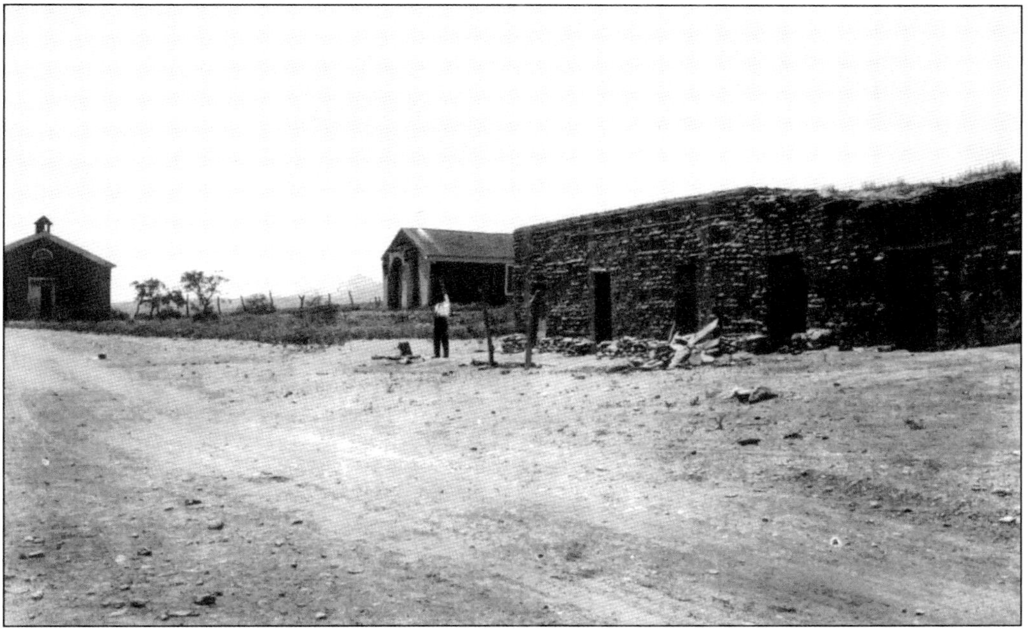

This 1915 photograph from Robert Forbes's book, *The Penningtons*, shows the Pennington house in Tubac. Made of sun-dried adobe bricks and roofed with sod, the building dates from 1860 and is typical of early Tubac construction. The 1885 schoolhouse is visible on the left, and the Tumacácori Mountains are visible beside the old church. Today the Pennington house is the Hugh Cabot Gallery.

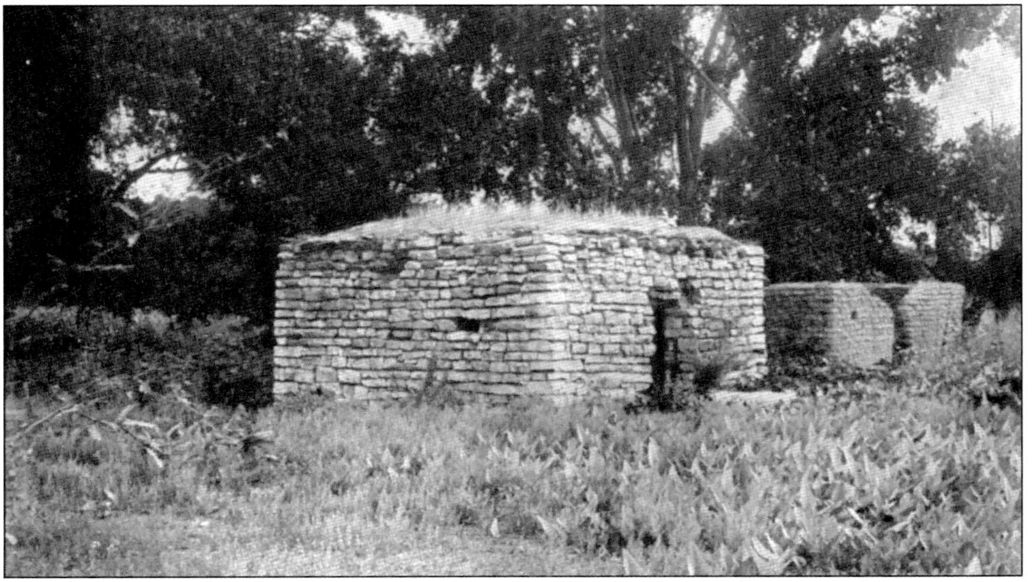

Before moving to Tubac, Larcena's father, Elias Pennington, built this fortress-like stone house overlooking the Santa Cruz River northeast of Nogales. The family, including 12 children, was headed for California, but an Apache raid drove off their livestock and forced them to settle in the area. Cabot Sedgwick purchased the property in the 1990s; it has since been included in the National Register of Historic Places.

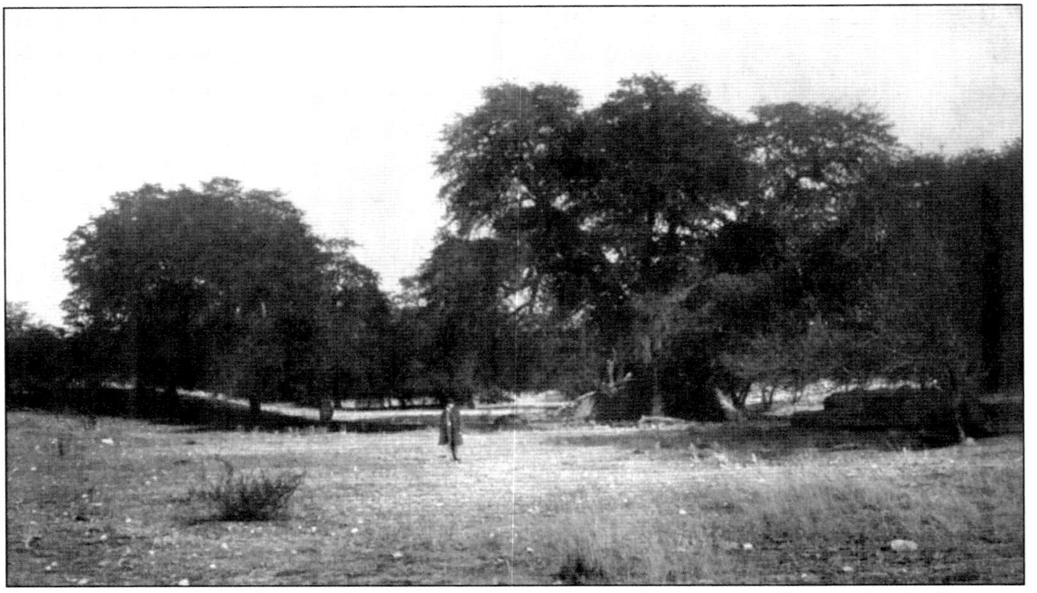

This photograph shows the site of Fort Buchanan in 1919. Established in 1857 at the head of Sonoita Creek, about 30 miles east of Tubac, it provided some protection for the miners and settlers from Patagonia to Calabasas to Tubac and Arivaca. It was abandoned in July 1861 when its supplies (and, alas, its records) were burned and the troops recalled to eastern battlefields.

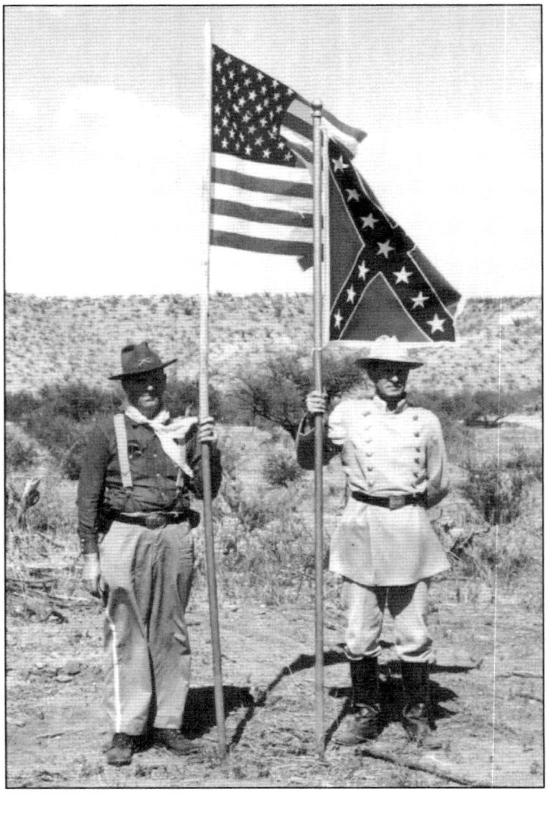

Before the Civil War, Tubac had a population of 300, but the withdrawal of Federal troops from Fort Buchanan left them without protection. Records state that 25 people remaining in Tubac attempted to hold out against a force of 200 Apaches, but they eventually moved to the safety of Tucson. In 1861, Col. John Baylor took possession of Arizona in the name of the Confederate States of America and organized a military government with himself as governor. This photograph shows a 1961 reenactment in Tubac.

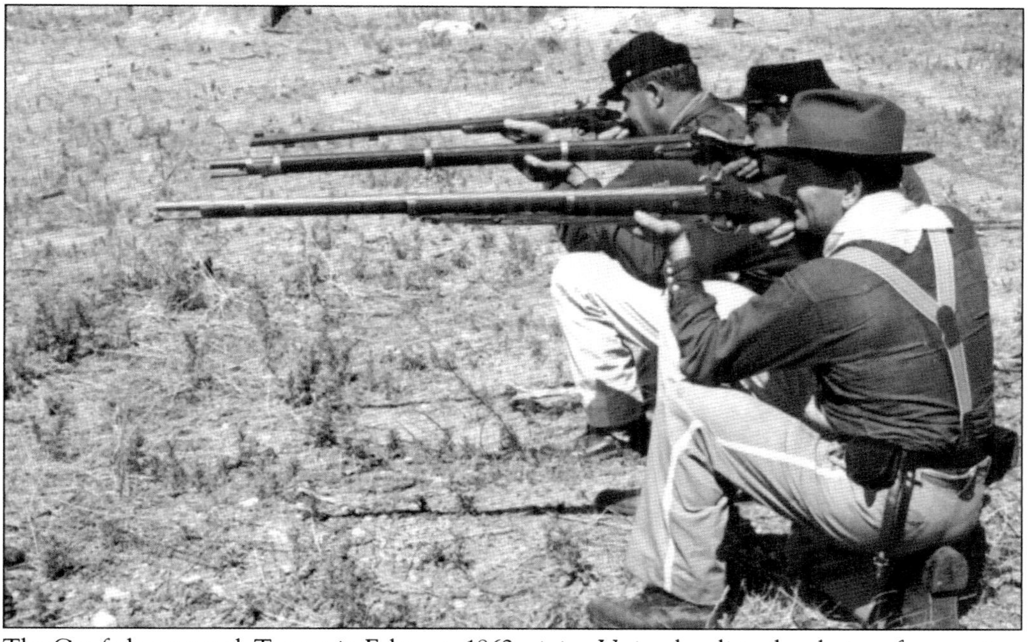

The Confederates took Tucson in February 1862, giving Union loyalists the choice of supporting the South or leaving. Few people remained in the upper Santa Cruz Valley. A detachment of Union troops under the command of Col. James H. Carleton engaged and defeated the Confederate troops at Picacho Peak. Carleton then established Camp Tubac, from which other camps were organized. This is another view of the 1961 reenactment.

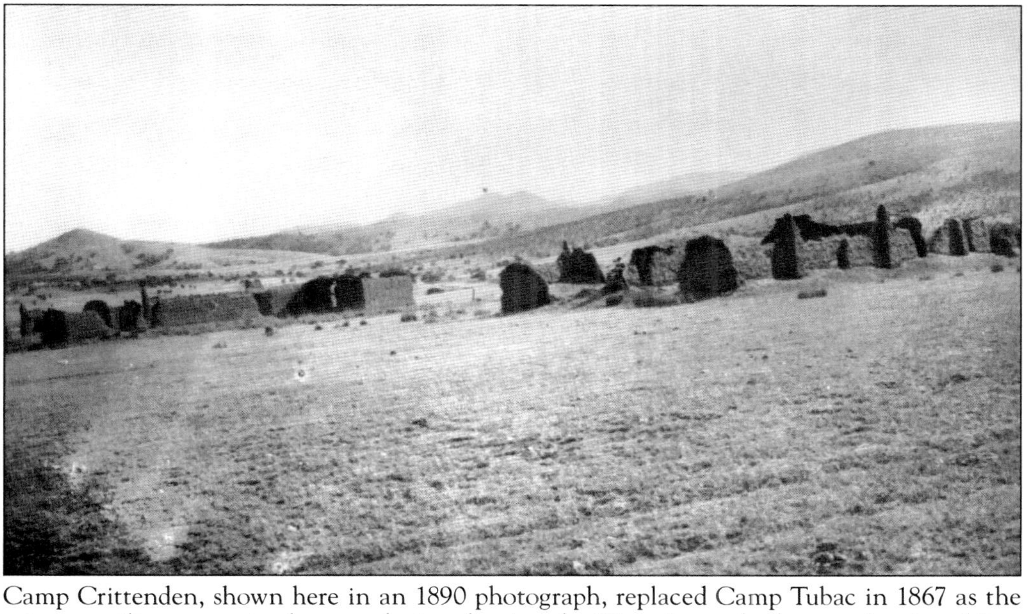

Camp Crittenden, shown here in an 1890 photograph, replaced Camp Tubac in 1867 as the primary military post in the area during the Apache Wars. It was built near the site of Fort Buchanan on Sonoita Creek near present-day Patagonia. The fort was closed in 1873 but four years later was replaced by Fort Huachuca, which continues in operation today as home for the U.S. Army Intelligence Center.

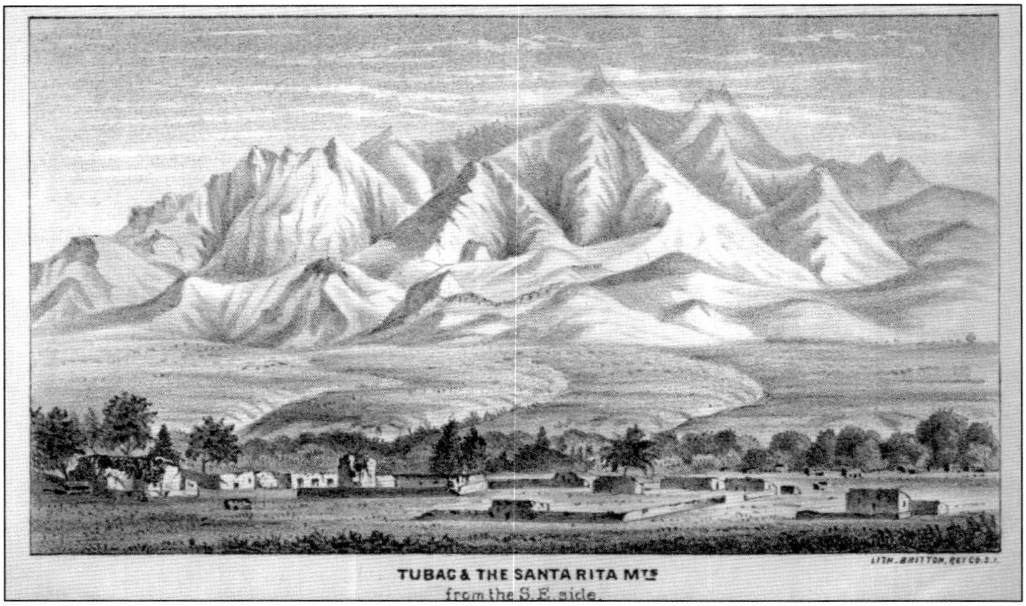

Richard J. Hinton wrote the illustrated *Hand-book to Arizona* in 1878 for "the general public, and especially to the intending prospector, emigrant, traveler, and tourist." Here he shows the peaks of Hopkins and Wrightson towering over the ruined presidio and a number of dilapidated buildings. He wrote lyrically of what we still see today: "The mist is flushed with gold, and the warm purple tints are enchanting."

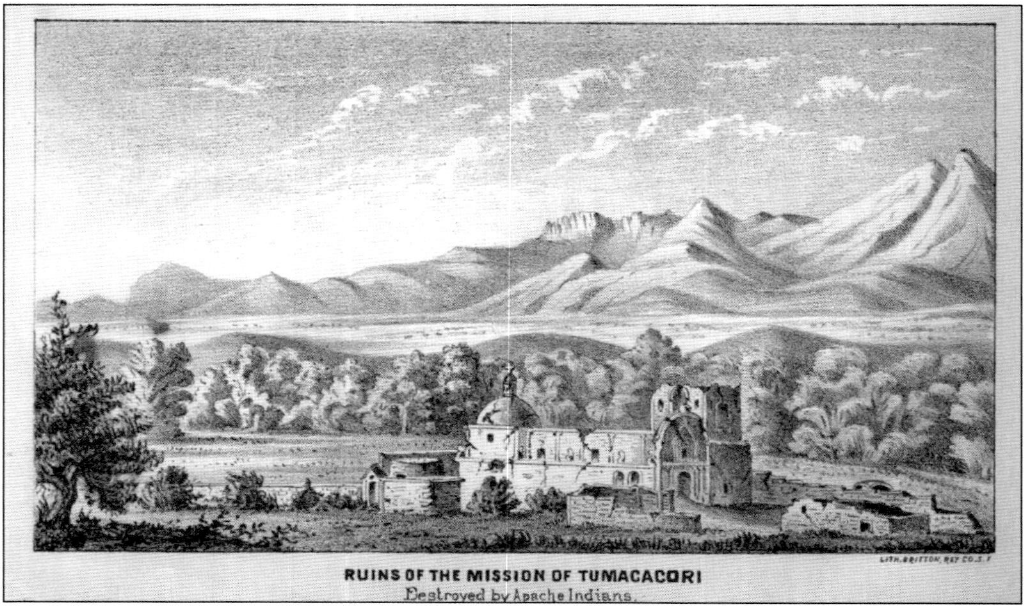

This is Hinton's view of Tumacácori with Elephant Head clearly visible in the background, above the tree-studded Santa Cruz River. He writes of "the lonely beauty everywhere visible, . . . scene[s] of busy life, but of death also, resounding with the harrowing yells of the . . . Apache." Hinton's book encouraged development by providing detailed information on the area's geology, history, mineral resources, climate, and Native American tribes.

A map in Hinton's book shows the Tyndal and Aztec Mining Districts. Camp Crittenden was positioned to protect the numerous gold, silver, and copper mines in the Santa Rita Mountains as well as the mines in the Patagonia Mountains to the south. King's Ranch near Tumacácori (where these mining districts were planned) and Kitchen's Place to the south are still familiar historical sites today.

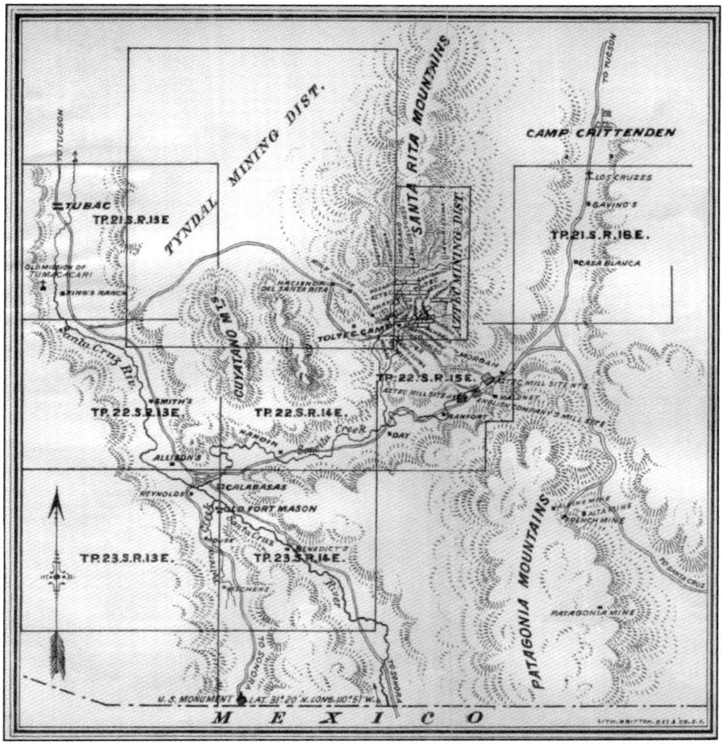

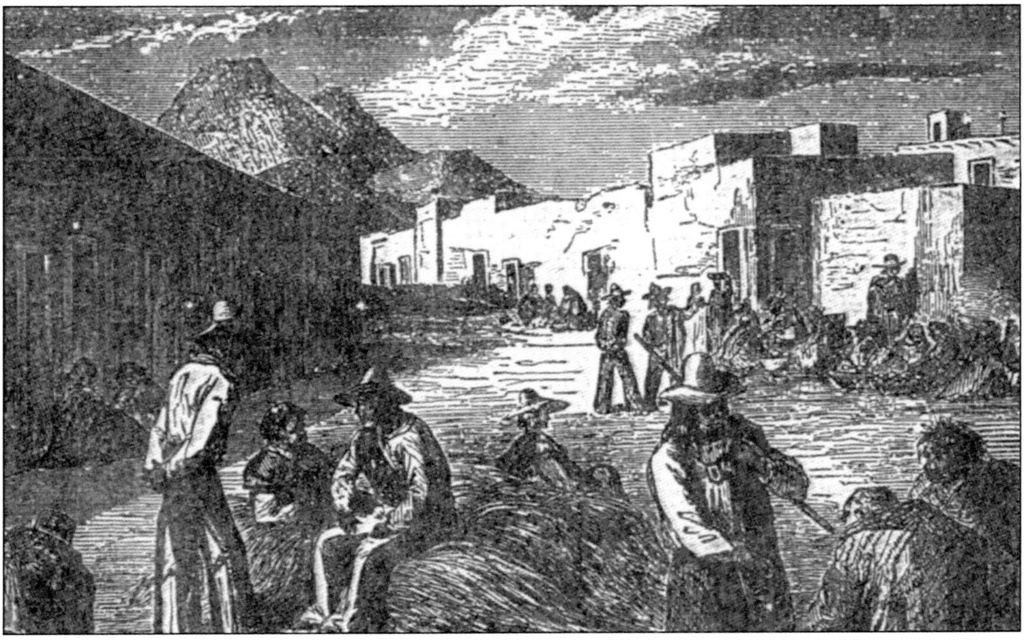

Enoch Conklin's book *Picturesque Arizona* (1878) was published in New York for an East Coast audience. Idealized illustrations like this one of "a street scene of adobe Spanish residences" were used to promote the beauty, fertility, and wealth of the Santa Cruz Valley. The peaks of Hopkins and Wrightson indicate the scene was set in Tubac.

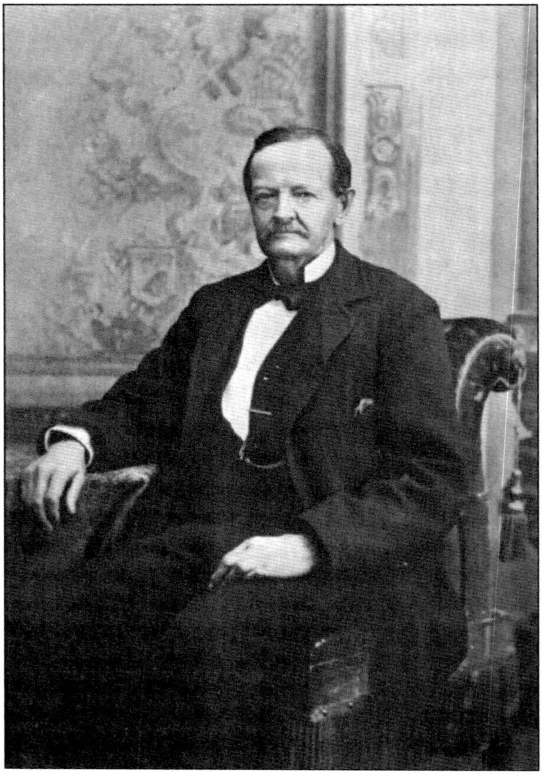

Poston's friend Pete Kitchen arrived in southern Arizona in 1854, setting up a ranching operation to supply beef to army garrisons. Apaches and Sonoran bandits drove out most settlers, but Kitchen's fortified ranch became a haven of security for travelers and area residents alike. In the 1950s, Gil Procter bought it and promoted the area's history and Kitchen's role in it by establishing a museum there.

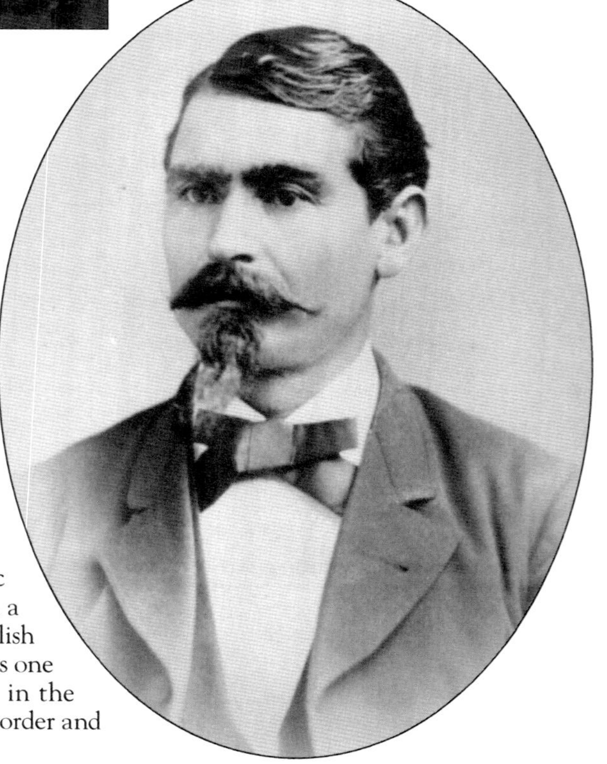

Sabino Otero was born in Tubac, on the land granted in 1789 to his great-grandfather that is now part of the Tubac Golf Resort. A friend of Charles Poston, a generous philanthropist who helped establish St. Mary's Hospital in Tucson, Otero was one of the greatest ranchers and stockmen in the area, owning land on both sides of the border and employing many vaqueros.

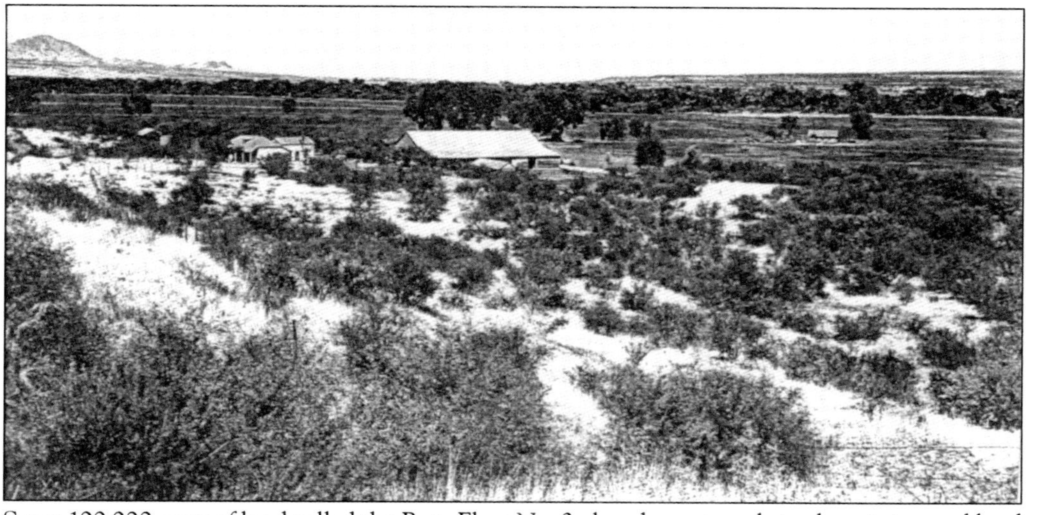

Some 100,000 acres of land called the Baca Float No. 3 played a major role in the mining and land speculation boom of the late 19th century. This 1905 photograph shows the Baca Float Ranch when it was owned by Joseph Wise. A later change in ownership brought about the series of land evictions that tore Tubac apart and temporarily stopped its development. (Cowbelles Museum, Ranchers' Heritage Center.)

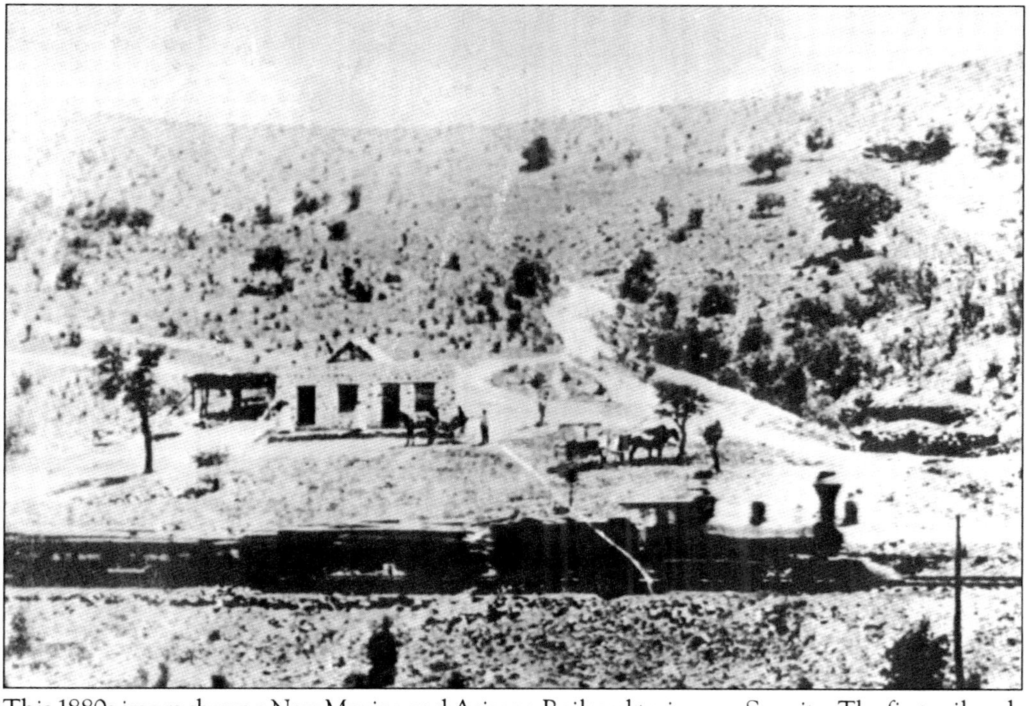

This 1880s image shows a New Mexico and Arizona Railroad train near Sonoita. The first railroads in the area were not extensions of the Southern Pacific line, which reached Tucson in 1880, but instead came from Benson to the east, via Fairbank, Elgin, Patagonia, and Calabasas, linking with a line coming up from Guaymas at Nogales. Calabasas was the closest rail link to Tubac until 1910, when the link from Tucson to Calabasas via Sahuarita was completed.

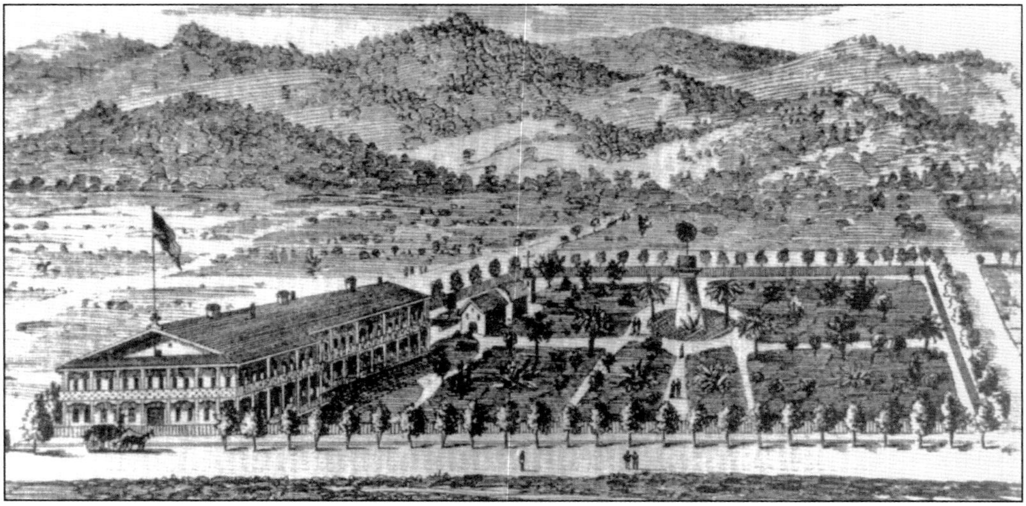

New York promoter Col. Charles Sykes gambled that Calabasas would become a shipping terminal for the nearly completed railroad linking the United States and Mexico. In 1880, he built the Santa Rita Hotel there, hoping it would become a vacation resort. The mining fortune he had made in Central City, Colorado, financed the lavish hotel with extensive gardens, two-story veranda, and running water in each guest room. (Hattie Wilson.)

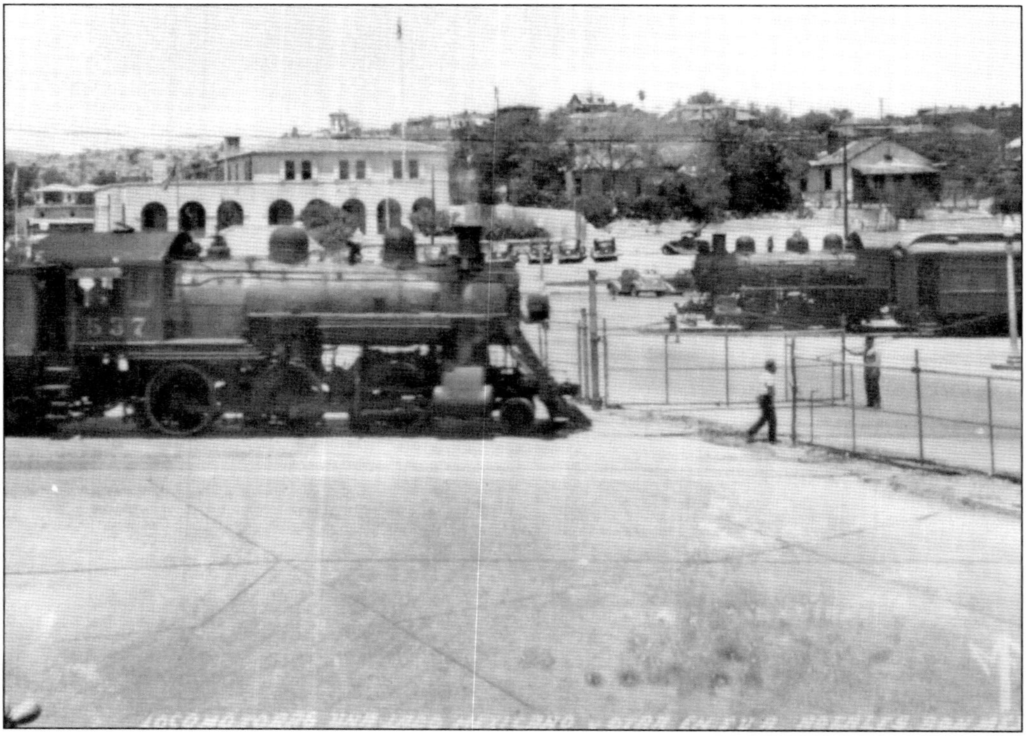

The Atcheson, Topeka, and Santa Fe line from Benson to Nogales via Calabasas was finished in 1882. In Nogales, the line met with the Compania Limitada del Ferrocarril de Sonora (owned and built by the Atchison, Topeka, and Santa Fe), which came north from Guaymas. In this view, two locomotives meet at the border of the United States (right) and Mexico (left). (Hattie Wilson.)

This Victorian cabinet holding 24 bird specimens was delivered from Boston on one of the first trains to Nogales in a crate marked, "Furniture for the grand opening of the Santa Rita Hotel, Calabasas, Arizona Territory." It stood prominently in the lobby for all of the years the hotel existed, then in the homes of Sykes's descendants, and now in the Pimería Alta Historical Society. (Shaw Kinsley.)

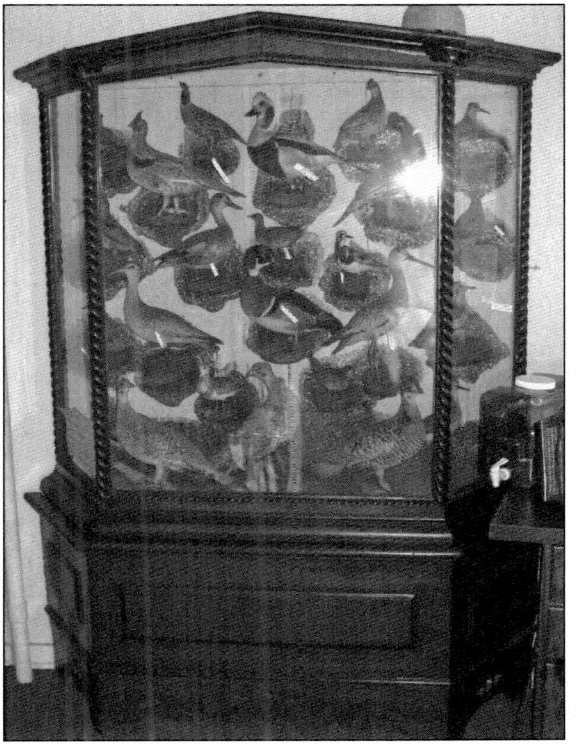

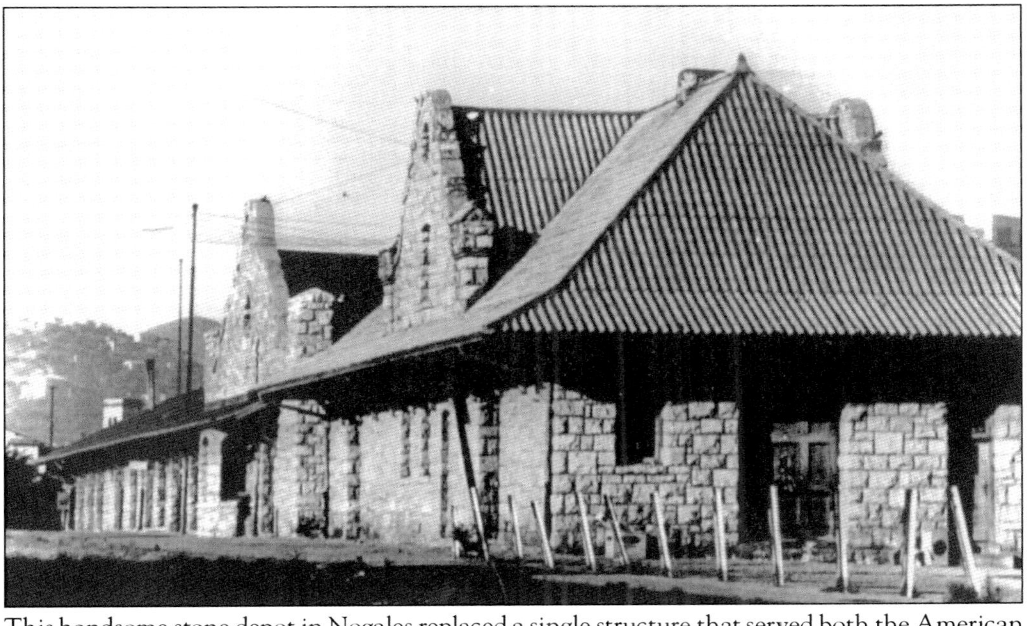

This handsome stone depot in Nogales replaced a single structure that served both the American and Sonoran railroads and straddled the international boundary until an 1898 edict by the United States cleared a 60-foot strip along the border. Both lines were operated by the Santa Fe Railroad. This view, looking south, was taken after 1906, when the station was built. The hillside in the distance is in Sonora. (Hattie Wilson.)

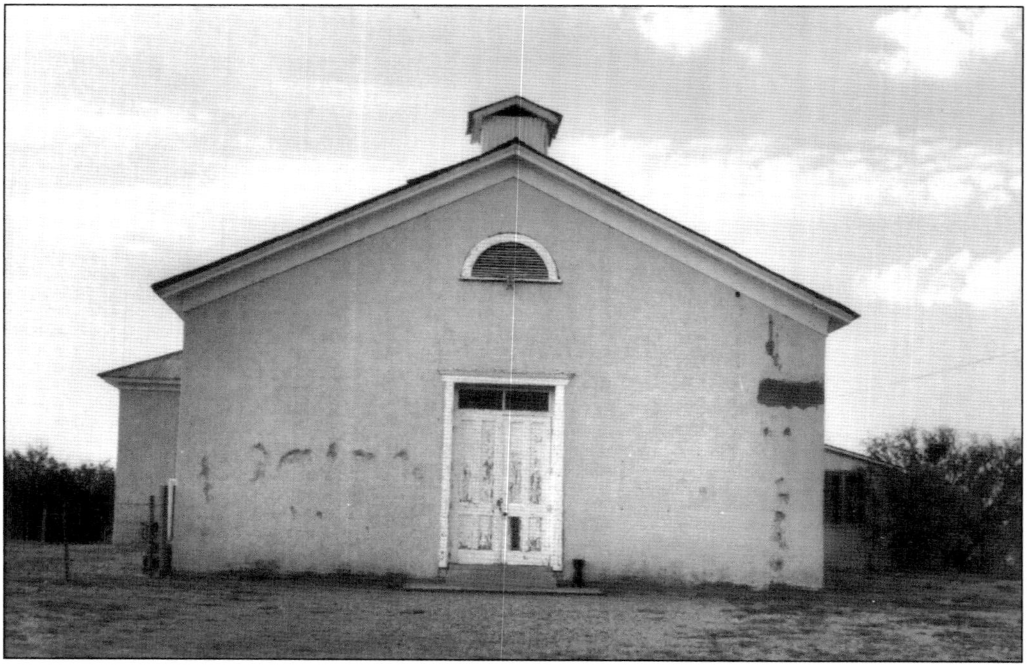

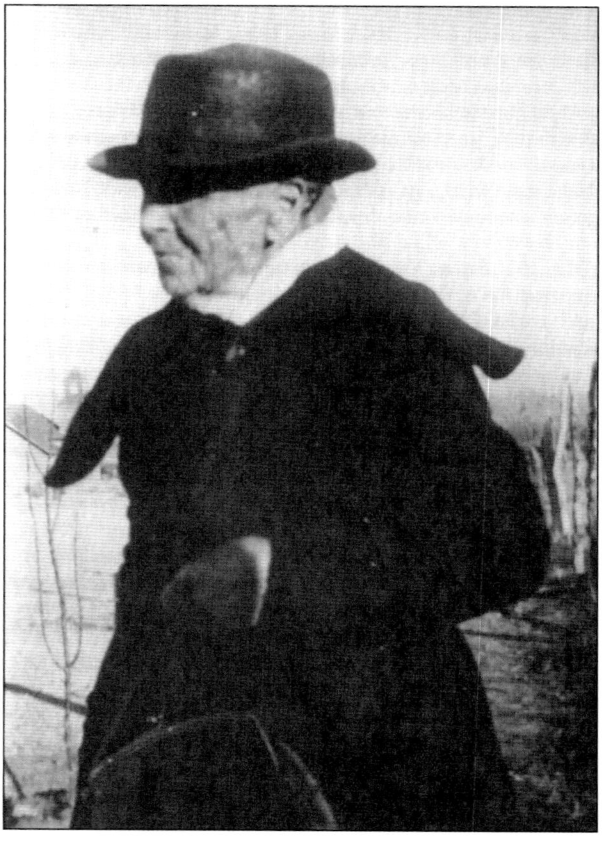

A school district was established in Tubac in 1876, but it didn't get a schoolhouse until 1885, when two distinguished locals, T. Lillie Mercer and Sabino Otero, funded the first one in the state of Arizona. It served the community temporarily as a church and meeting place as well as a school for 80 years, was saved from demolition by the community in 1969, and is now on the Register of Historic Places. (Tubac Presidio State Historic Park.)

Sarah and John Black came to Arizona from Maine by way of California. In 1884, she was teaching school near the Oro Blanco mine, south of Arivaca. When they heard of a teaching job in Tubac, the couple moved to the area. Sarah taught several generations of Tubac children. Before the schoolhouse was built, classes were conducted at one end of Mercer's store. Classes of 40 to 50 pupils received instruction in both English and Spanish from Sarah Black.

From 1914 until 1928, Samuel Beattie was teacher and principal at the Tubac school. His interests in botany and natural history influenced a number of Tubac students, and he is fondly remembered for riding a bicycle around town. Widowed many years before coming to Tubac, he lived in a small adobe structure built in 1910 by Manuel Sinohui and cooked for himself over a wood fire.

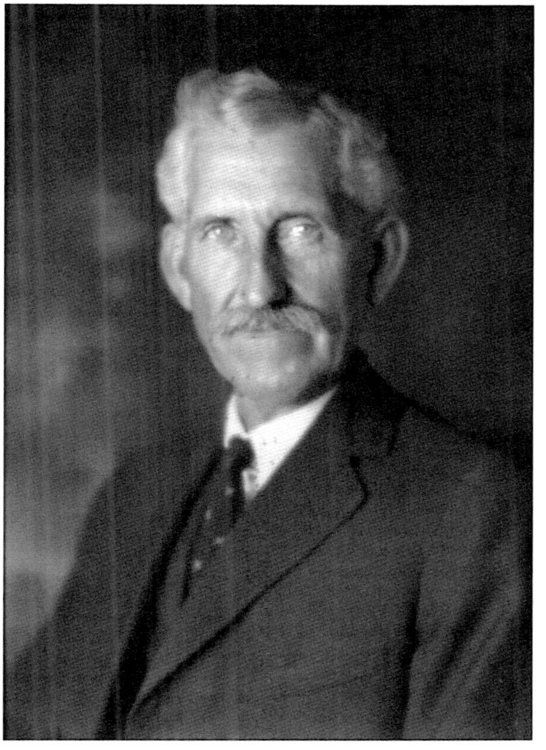

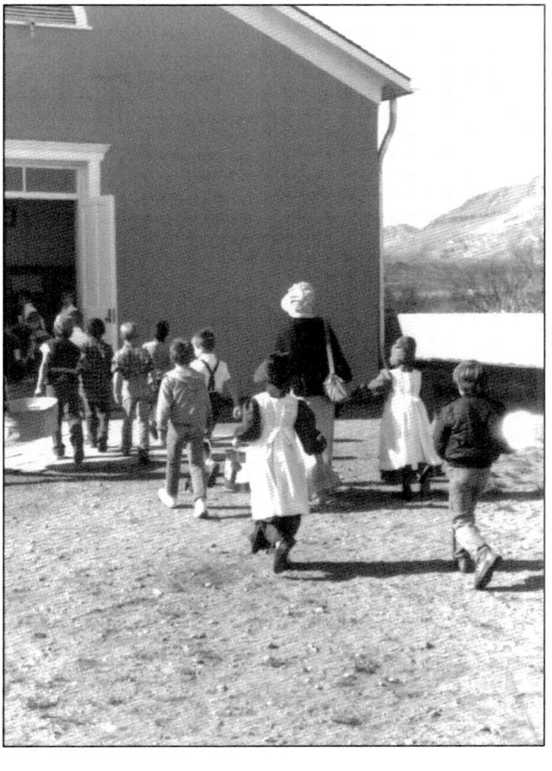

Schoolchildren of the 21st century can experience what education was like in the territorial period through "reenactment" field trips to the Tubac 1885 schoolhouse. In this photograph, park rangers, teachers, and students dress in period costumes and wear the names of students enrolled during the school's first years. Sarah M. Black taught several generations of Tubac children and received one of the first Arizona teacher's pensions. (Tubac Presidio State Historic Park.)

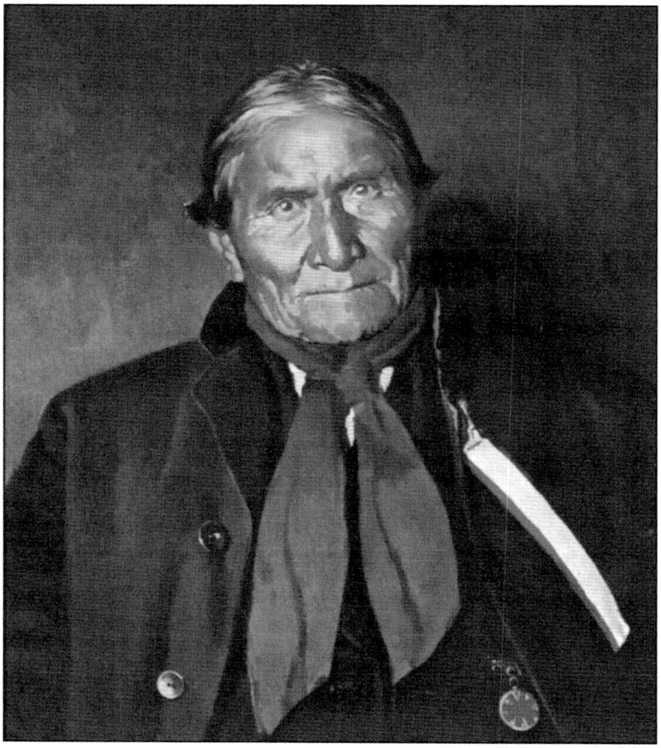

Geronimo staged one of his last raids on April 27, 1886, at Peck Canyon just south of Tubac. This humanistic depiction of the famous Chiricauhua Apache leader was painted by artist Francis Beaugureau, noted for his western landscapes and genre scenes and a series of 12 oil paintings of military operations in Arizona. Beaugureau lived in Tubac from 1973 until the late 1980s.

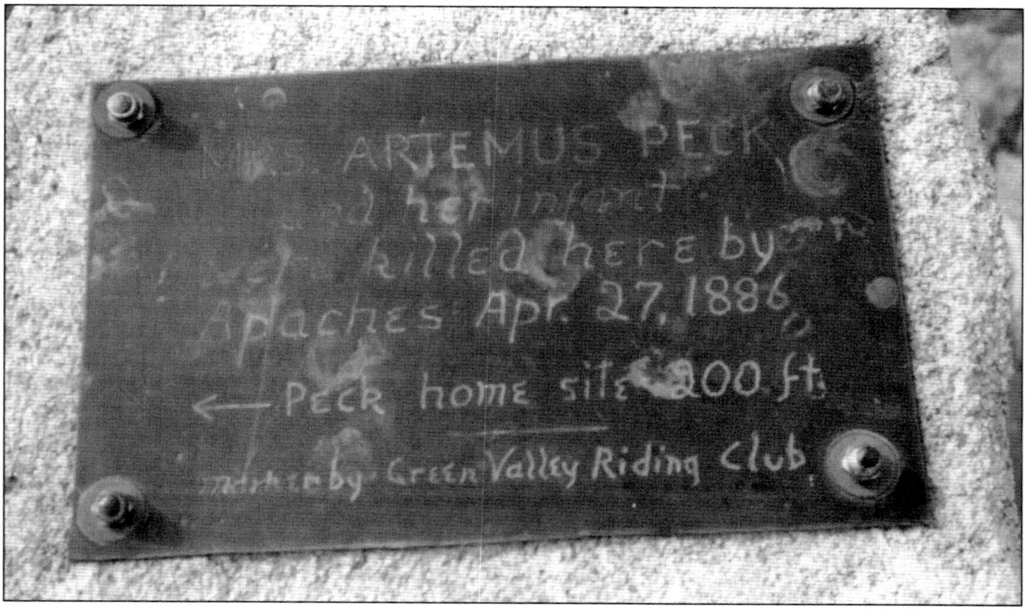

Although today a plaque marks the site of the so-called Peck Ranch Massacre of 1886, no one can confirm what really took place that day. Reports of atrocities committed by Geronimo's warriors against Petra Peck, her son, and her young niece were contradicted by eyewitnesses. Anti-Apache hysteria was being fueled by the popular press at a time when the Apaches fought a losing battle against the inexorable expansion of settlements, the U.S. military, and ranching interests.

Capt. Thomas Lebo left Calabasas with K Troop of the 10th Cavalry (a unit comprised of black soldiers) in pursuit of Geronimo and his followers after the Peck massacre. After a chase over brutally harsh terrain, the Apaches occupied an impregnable cliff top. Lebo was forced to withdraw until reinforcements arrived and eventually lost the trail after five days of searching the area. The Apache Wars continued until August 1886, when Geronimo surrendered to Gen. Nelson Miles.

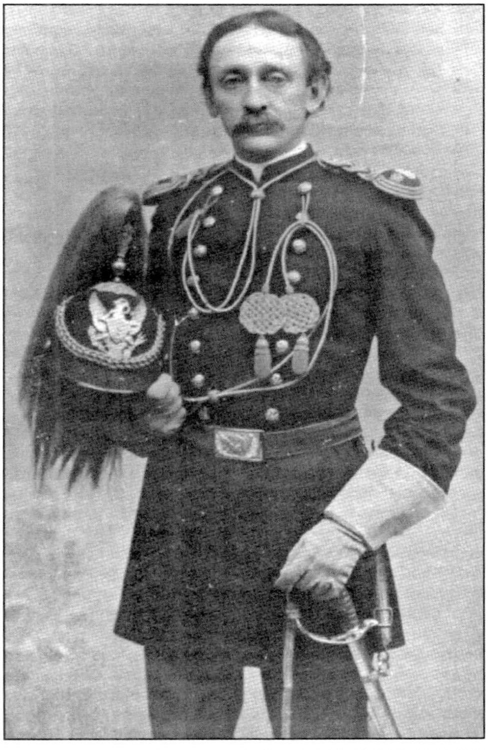

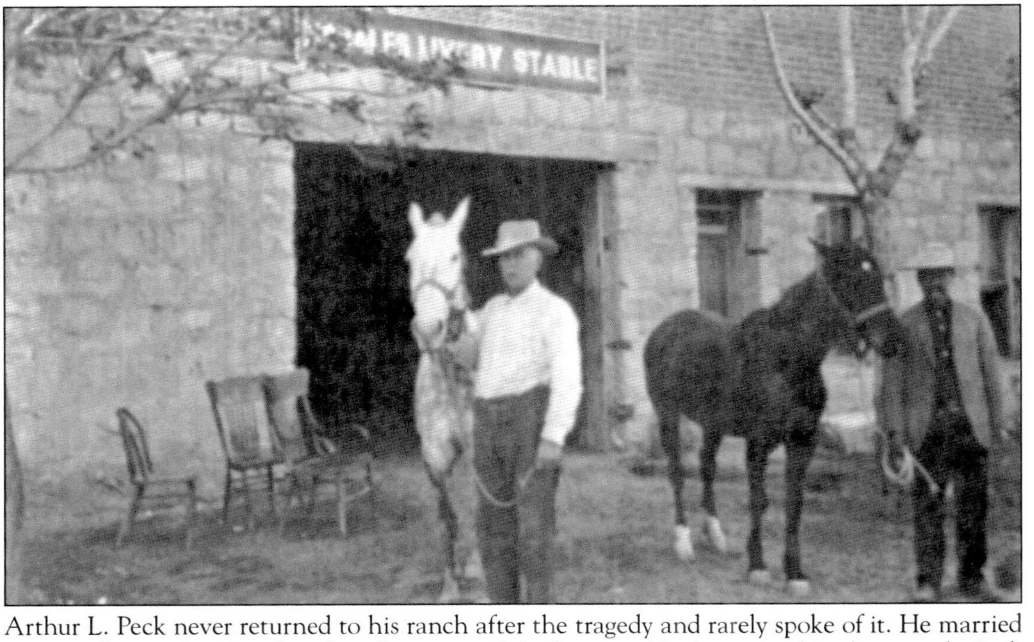

Arthur L. Peck never returned to his ranch after the tragedy and rarely spoke of it. He married again and moved to Nogales where he operated the livery stable shown in this photograph. Peck served as a member of the city council and, after Santa Cruz County was created in 1899, was a member of the board of supervisors. He lived to the age of 94 and died in 1939. (Pimería Alta Historical Society.)

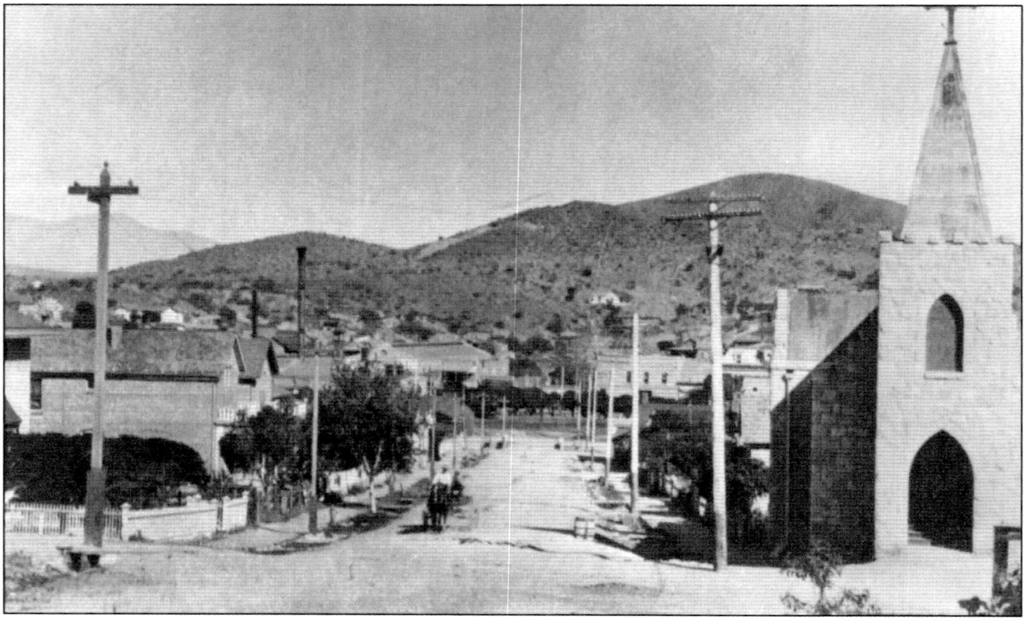

This view of a sleepy street in Nogales, Arizona, gives no hint of the armed battle of the Mexican Revolution fought near here on March 13, 1913. The fighting between Revolutionists and the Rurales was heard on Crawford Street, shown here with St. Andrew's Episcopal Church on the right. Curious spectators including Harriet Garrett from Tubac looked on, and several civilians and one soldier were injured by gunfire. When Interstate 19 was built, the church was demolished and a new St. Andrew's was built on Country Club Drive. (Pimería Alta Historical Society.)

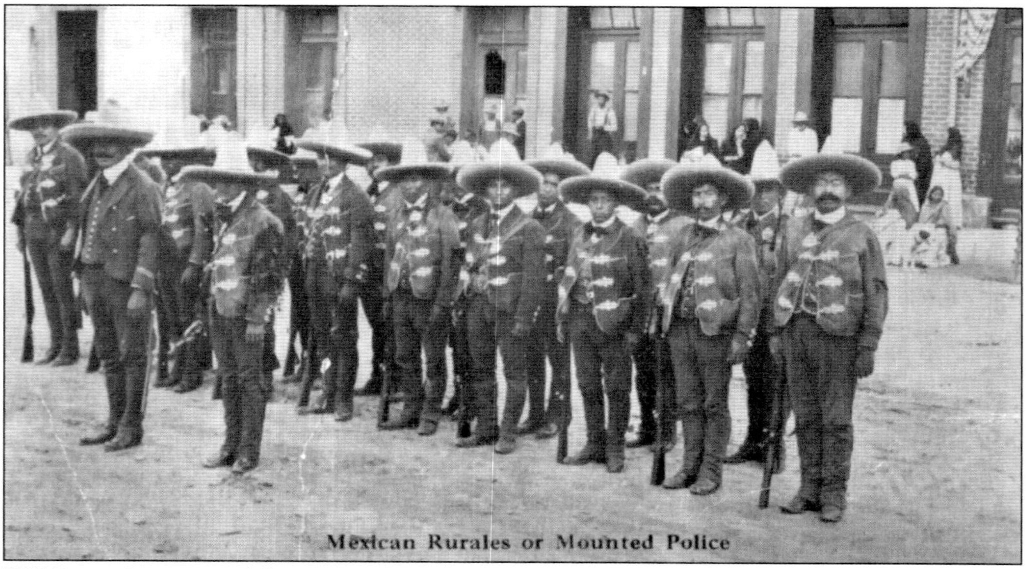

Will Rogers Jr. presented this vintage photograph of the Mexican frontier guard known as the Rurales to the Tubac Historical Society in the 1970s. Under the command of Col. Emilio Kosterlitzky, the unit firmly and sometimes brutally put down disorder in the first two decades of the 20th century. The photograph shows the heavily armed Rurales in their sun-shielding sombreros and distinctive silver-trimmed gray uniforms carrying sabers, carbines, and pistols.

Russian-born Emilio Kosterlitzky joined the Mexican army in its fight against the Apaches. While he was stationed on the border, he dealt frequently with U.S. troops who called him the "Mexican Cossack." During the Mexican Revolution, he was captured by revolutionaries and imprisoned until 1914, when he and his family were permitted to immigrate to the United States. This studio photograph shows the colonel and his young family in earlier, more peaceful days. (Pimería Alta Historical Society.)

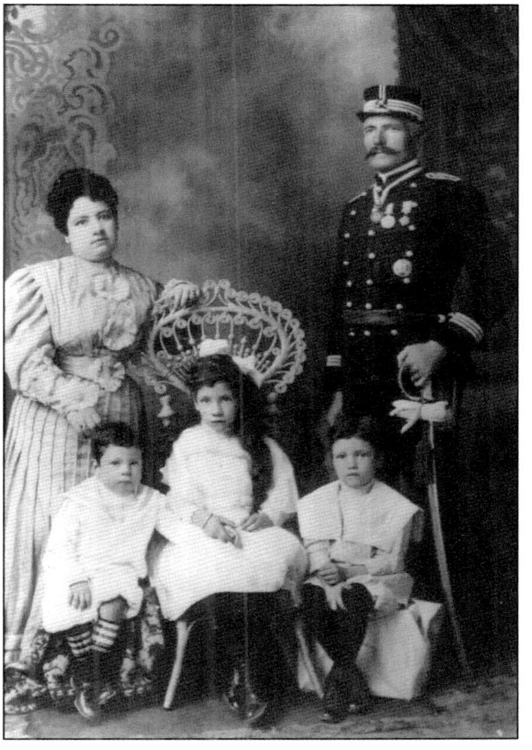

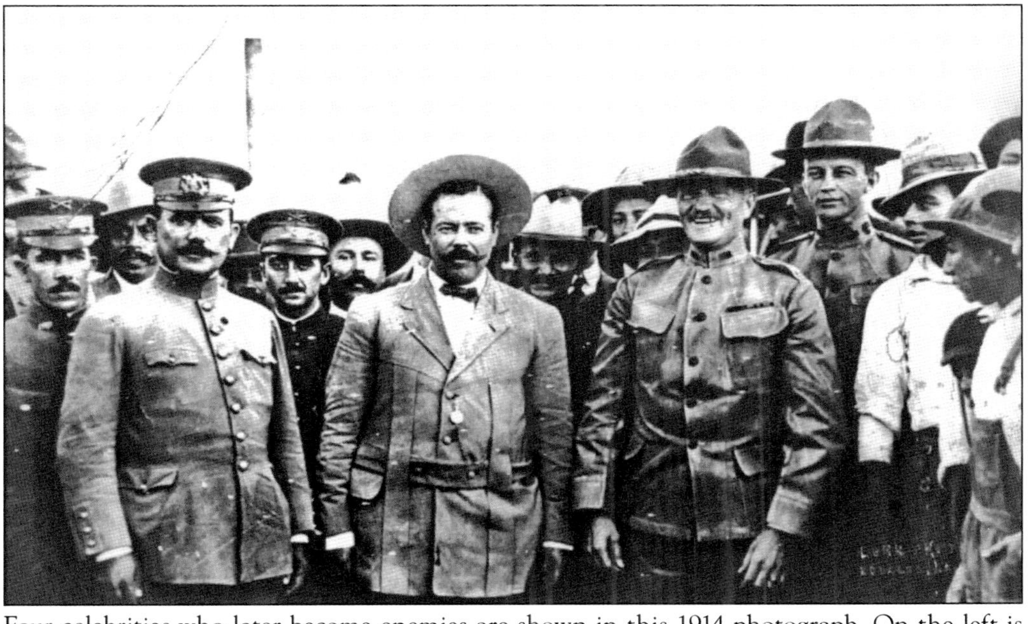

Four celebrities who later became enemies are shown in this 1914 photograph. On the left is Mexican general Alvaro Obregon, who in 1920 became president of Mexico. Next to him is a hero of the Mexican Revolution, Francisco "Pancho" Villa, assassinated in 1923. To the right of Villa is Gen. John J. Pershing and to Pershing's right is Lt. George Patton, who both later unsuccessfully attempted to capture Villa and stop his destructive raids on U.S. border towns.

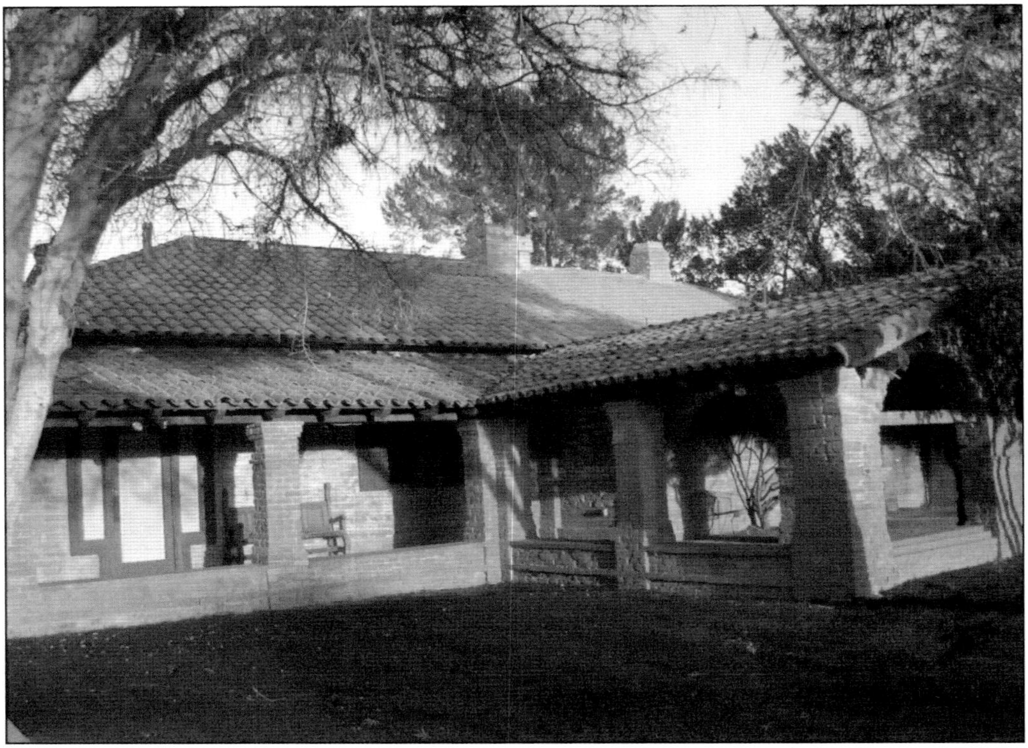

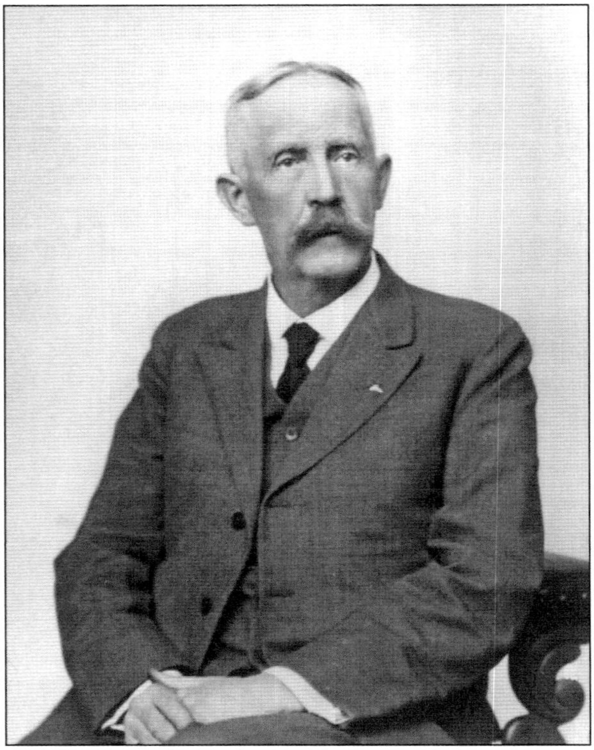

The Otero family has been in Tubac since at least 1789, when they were given a grant of land by the Spanish crown. With relations on both sides of the border, many Sonoran Oteros moved to the safety of Tubac during the Mexican Revolution. The main hacienda of the Otero Ranch (above) was built around 1912 to accommodate the newcomers. (Shaw Kinsley.)

Capt. Leander W. Mix was the first fire chief of Nogales in 1895 and later became its mayor. He was successful in efforts to have a battleship of the U.S. Navy named for the 48th state. The USS *Arizona* was commissioned in 1916 and along with much of the U.S. Pacific Fleet was sunk in Pearl Harbor by Japanese aerial attacks on December 7, 1941. Prominent Tubac citizens Judy England and Jean England Neubauer are direct descendants of Mix. (Pimería Alta Historical Society.)

Three

Agricultural Tubac

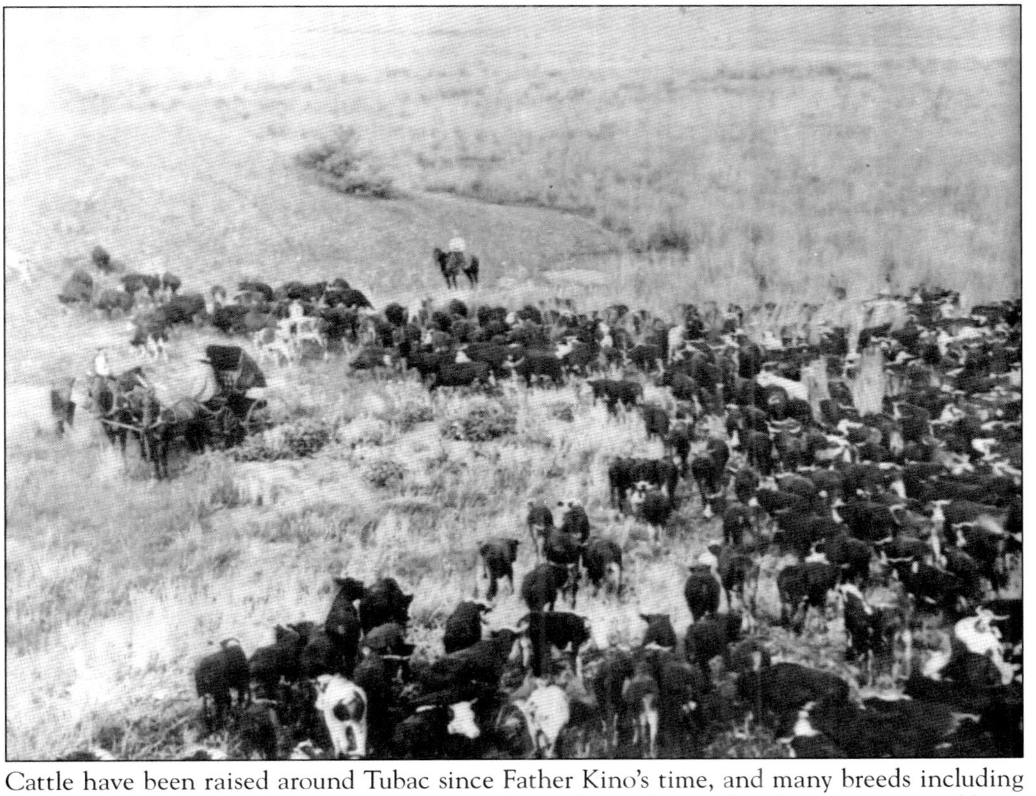

Cattle have been raised around Tubac since Father Kino's time, and many breeds including Hereford, Charolais, Brahman, Angus, Santa Gertrudis, and Texas longhorn have grazed here. After Juan Bautista de Anza's expeditions passed through, remnants of his herds continued to roam wild. Once ranching began, everyone's cattle ran loose in the valley, changing the landscape for decades to come. Round-ups were cooperative affairs shared by the Sopori, Arivaca, Otero, Gastelum, Salcido, Trujillo, Alegria, Megariz, Casanega, Canoa, Calabasas, and Garrett cowboys. This photograph shows a herd of yearling steers headed for market in the 1920s.

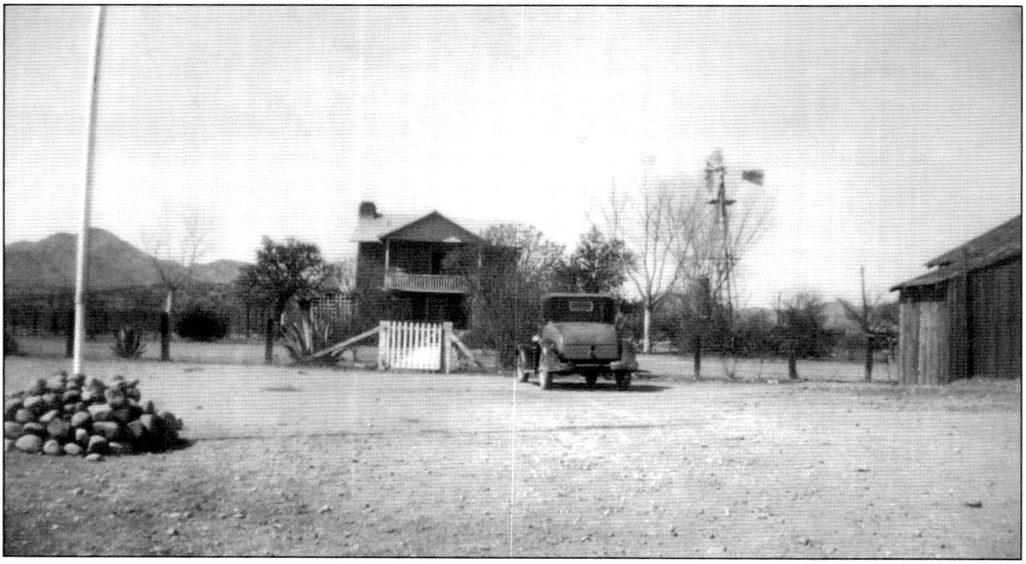

The Garrett family arrived from Knickerbocker, Texas, in 1913, making all of modern Tubac their cattle ranch, from Burruel Street west to the Tumacácori Mountains and from Tubac Road north to where the Golf Resort is now. The headquarters of their ranch, as seen in this 1932 photograph, was the first two-story house between Tucson and Nogales. Built of sun-dried adobe bricks made by Pedro Salcido and his family, it had dressed lumber floors and a second-floor sleeping porch for hot summer nights.

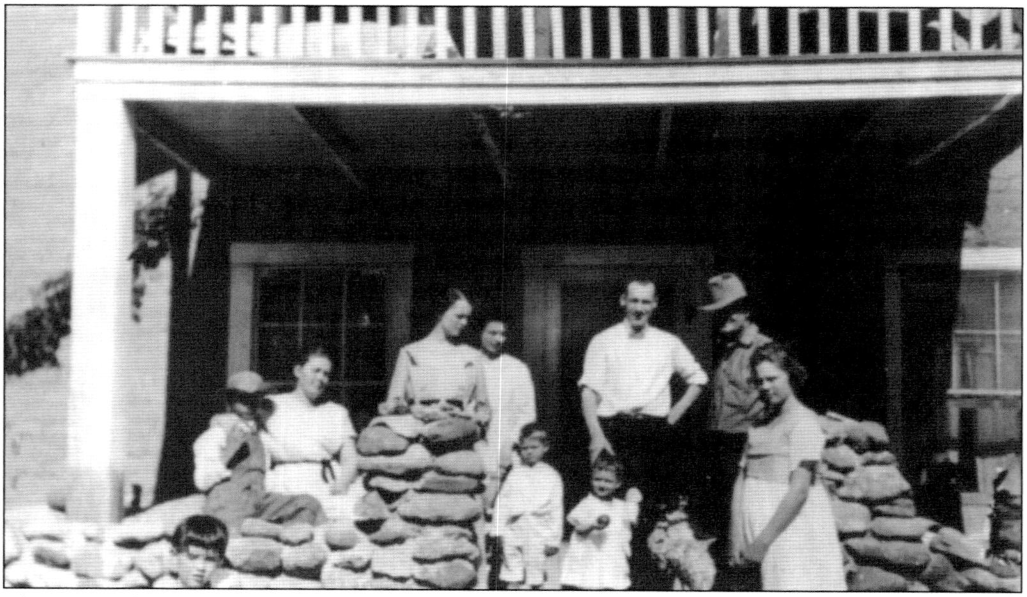

The Garret family welcomes visitors Mr. and Mrs. Beal and their children in the shady entrance to their home in 1918. Daughter-in-law Lillian Garrett later wrote, "Mother Garrett never knew how many there would be for any meal; the table was always ready. Every morning she baked biscuits, cooked meat, gravy, hot cereal, hot cakes, eggs, and coffee." Seven Garrett children—Pauline, Jessie, Marcella, Jim, Stan, Jim Thomas, and John—attended the Tubac school.

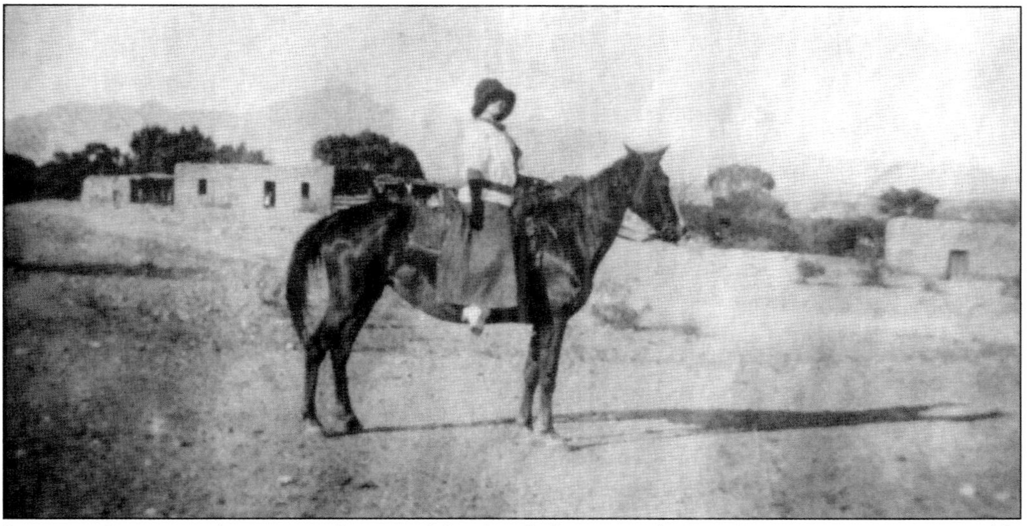

Beatrice Garrett is shown astride one of the family horses with San Cayetano Mountain visible in the distance. The long adobe structure on the right served as the Garretts' first home and storeroom. (Hattie Wilson.)

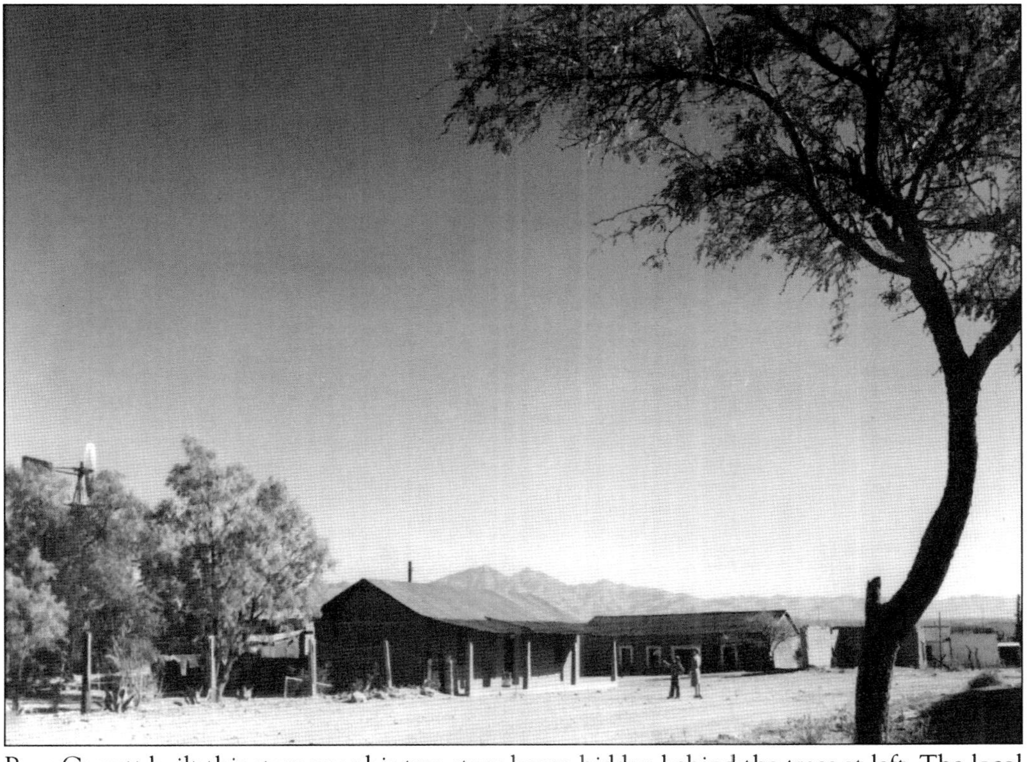

Papa Garrett built this store near his two-story house hidden behind the trees at left. The local community relied on the store for Levis, shirts, hats, and boots for men, women, and children; for lariats, spurs, and bridles for cowboys; and for miners' tools and tobacco. It also sold fabric, thread, and buttons and candy that came in wooden buckets shipped by train from Tucson.

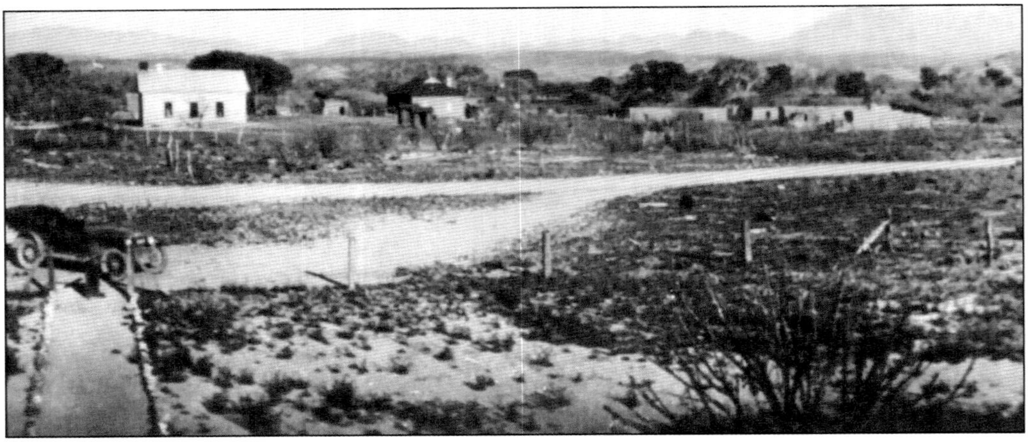

Looking east from the second floor of the Garretts' house, this 1917 photograph shows Tubac's original 1885 schoolhouse with its two privies at right. Newly completed Otero Hall, where the younger children were taught, is beyond the privies to the right. The main road between Tucson and Nogales (now Burruel Street) runs across the middle of the view. The buildings at right were part of a complex of apartments for teachers called the "teacherage."

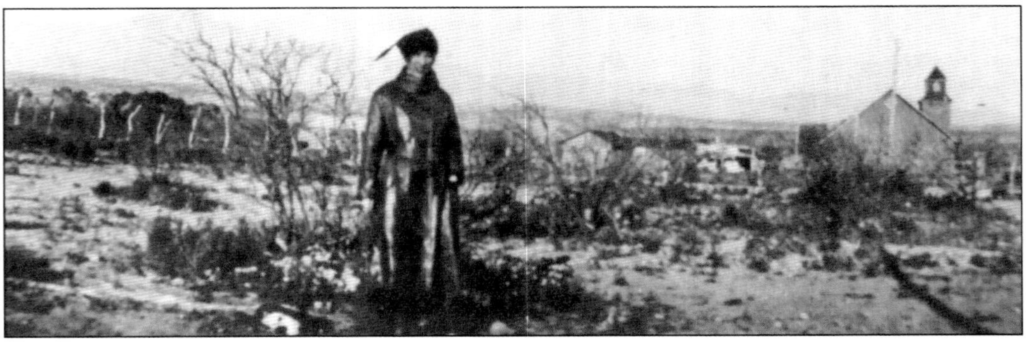

The identity of this woman wearing a stylish hat is unknown, but clearly visible in the distance is St. Ann's Church and tower, completed in 1917 and shown here before it received a coating of stucco. No one knows who the builder was or why the Tyrolean architectural style was chosen.

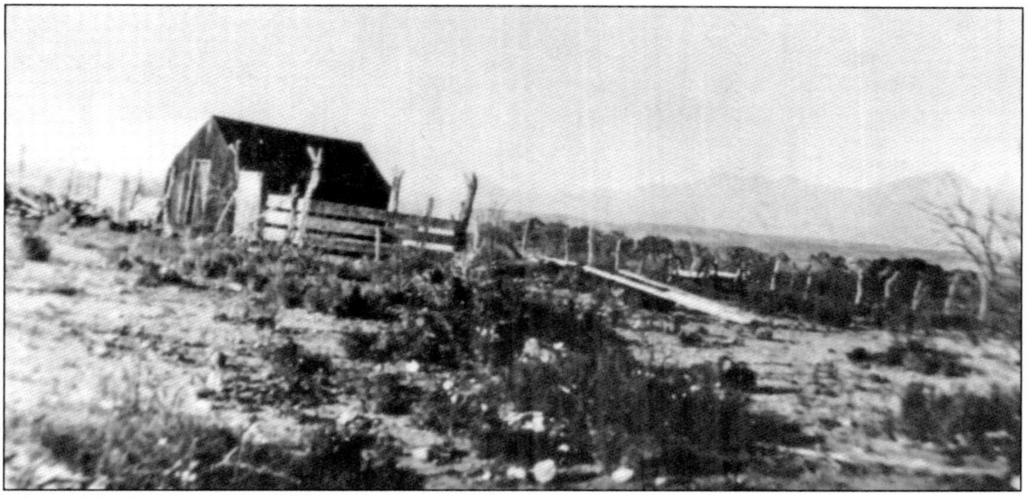

This adobe barn and corral belonged to Bird Yoas, who had a cattle ranch near Agua Caliente Canyon east of Tubac. It was used by the Garretts for the Guernsey cows they brought from Texas. The thick growths of cottonwoods beyond the corral attest to the vitality of the Santa Cruz River at this time. Faintly visible in the distance are the Santa Rita Mountains.

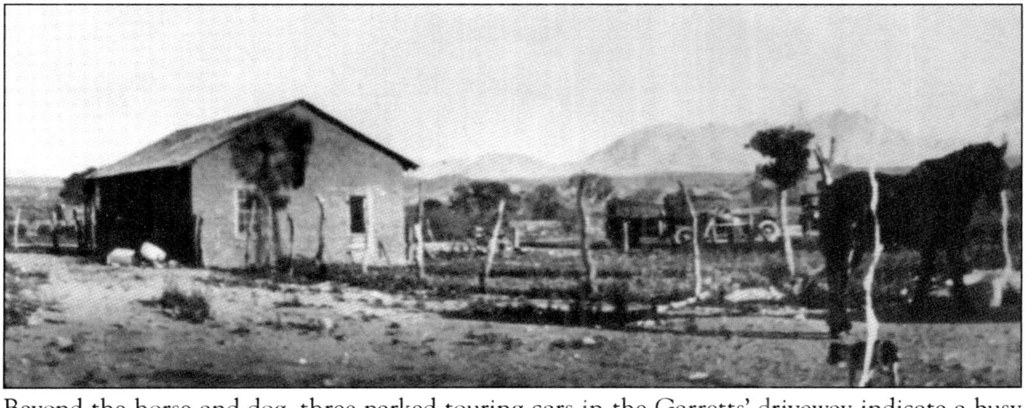

Beyond the horse and dog, three parked touring cars in the Garretts' driveway indicate a busy day at the ranch. From 1926 to 1929, the old Garrett Store was also used by the U.S. Immigration Service as a headquarters for the newly established Border Patrol.

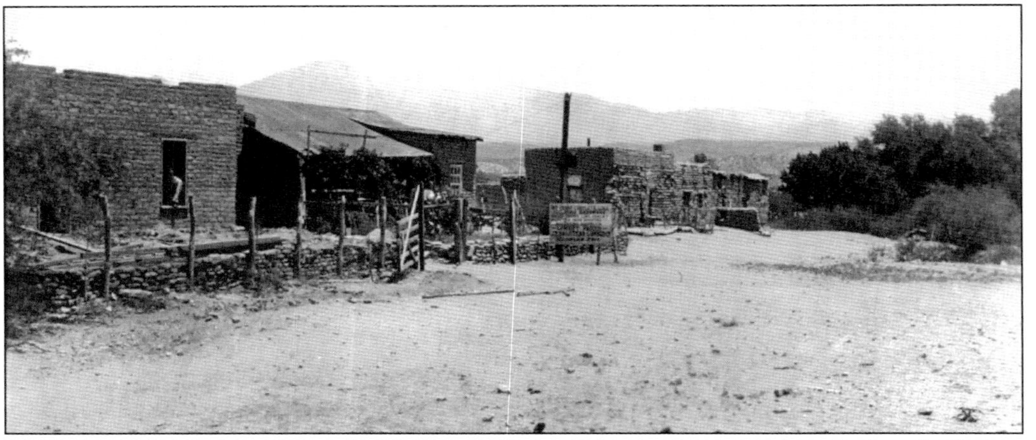

This view looking east on River Road (now Calle Iglesia) was taken in 1915 by Robert H. Forbes, Larcena Pennington's son-in-law. It shows Tubac's post office at the far left, as well as the Lowe family residence and an early structure thought to have been built by Charles Poston in the late 1850s. Evidence of local commercial enterprise is visible in the advertising sign for the J. D. Halstead Lumber Company of Nogales. (Tubac Presidio State Historic Park.)

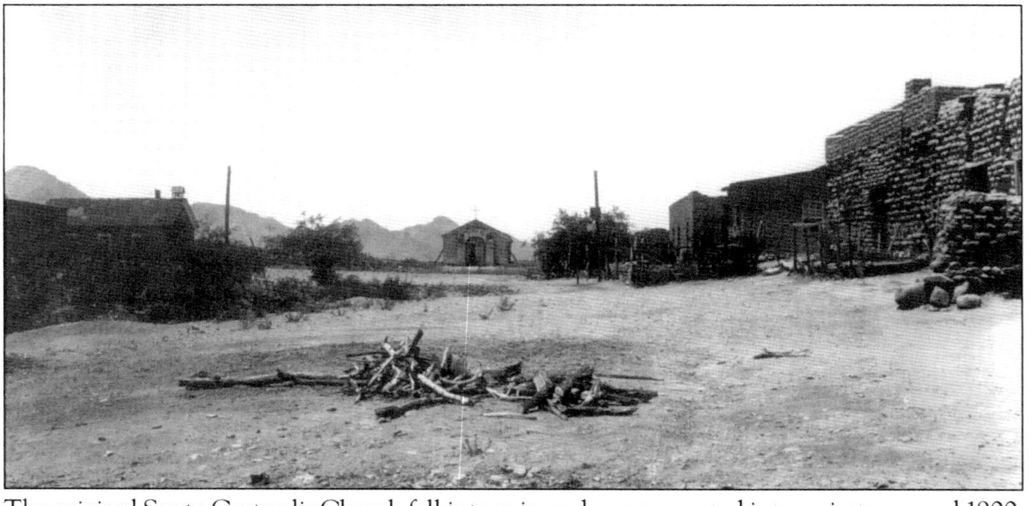

The original Santa Gertrudis Church fell into ruin and was converted into a pigsty around 1900. A new church was built in 1912, but winter storms soon damaged the adobe structure. This 1915 photograph by Robert Forbes looks west on River Road to the Tumacácori Mountains, showing the Poston and Lowe houses and post office. Storm-damaged church walls and schoolhouse roof are clearly visible. (Tubac Presidio State Historic Park.)

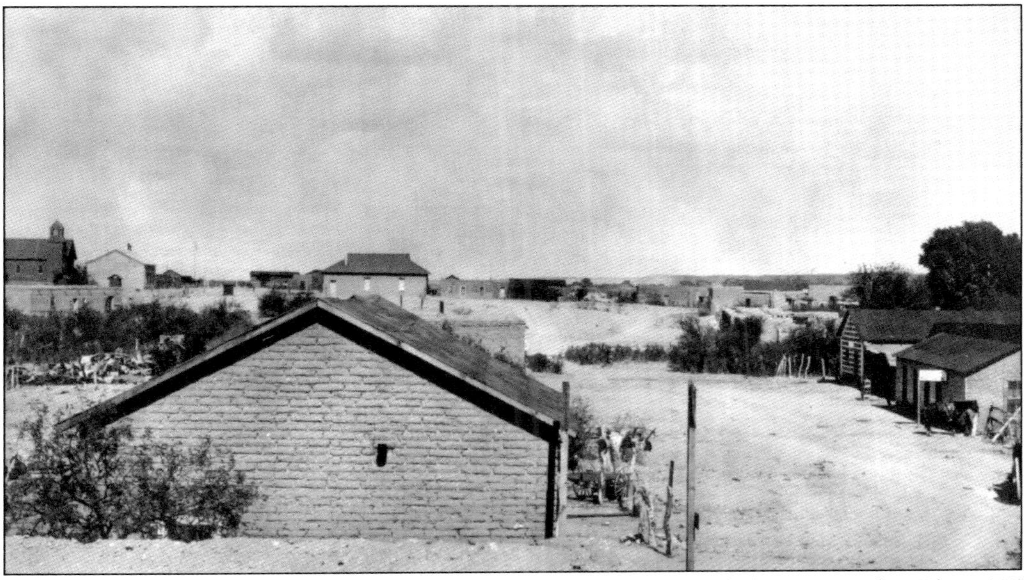

Before 1920, Tubac's commercial area was located to the southeast of where it is today. This 1915 image shows the old road from Tumacácori lined with buildings, including Luis Lim's grocery store and the residence of Tubac's midwife. The 1885 schoolhouse and St. Ann's Church are visible beyond the roof of the cantina in the foreground. (Tubac Presidio State Historic Park.)

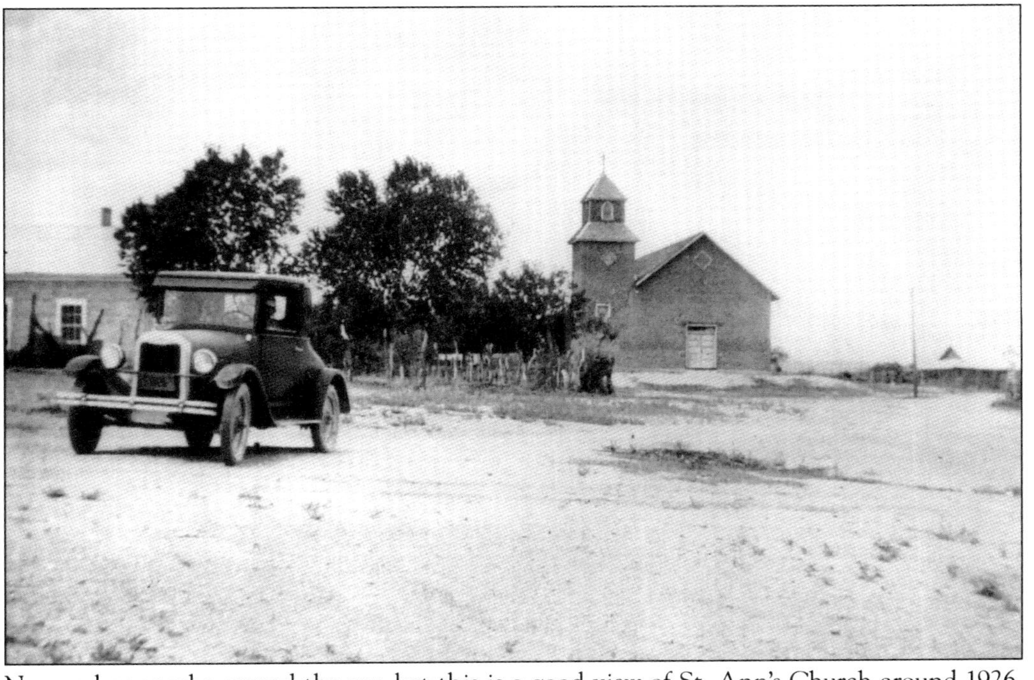

No one knows who owned the car, but this is a good view of St. Ann's Church around 1926. Construction was begun in 1916 and supposedly finished by 1917 for the baptism of Bennie Lowe. Structural problems are already evident in the building before it received its stucco coating in 1929. (Tubac Presidio State Historic Park.)

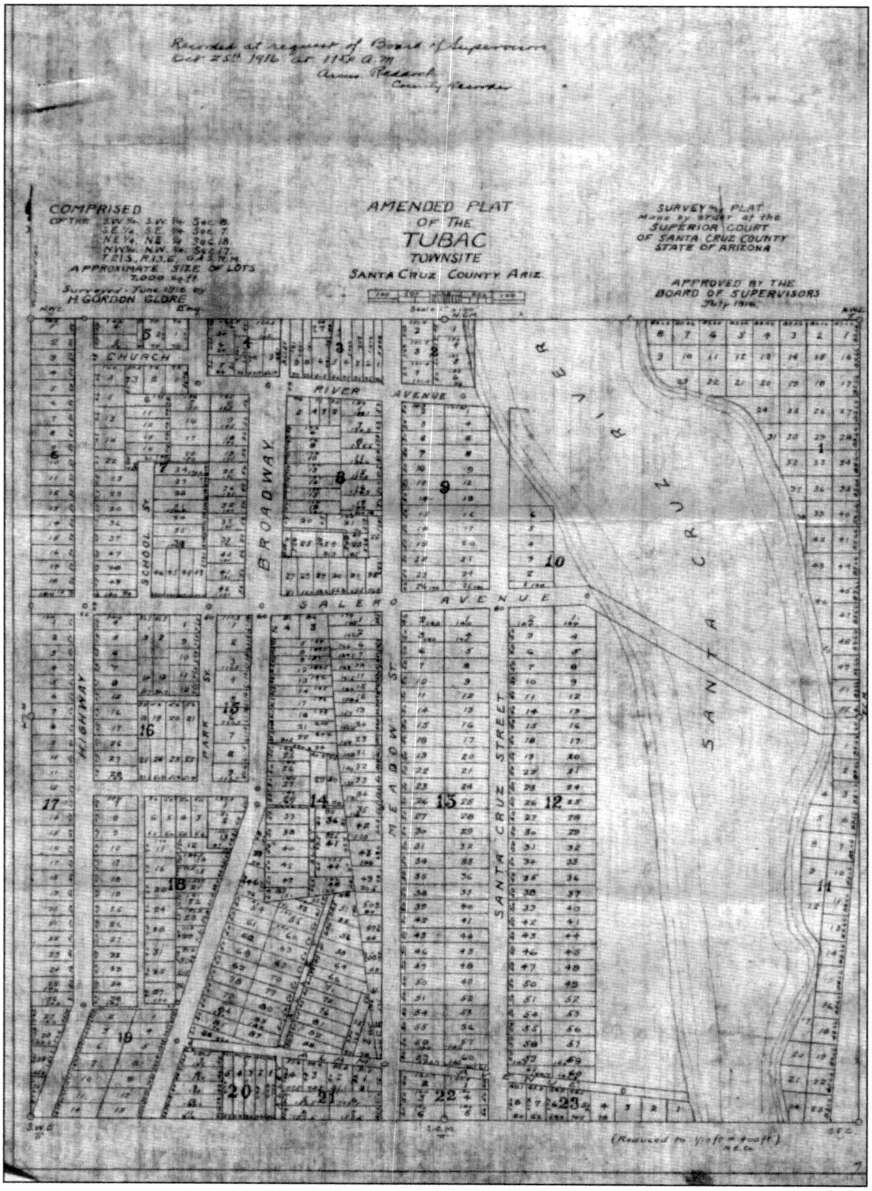

The story of the parcel of land called the Baca Float No. 3 is complex, full of legal maneuvering and heartbreak. One of five 100,000-acre grants originally awarded to the family of Luis Maria Baca of New Mexico, it stretched from what is now the southern boundary of the state park all the way to Nogales, completely encompassing what is now Rio Rico. Claims to the land were purchased by second parties, and subsequent litigation raged for decades; ultimately the U.S. Supreme Court awarded the land to speculators, and in 1918, families that had fought for it, farmed it, and lived on it for generations were forcibly evicted. The amended plat of Tubac showed here projected an investor's dream of hundreds of building lots on new streets. If realized, this expansion would have completely destroyed archaeological sites in the state park and the current Archaeological Preserve. The Baca Float decision serendipitously (and unknowingly) stopped the development and preserved much of Tubac's history for future generations.

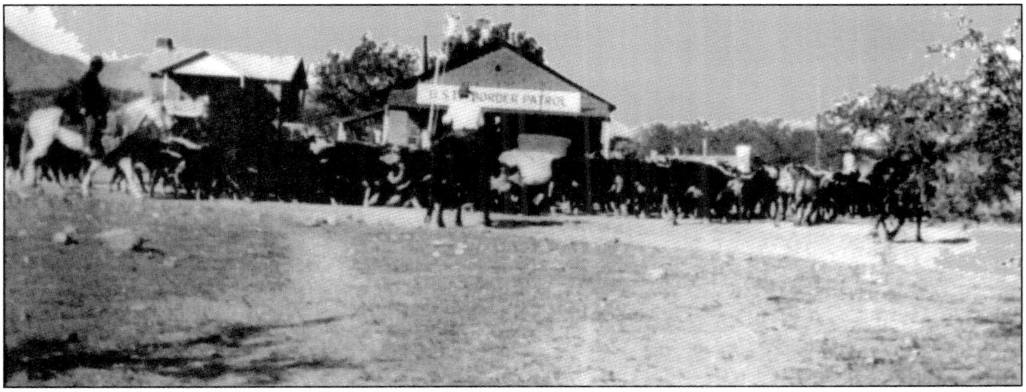

The Baca Float decision caused the Garretts to lose a store and some of their cattle land, although their two-story house and former store were outside the affected area. This undated photograph shows cowboys moving a herd of cattle north on the main road to Tucson (now Burruel Street), off the Baca Float lands, past the old store, and into what is today modern Tubac.

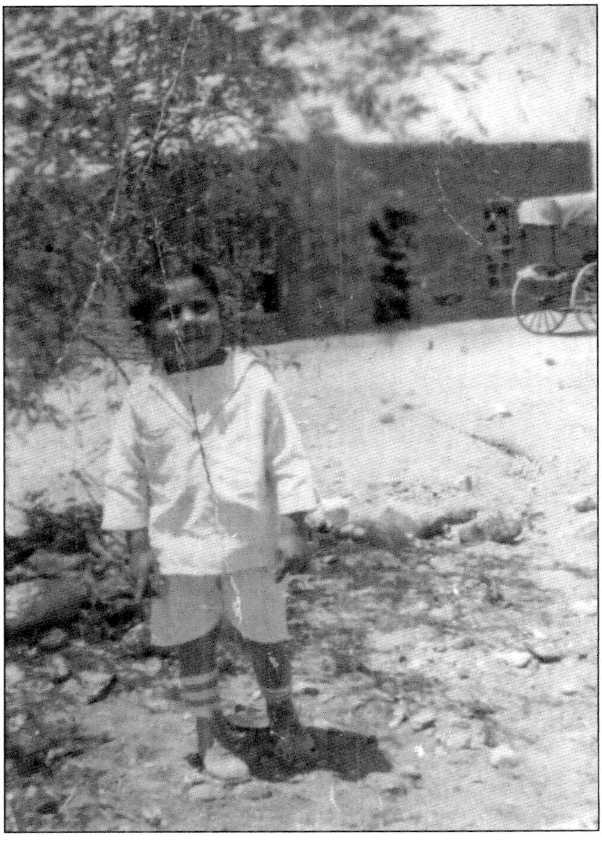

This 1916 photograph shows four-year-old Luis Acuña Gastelum during the Baca Float evictions. The Acuña family had spent 30 years improving their 120-acre homestead. The Baca Float decision should have affected only 20 of their acres, but their entire holdings were taken because of a surveying error. Denied the opportunity to appeal the eviction, the family permanently lost the land.

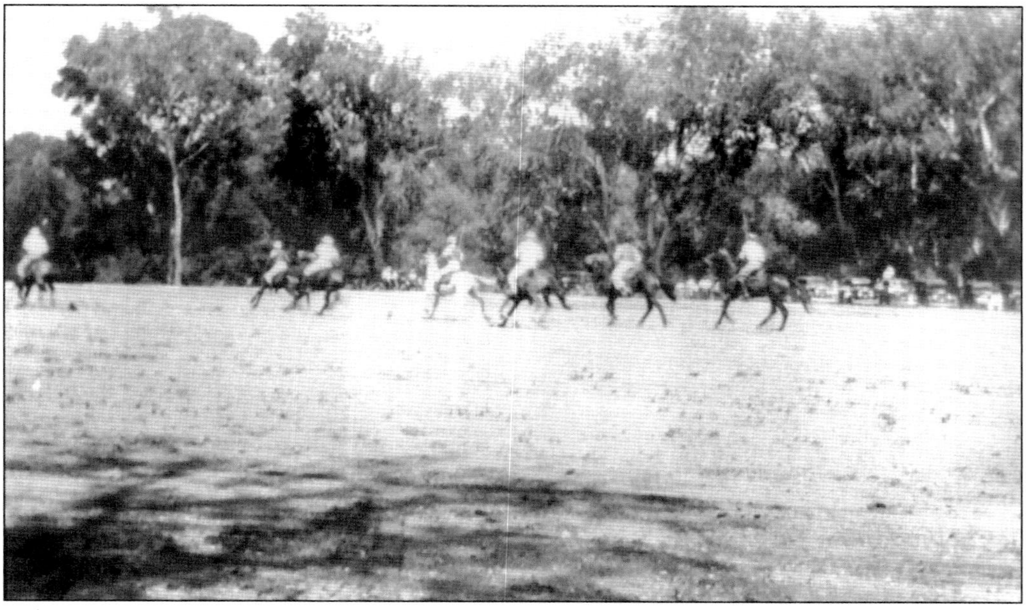

Riders and mounts engaged in a polo chukka at the Circle Z Ranch on Sonoita Creek, southeast of Tubac, are shown in this 1928 image. Dude ranches attracted wealthy Easterners, many of whom fell in love with the western way of life and ended up purchasing land nearby. Setting themselves up as gentlemen (and lady) ranchers, they raised high-grade cattle, Thoroughbred horses, cotton, and, later, pecans. (Pimería Alta Historical Society.)

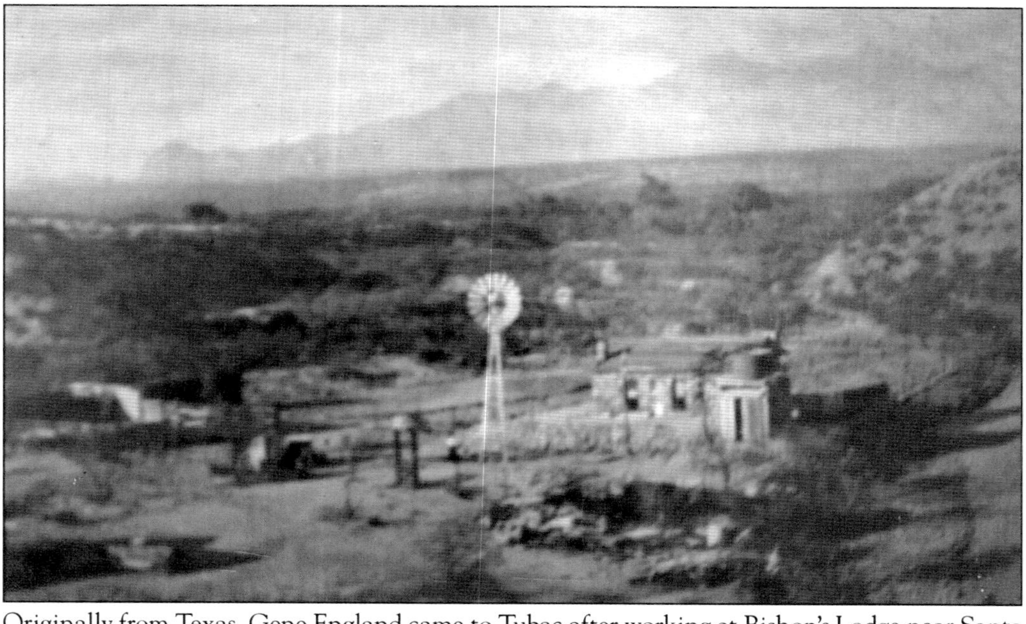

Originally from Texas, Gene England came to Tubac after working at Bishop's Lodge near Santa Fe. He purchased the homestead relinquishment on the Rock Corral Ranch from A. T. Spence and his wife, the former Marcella Garrett, in 1931. One of the prettiest ranches in the valley, it nestles into the lower slopes of the Tumacácori Mountains with sweeping views of the Santa Ritas and Elephant Head Butte. (Jean England Neubauer.)

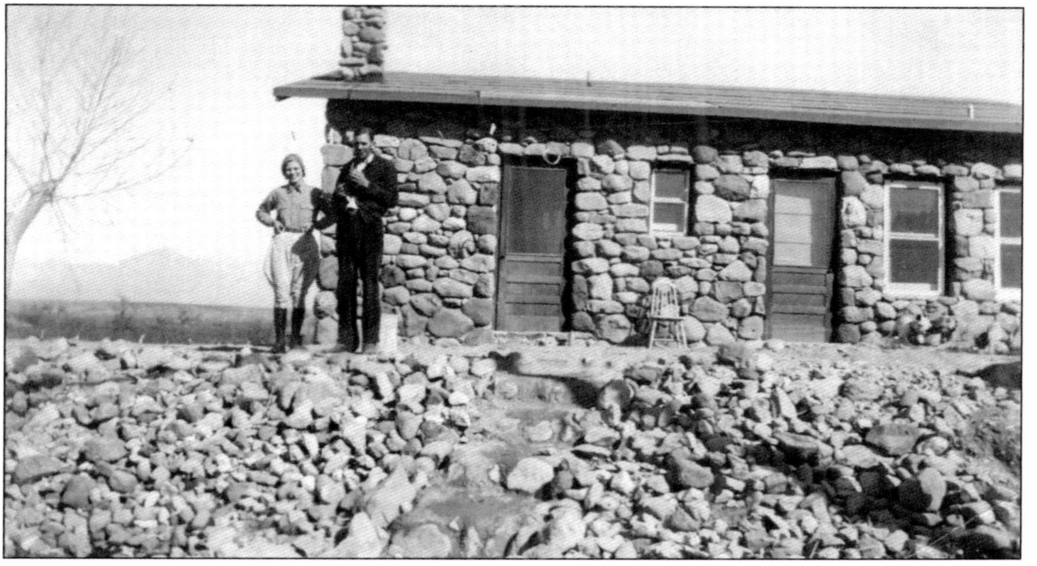

A. T. Spence's original house on his working cattle ranch was small, but the structure of carefully fitted river rocks included a living/dining room, kitchen, bedroom, bath, and no electricity. The new owner, Gene England, is shown here visiting with jodhpur-clad Mrs. Pond, who owned a laundry in Nogales. (Jean England Neubauer.)

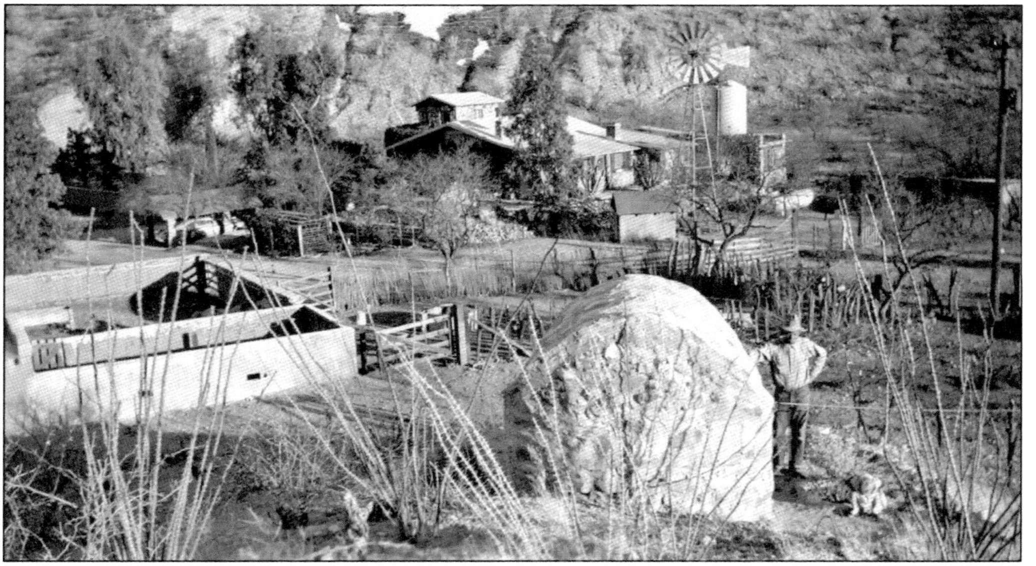

Before marrying Juliet ("Judy") Kibbey in 1941, England added electricity and hardwood floors to the Spence house, another bedroom and bath, and an upstairs known as the Ivory Tower. This 1945 image shows Nacho Flores, the Englands' ranch foreman, leaning on a shrine to La Purísima Concepción. Nacho's daughter Margaret assisted the Englands at the Santa Cruz Chili Company. His daughter Gumecinda married the current ranch foreman, Arnulfo Gomez. (Jean England Neubauer.)

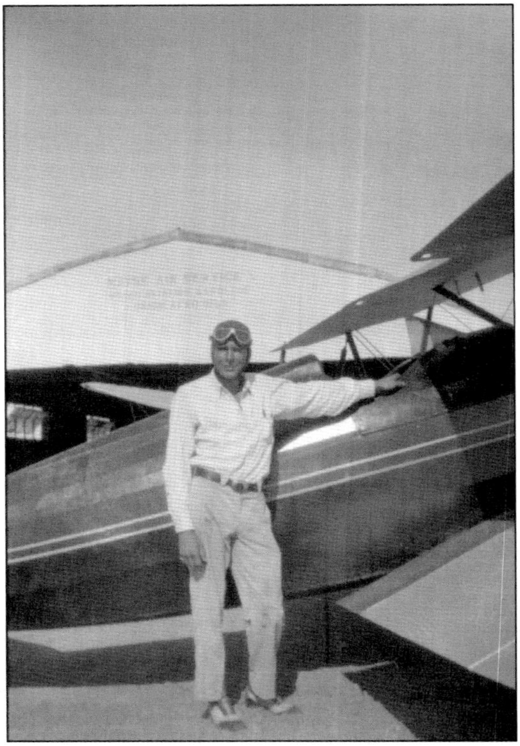

England was an aviation pioneer and, like others, was attracted to the high visibility and good flying weather of the desert. He learned to fly with Charley Mayze, who ran an airfield near what is now the Tucson Rodeo Grounds. England bought this Great Lakes 2 T-1 biplane in 1930 and eventually used it as down payment on the Rock Corral Ranch. (Jean England Neubauer.)

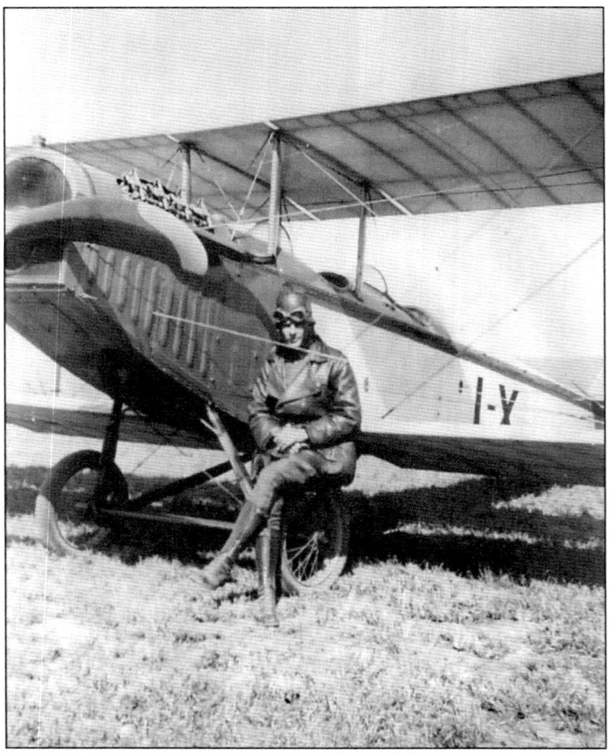

Joan Fay Shankle, the first woman to earn a Private Pilot's License in Massachusetts and the first woman to fly solo coast-to-coast, is shown sitting on the landing gear of a biplane. She and her husband, Clarence "Dutch" Shankle, bought a 400-acre farm north of Tubac from Thomas Casanega in 1931. They named it Pajaritos Migradores ("Migratory Birds") and immediately added a hangar and runway. (Pima Air and Space Library.)

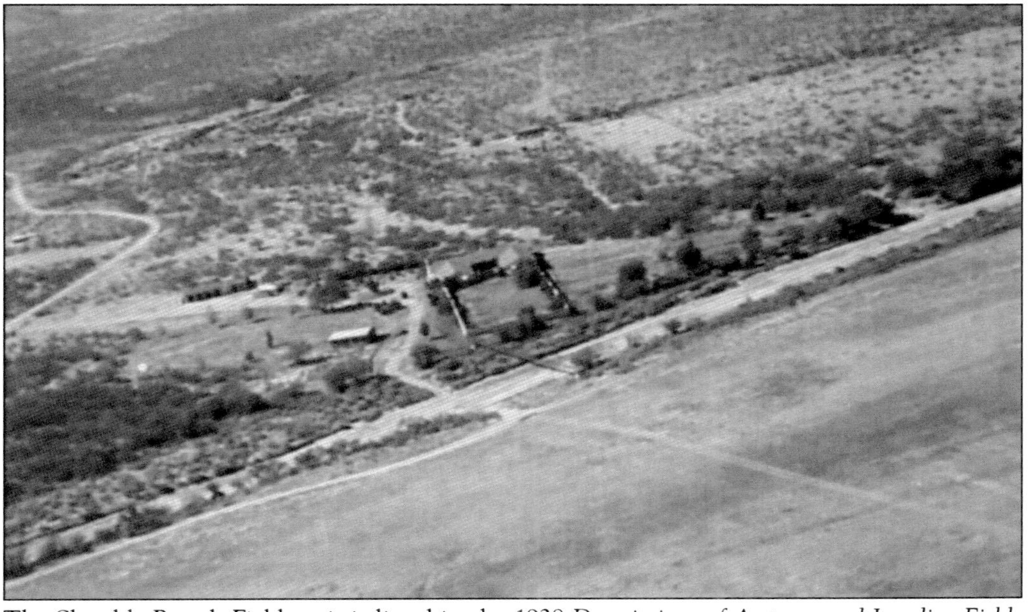

The Shankle Ranch Field, as it is listed in the 1938 *Descriptions of Airports and Landing Fields in the United States*, is shown in an aerial view. It had three landing strips with clear approaches and was located on the east side of the river west of the railroad tracks. Both Joan Fay and Dutch Shankle entered the First Annual Tucson Air Show in 1933, winning awards in their Stearman J-5 and Lockheed Sirius airplanes. (Pima Air and Space Library.)

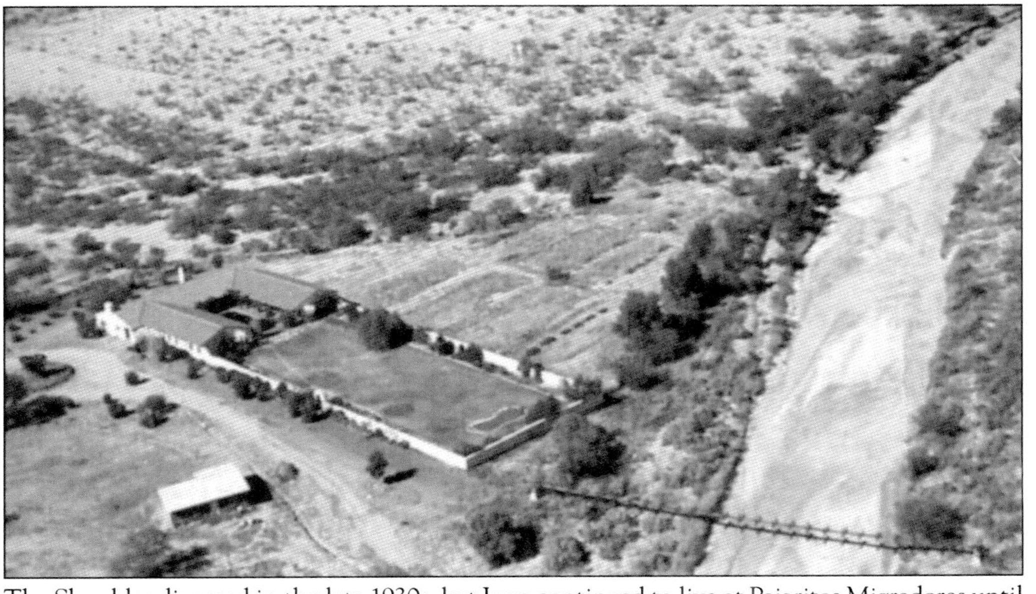

The Shankles divorced in the late 1930s, but Joan continued to live at Pajaritos Migradores until 1942. Her property is shown in this undated aerial view, which shows that the runway's location on the east side of the Santa Cruz River meant a harrowing trek across a footbridge to reach home. In 1948, Joan married Walter Davis and purchased the Otero Ranch. Chester Crebbs bought the old Shankle property in 1949, and it is still known as the PM Ranch today. (Pima Air and Space Library.)

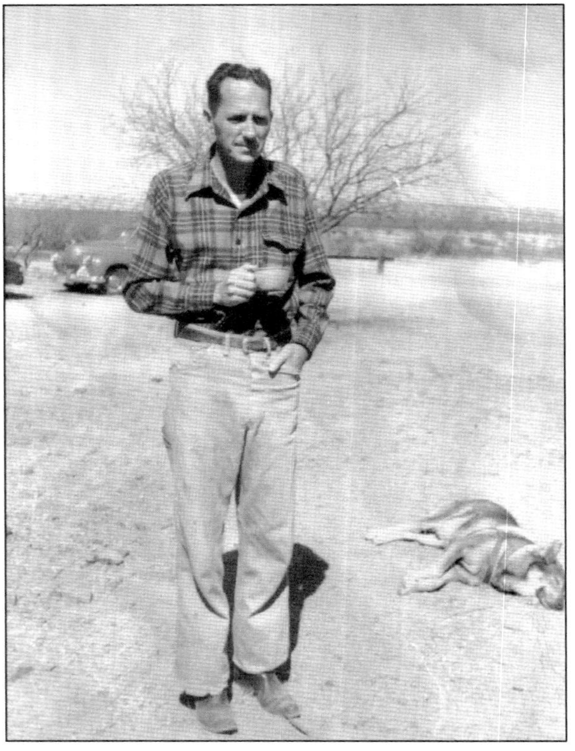

For many years, Bob McDowall (left) visited the Circle Z Ranch with his friends William and Sis Allen. This experience inspired them to start the first dude ranch in Santa Cruz Valley, the Kenyon Ranch, named for Bill Allen's Ohio alma mater, in 1937. The partnership purchased just less than 1,000 acres of land and built a complex of attractive stone buildings west of Tubac. (Peggy Vanderventer.)

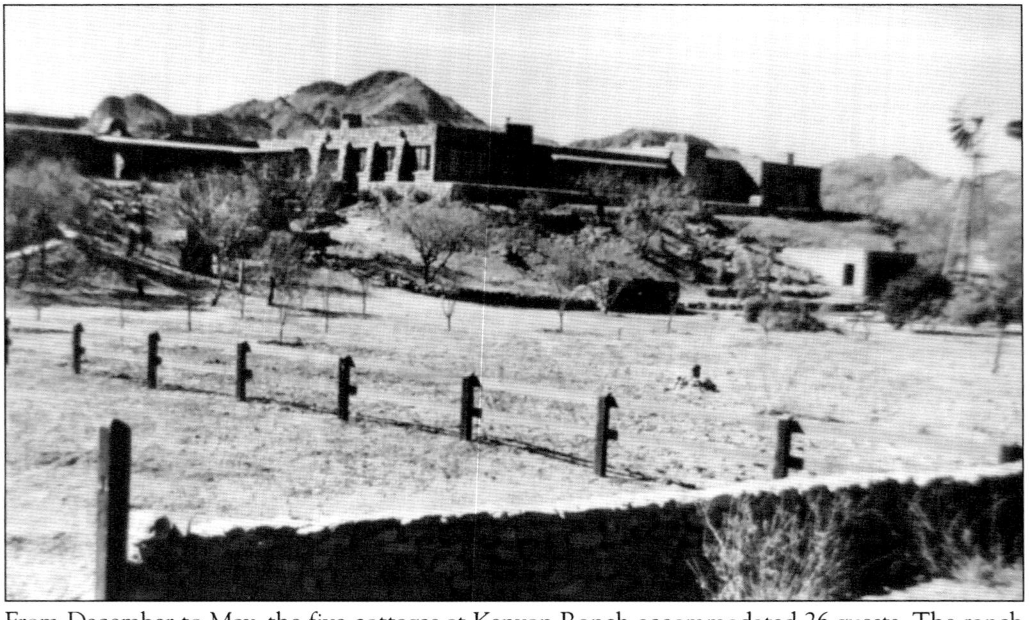

From December to May, the five cottages at Kenyon Ranch accommodated 26 guests. The ranch attracted prominent businessmen and their families from the Midwest with the lure of excellent food, fun, camaraderie, and a special atmosphere created by the Allens. Guests became regulars, coming year after year, sometimes leaving no room for newcomers. Many Kenyon guests including the Reid, Jarvis, Liverance, and Vanderventer families eventually purchased property in the area.

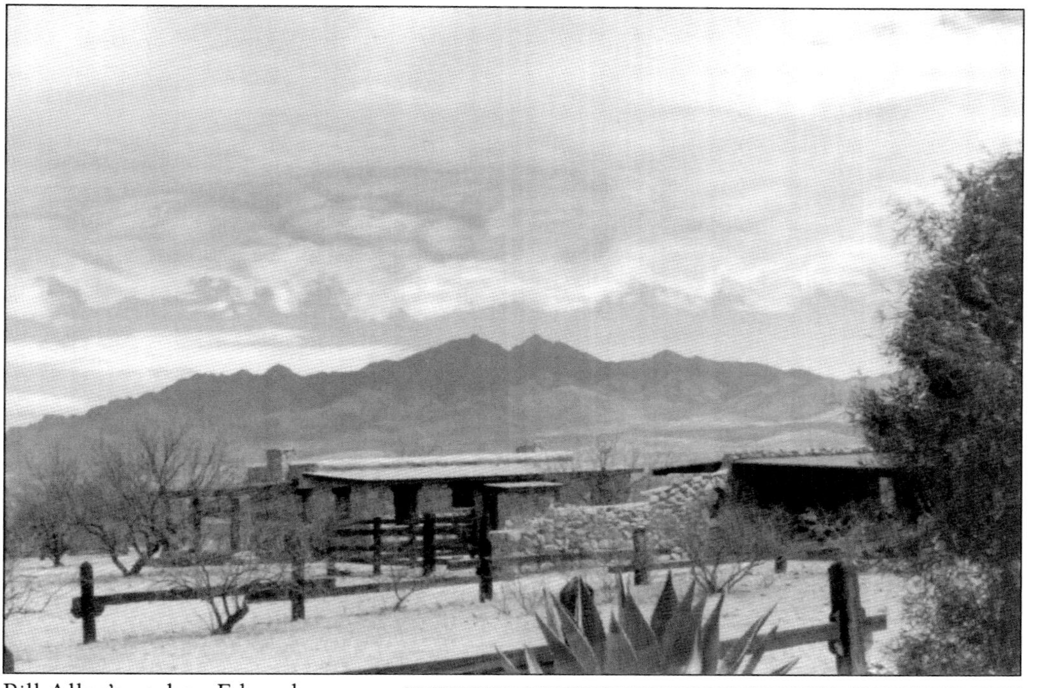

Bill Allen's nephew Edward Danson helped open Kenyon Ranch in 1937 and was so enchanted by the area that he left Cornell and finished his B.A. at the University of Arizona. His career as an anthropologist got its start when he became friends with Louis Caywood, the custodian of Tumacácori National Monument, and the two explored the area's abundant archaeological sites.

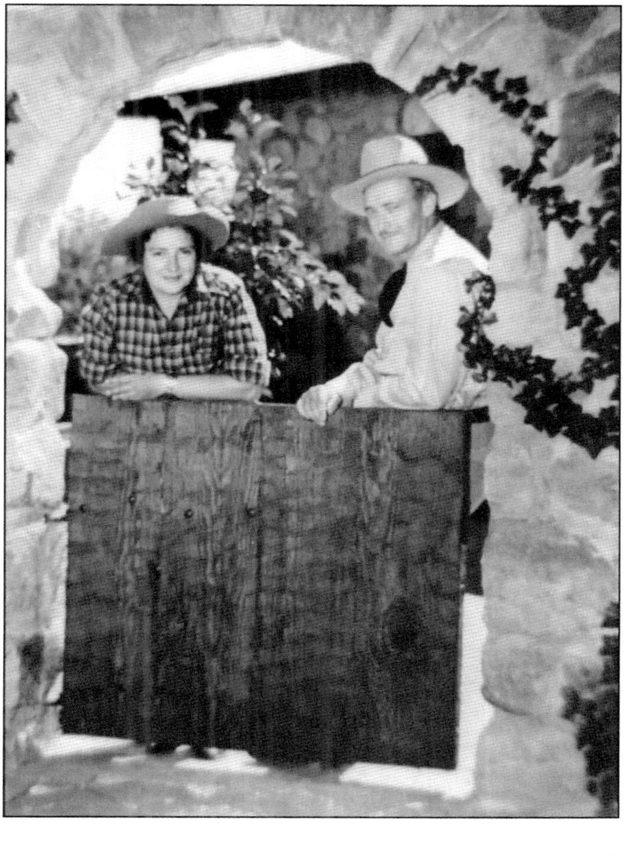

Bill and Sis Allen, shown at Kenyon Ranch gate, maintained this winter destination for "snowbirds" for 40 years. Together with daughter-in-law Ann Nichols and a staff of 30, they provided all services, including the cottages, horses, pool, badminton, croquet, tennis, and meals, for only $10 per day. Raised to $18 in 1952, rates peaked at $50 in 1974. They were also founding members of the Santa Cruz Valley Arts Association and the Tubac Historical Society.

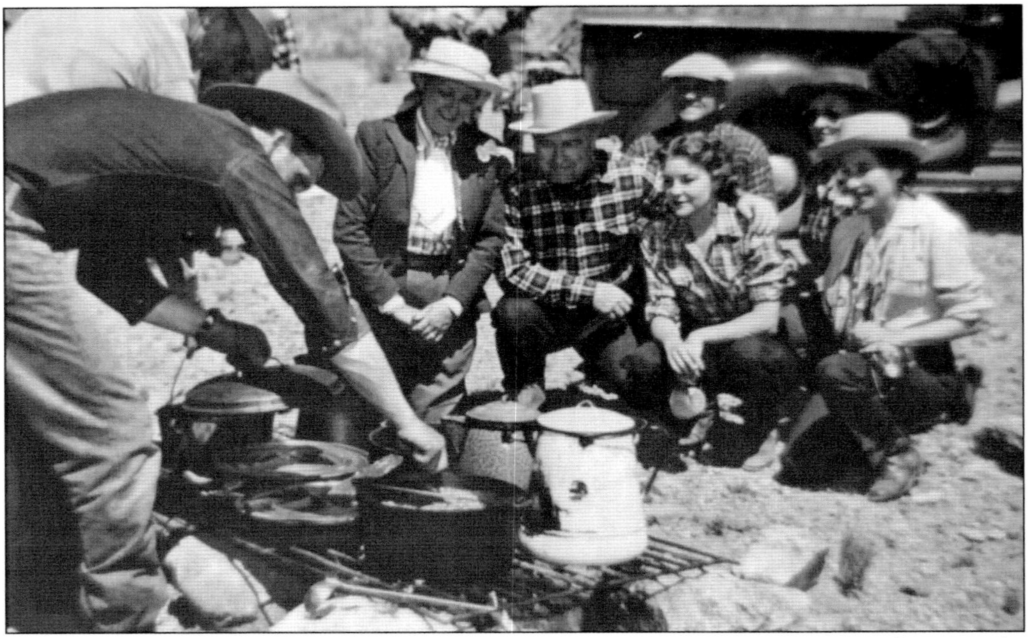

Food at Kenyon was first rate, and the ranch employed only five cooks in its 40-year history. The staff enjoyed the same menu as the guests. Real trail cookouts as shown in this photograph were popular, featuring bacon, eggs, toast, and Kenyon's famous hotcakes. Sis Allen tells of one cookout that featured javelina—with many guests choosing the optional chicken.

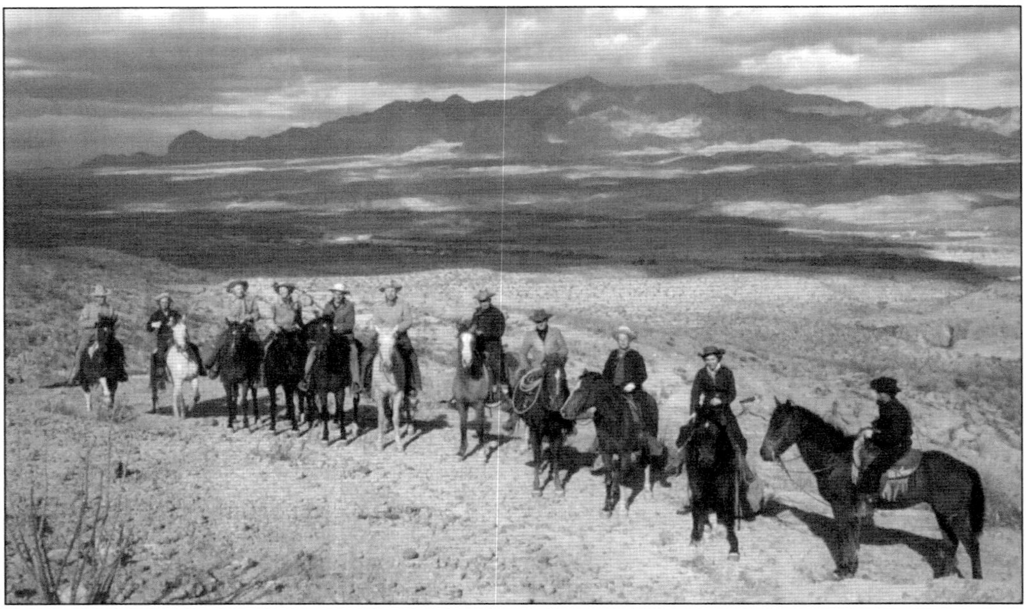

The Allens were proud of their good horses and the three "real" cowboys employed to lead fast, medium, and slow rides in all directions. This view of a spectacular cloud-shadowed valley shows a terrain undefined by fences. Later when the barbed wire appeared, the Allens negotiated to have keys to any locked gates. Tubac-area residents Beth Aycock and Al Donau worked at Kenyon as wranglers.

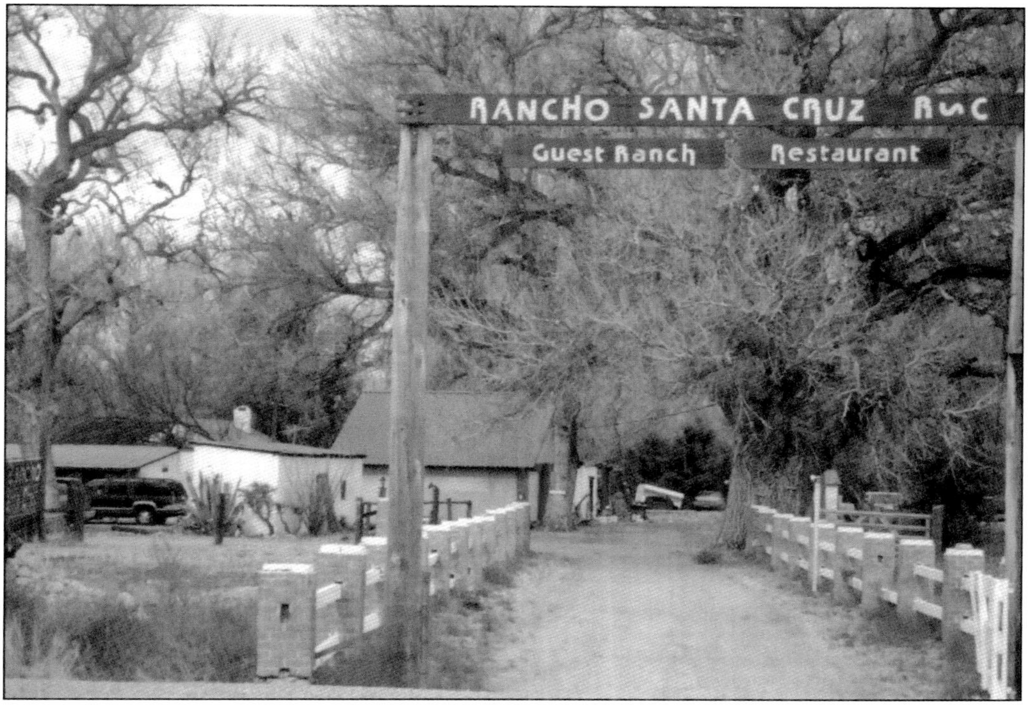

Originally the headquarters for the Baca Float Ranch when it was owned by World War I aviator Tol Pendleton, these buildings were sold in 1939 with 100 acres to Doris Oesting, a friend of Bill and Sis Allen, who suggested the name Rancho Santa Cruz. Many of the buildings were built with bricks from the demolished Santa Rita Hotel when the land in Calabasas was planted with cotton. (Cowbelles Museum, Ranchers' Heritage Center.)

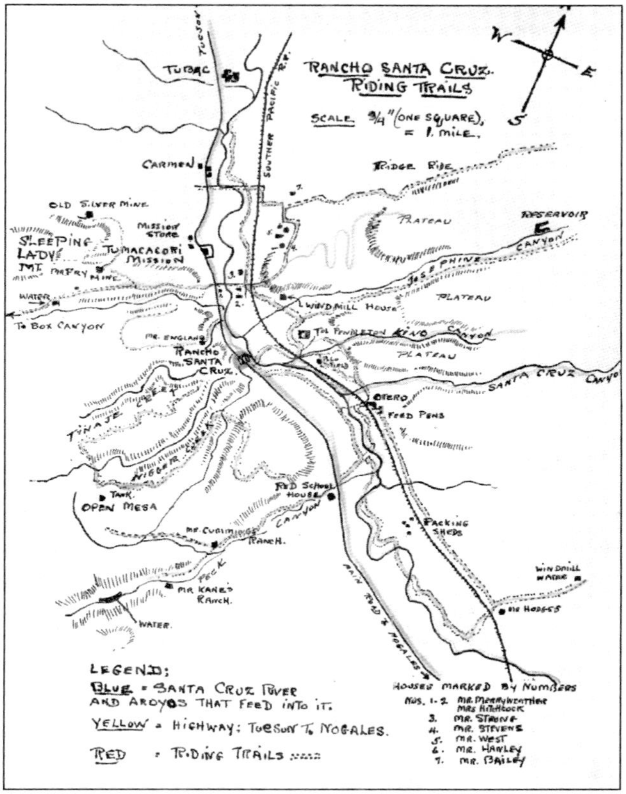

This riding trail map of Rancho Santa Cruz dates from the 1950s and shows a number of landmarks that are only memories today. Note the polo field south of Tol Pendleton's place and the old silver mine west of Tumacácori. The ruins of the feed pens by the Otero train stop can be seen today east of the river on Palo Parado Road, but nothing remains of the packing sheds farther south. (Wendy Williams.)

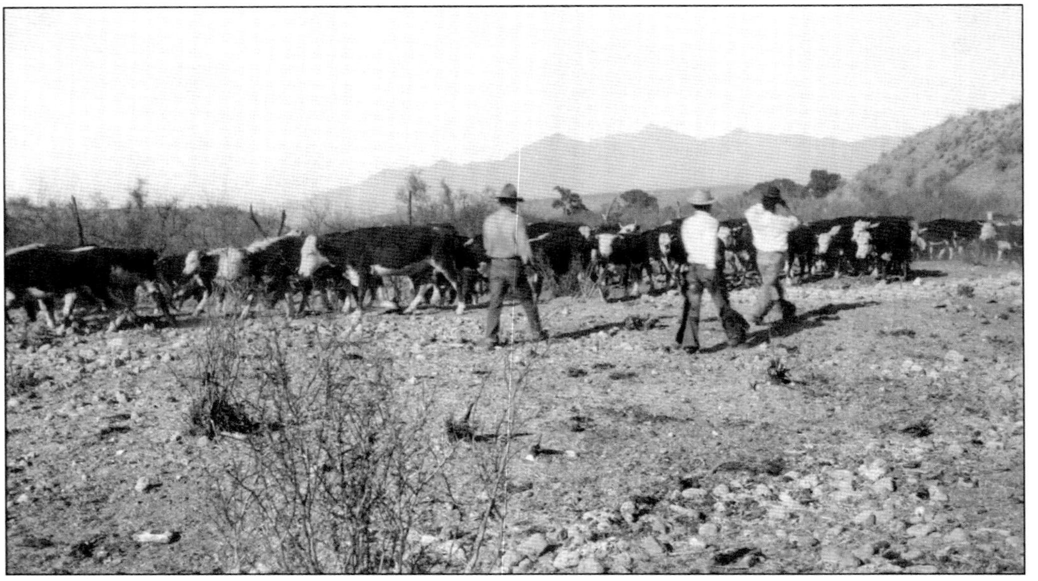

Cattle ranches around Tubac continued to flourish. The Rock Corral Ranch was a cow-calf operation, maintaining a herd of mother cows and selling an annual crop of calves. In addition to their own land, many ranchers leased state and federal land for grazing. Here cowboys are shown encouraging a herd of Rock Corral Ranch Herefords to move from the Santa Cruz River to higher ground. (Jean England Neubauer.)

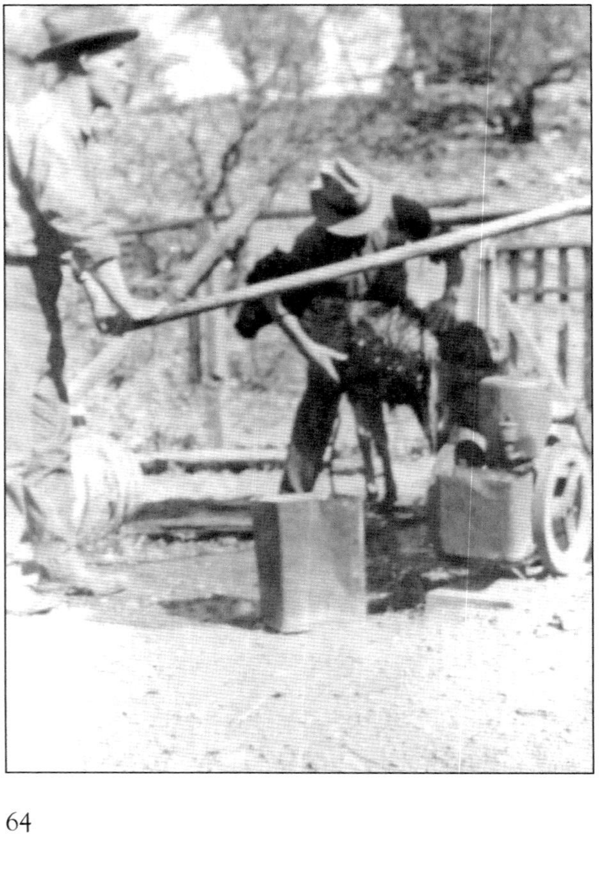

Battling the spread of deadly hoof-and-mouth disease, the U.S. government required all cattle coming in from Mexico to be dipped in an arsenic solution, but the dip was so toxic that it killed many animals. Jim Garrett in Tubac alone lost over 50 head. The solution was made safer, but arsenic can still be found in soil samples near dipping areas. This undated photograph shows two men engaged in the messy task. (Pimería Alta Historical Society.)

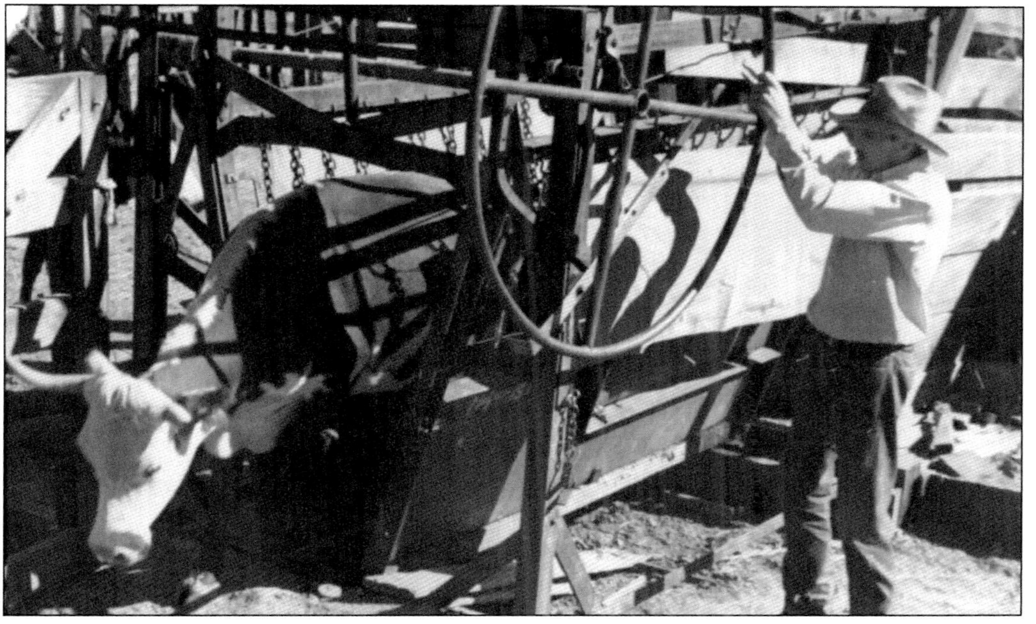

This 1940 image shows Gene England with a cattle squeeze he made himself. An innovation that saved labor and reduced injury and stress to the animals, squeezes were meant to replace roping and tying. A cow entered the squeeze from a chute; the squeeze was tightened, immobilizing the animals so that they could be de-horned, branded, inoculated, or castrated. Rock Corral cowboys no longer use the squeeze and now catch their cows in the traditional way. (Jean England Neubauer.)

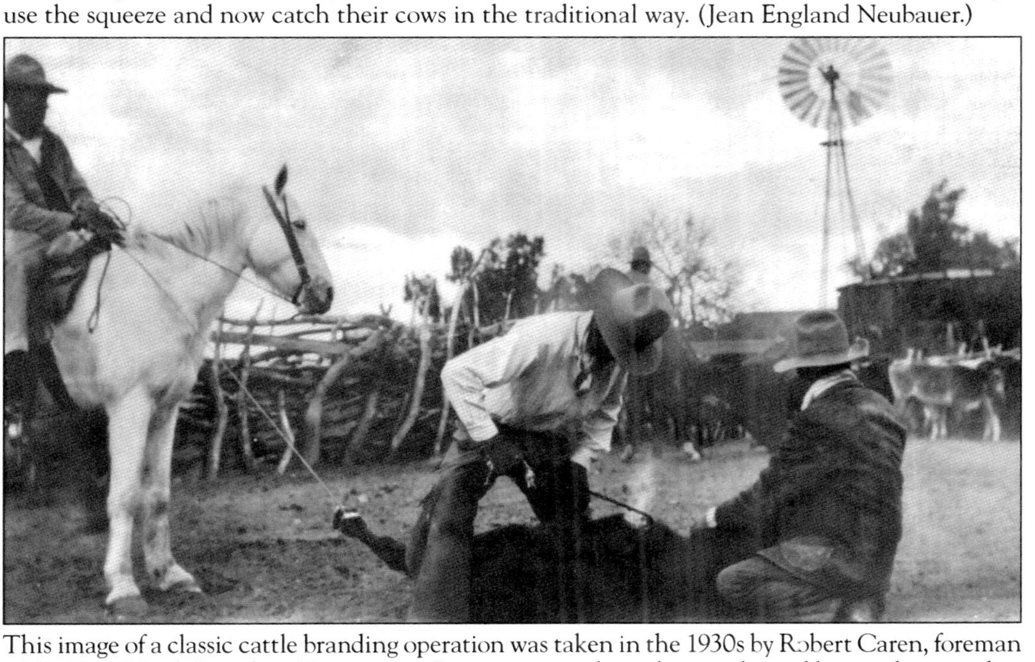

This image of a classic cattle branding operation was taken in the 1930s by Robert Caren, foreman of the Four Winds Ranch in Tumacácori. Distinctive markings have indicated livestock ownership from the earliest times. Some of the earliest brands in the New World were Mexican, registered with the king of Spain's governing agency, the Mesta. Since 1898, the Live Stock Sanitary Board of Arizona has kept records of brands on cattle, horses, sheep, goats, and hogs.

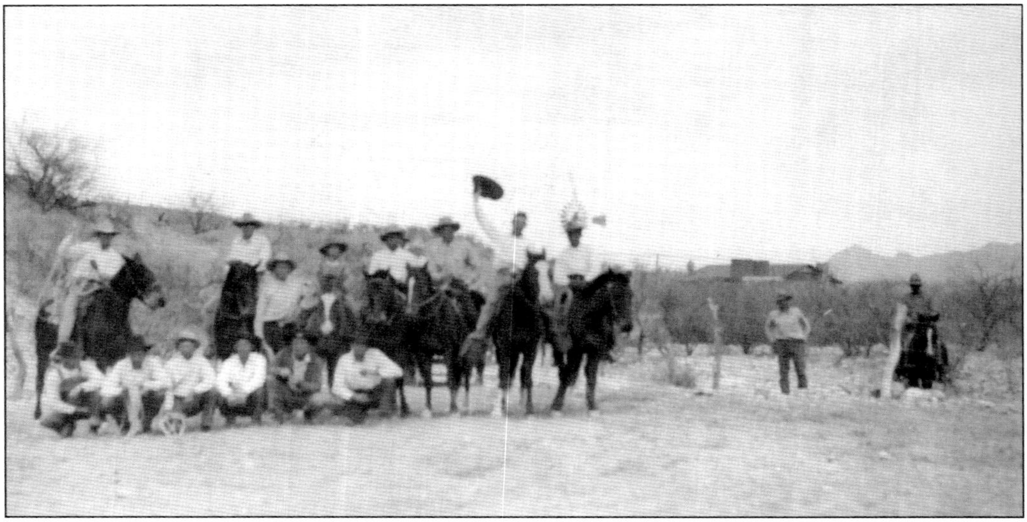

The hard work of the roundup involved many skilled hands for gathering, sorting, tagging, and branding hundreds of calves. The man waving his hat in this photograph is thought to be Howard Wisdom Sr., employed by Tol Pendleton on his Baca Float Ranch but in this instance helping out with a Rock Corral Ranch roundup. (Jean England.)

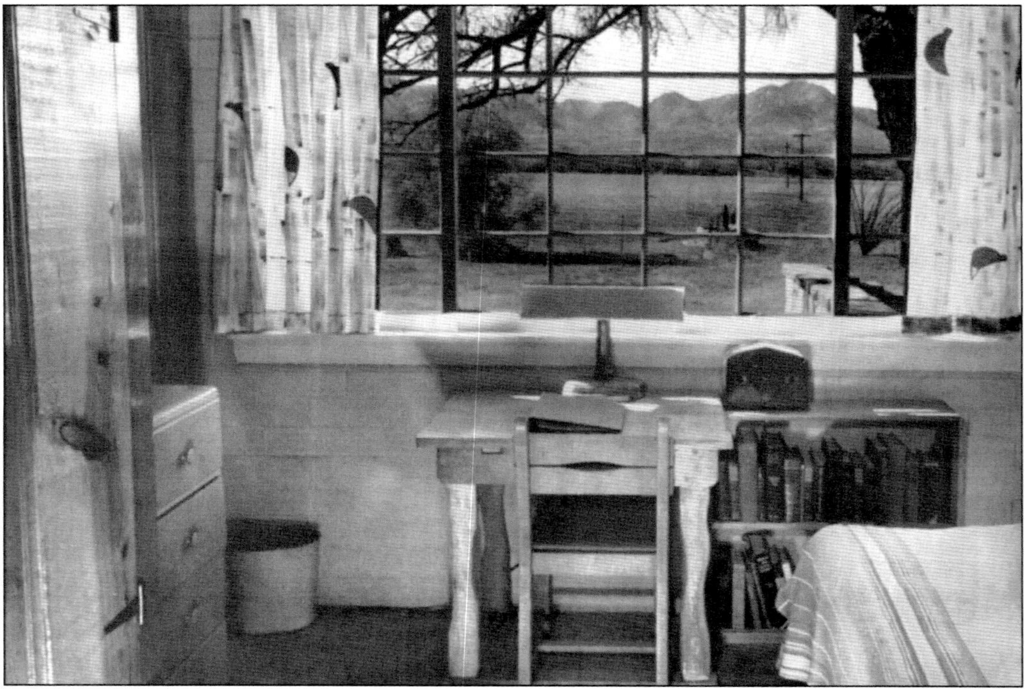

This image shows a boy's private room when Ann Kennedy Huntoon's La Querencia Ranch was home to Wally Whitcombe's Santa Cruz Valley School in 1950. The private coed boarding school added several buildings and facilities, including a tennis court before it moved to Tucson. Ann established one of the first horse farms in the valley here, today managed by Jean Burke. Named for the homing instinct in animals, La Querencia was Ann's passion for more than 40 years. (Ann Kennedy Huntoon.)

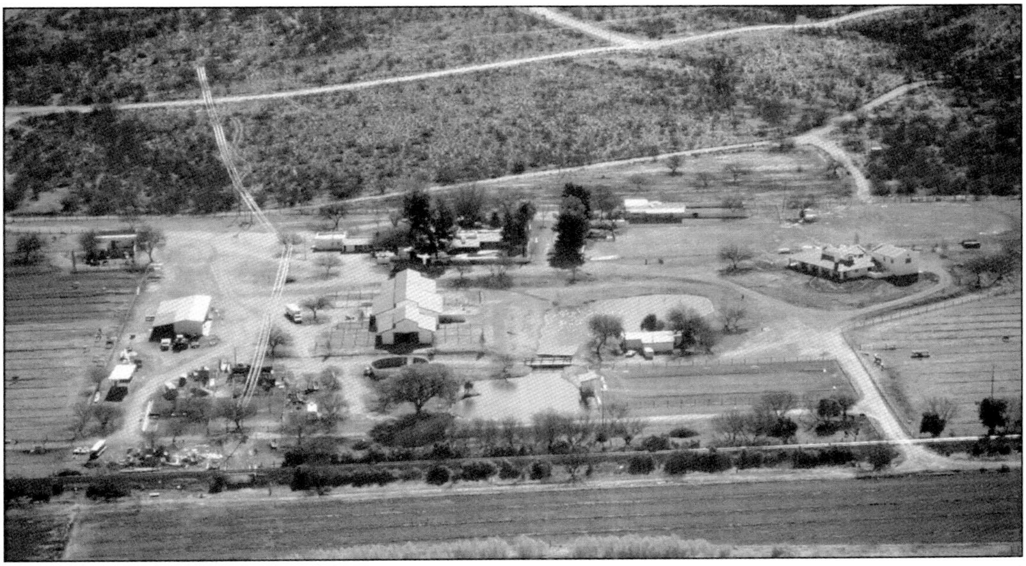

The Potreras Ranch, shown in this aerial photograph, was purchased by E. T. Strong, the retired president of Buick, in 1937. He ran it as the El Canto guest ranch for three years. It was later owned by the Joffroy family of Nogales. When the 1983 flood washed their house away, they sold the property to Ann Orell, who raised Andalusian horses here. It is now owned by the Global Community Communications Alliance. (Jennifer Tougas.)

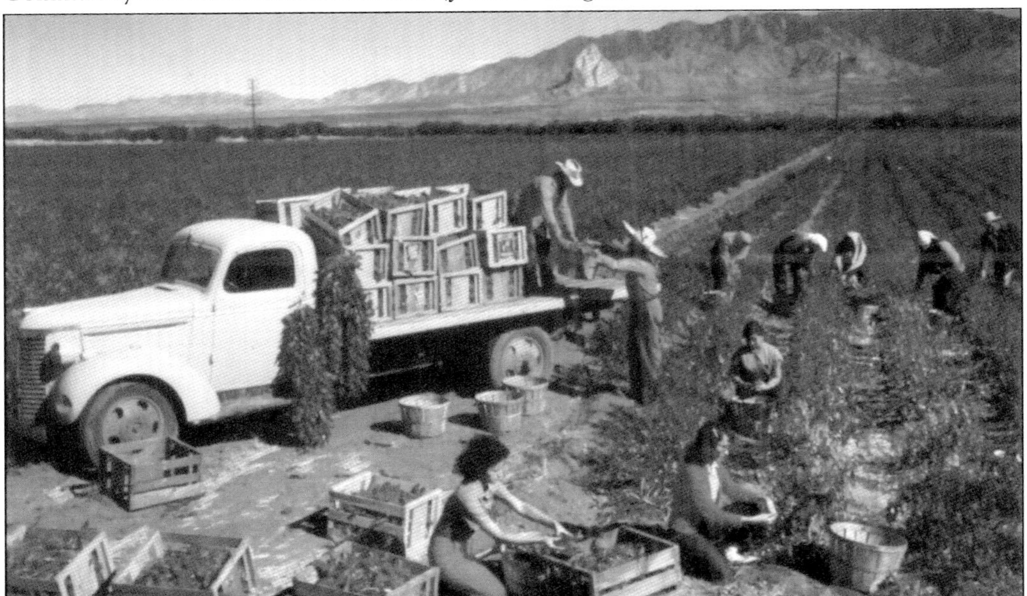

The Santa Cruz Chili and Spice Company was founded in 1943 by Gene and Judy England. Gene's land in Amado was perfect for growing the poblano, chipotle, guajillo, serano, habanero, and other chili pepper varieties. This staged photograph does not show the hard, hot work involved in handpicking chilies, but it conveys pride in a family-owned business. The Englands expanded their market and product line in the 1960s and today are an internationally celebrated chili and spice company. (Jean England Neubauer.)

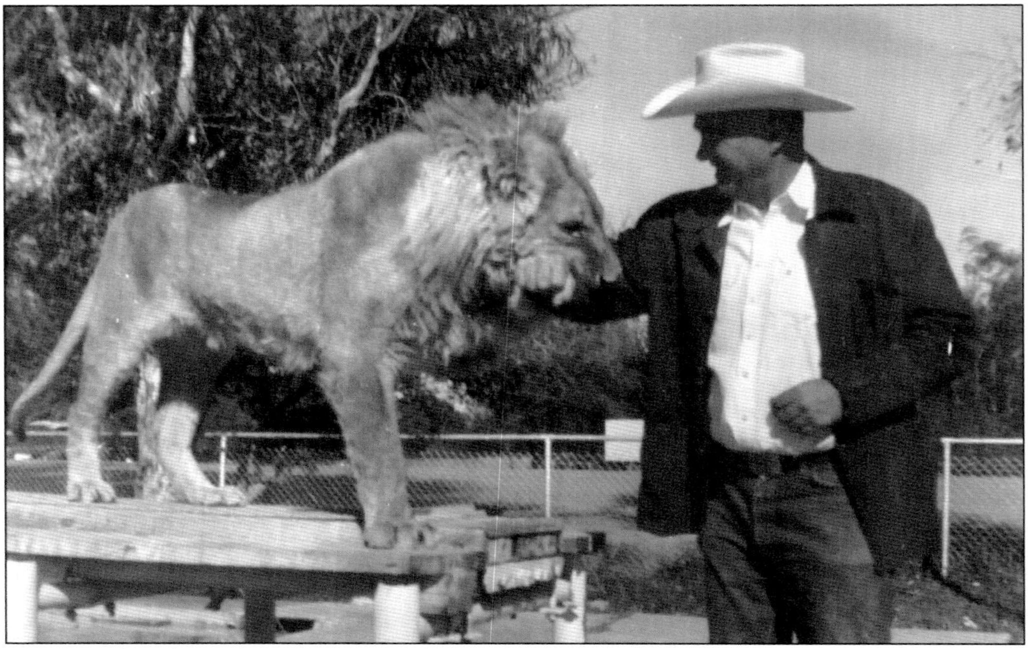

Otho Kinsley, shown here with one of his pet African lions, developed a 600-acre ranch north of Tubac into a popular recreation area. In addition to his general store, restaurant, and dance hall, people could fish in his man-made lakes and watch movies projected onto a wall during balmy evenings. The eucalyptus trees surrounding the present Cow Palace restaurant once shaded Kinsley's large swimming pool with its notorious ice-cold water. (Frank Bertolino.)

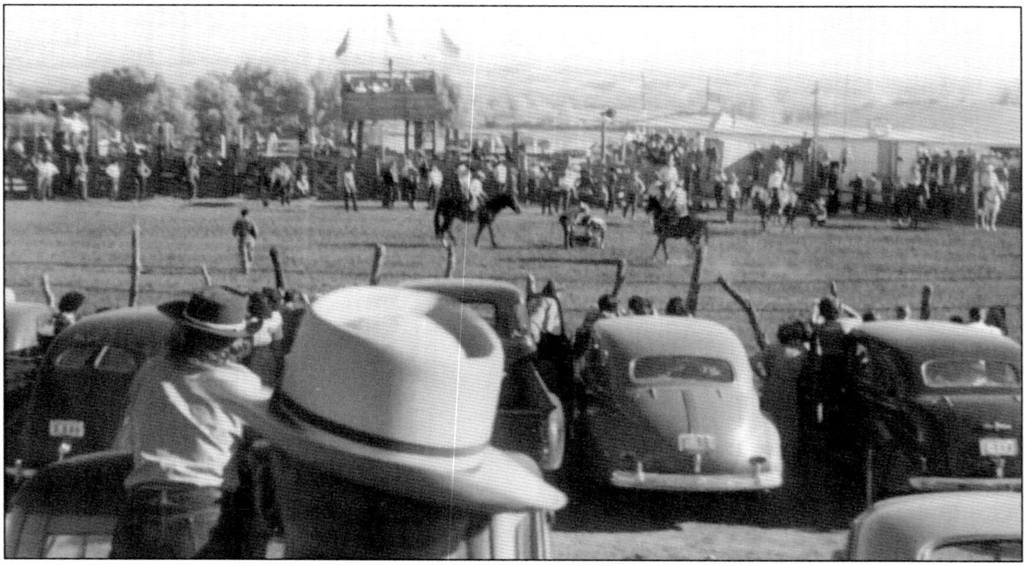

Kinsley sponsored rodeos and roping contests. The first were informal affairs in a dirt arena circled by cars. These were so popular that formal wooden chutes for the animals were constructed in 1950. This photograph shows a large crowd directly across from the chutes watching the many cowboys and horses in competition. Postwar prosperity is reflected in the shiny, early-1950s Chevrolet truck surrounded by older sedans. (Randy Williams.)

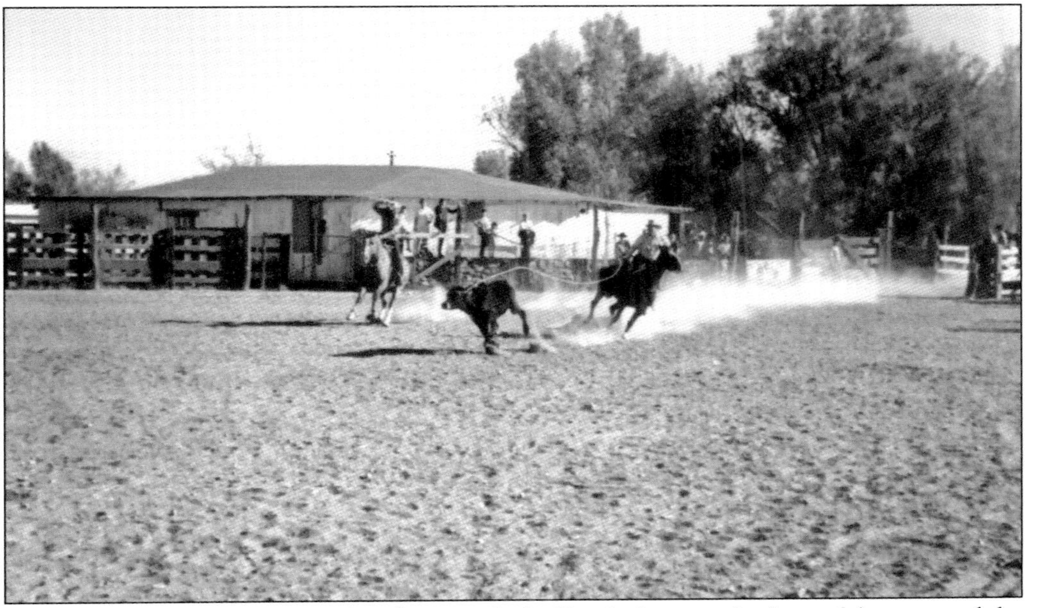

Team roping at the Kinsley Ranch is shown with the "header" roping the front of the steer and the "heeler" roping the hind feet. The building beyond the action is the original restaurant and dance hall, subsequently burned in a 1950 fire. The dense growths of trees behind allude to Kinsley's ability as a water-witcher and to the reportedly 900-gallon-per-minute well that filled his lakes and pool. Kinsley Ranch sold for $420,000 in 1959 to a group of developers. (Peggy Vanderventer.)

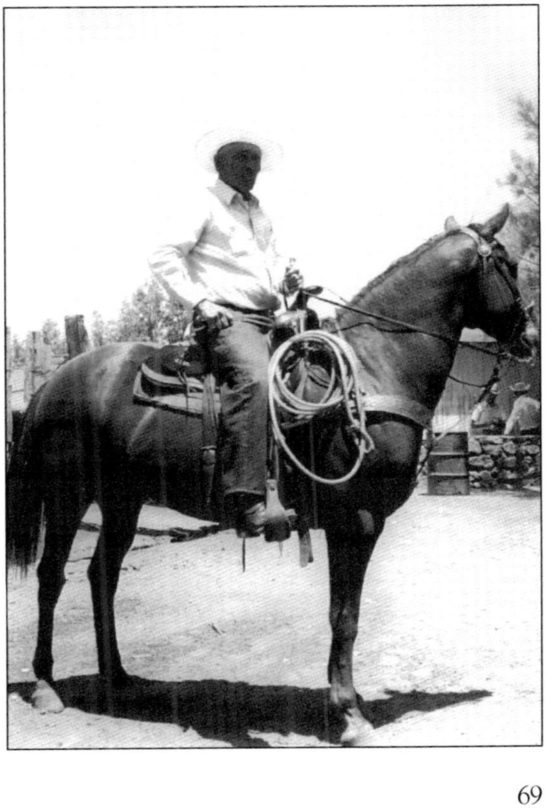

Santiago Gastelum, shown here on his mare Flicka at a roping contest at Kinsley's in 1959, had a ranch in Tubac east of the Santa Cruz River. He was a superb horseman and was elected to the Cowboy Hall of Fame. Originally from Tubutama, Sonora, Gastelum married his wife, Santos, in Tubac. Most area ranchers belonged to the Turtle Association, which later became the Professional Rodeo Cowboys Association.

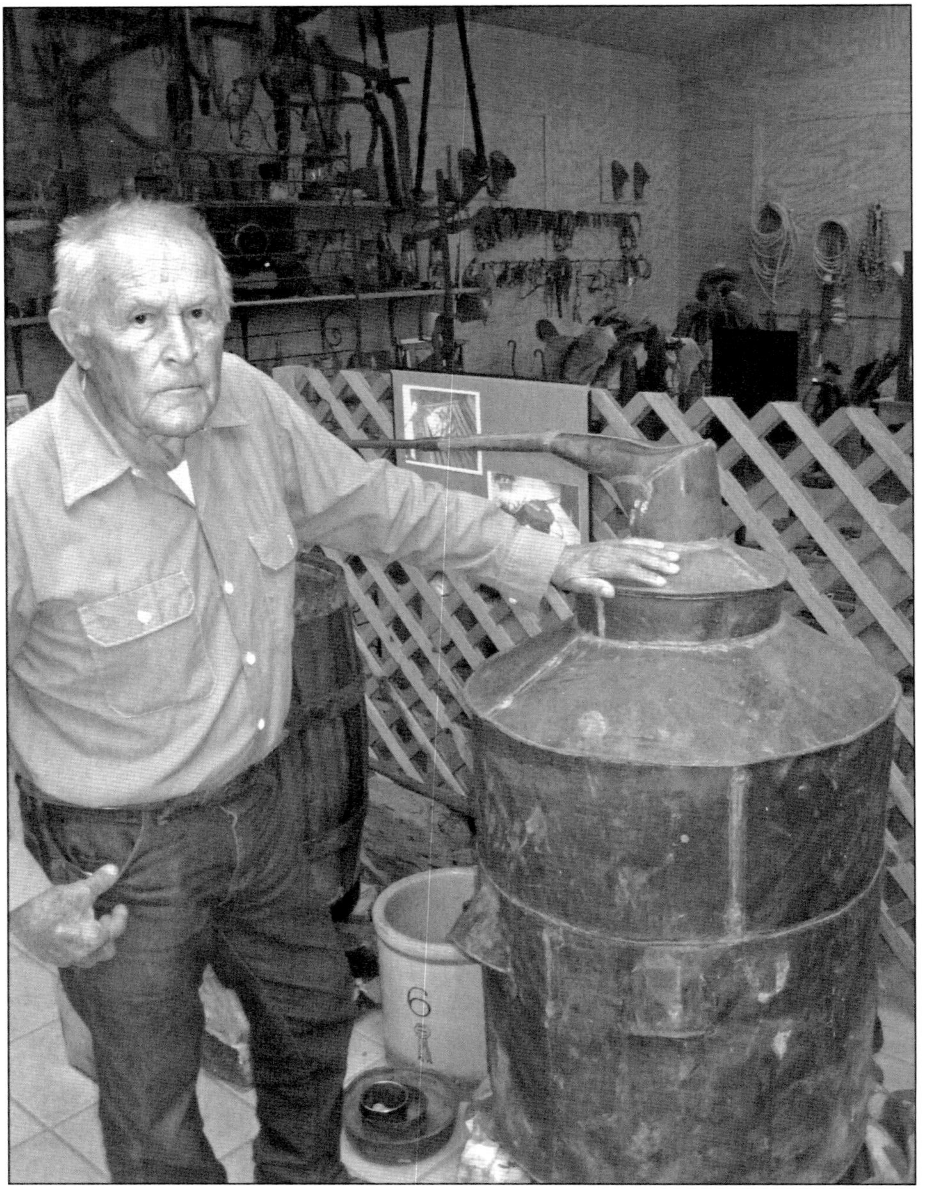

George Proctor of Patagonia stands next to the copper still his father, Charles Proctor, used to make moonshine mescal in the Santa Rita Mountains during the 1920s. Mescal was popular not only with miners and ranchers but also with the people who made it because of its low overhead and the ready availability of the main ingredient, *Agave americana* or maguey. Tequila is made from blue agave or *Agave tequilana*. The procedure was to select a number of big maguey heads, chop off their roots and leaves, and then roast them in a pit over several days. The baked heads were mashed in a wooden trough and put in a 40-gallon barrel with water for fermentation. The fermented liquid, called biguata, was transferred to a copper still like the one pictured here. A slow fire distilled the mescal, which dripped through a copper coil into waiting bottles. Even after the repeal of the 21st Amendment, illicitly made mescal remained popular in this area. (Shaw Kinsley.)

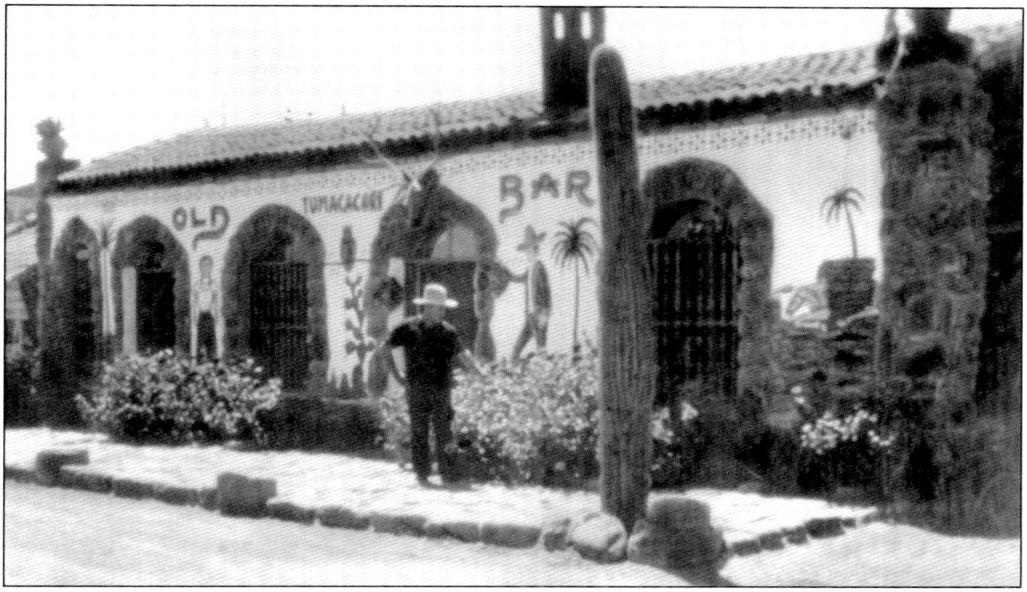

Abe Trujillo's colorful Old Tumacácori Bar has been a famous Santa Cruz County saloon since the repeal of Prohibition in the 1930s. Located across the street from Tumacácori National Historic Park, it was originally next door to a family-run grocery and general store. Generations of park visitors, dignitaries, ranch hands, tycoons, and travelers have enjoyed Abe's hospitality. (Abraham Trujillo family.)

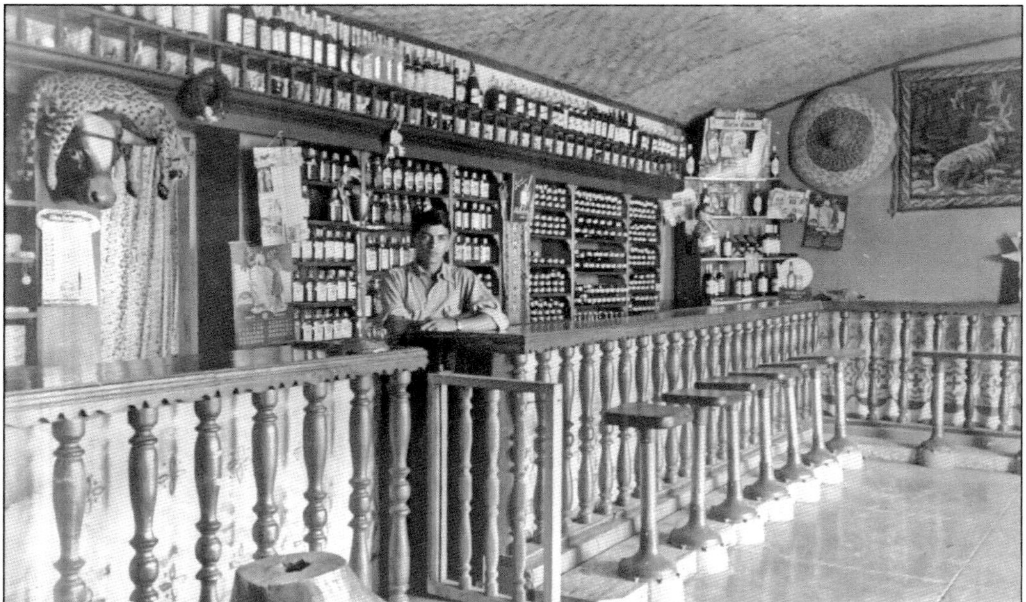

This young man is readying Abe's Tumacácori Bar for another busy night in December 1941. Today the countertop is still supported by these graceful balusters, but the barstools are no longer half axles of Model T Fords bolted to the floor. The oak tree trunk in the foreground came from the hills near Ruby and served as a table when turned upside down. (Abraham Trujillo family.)

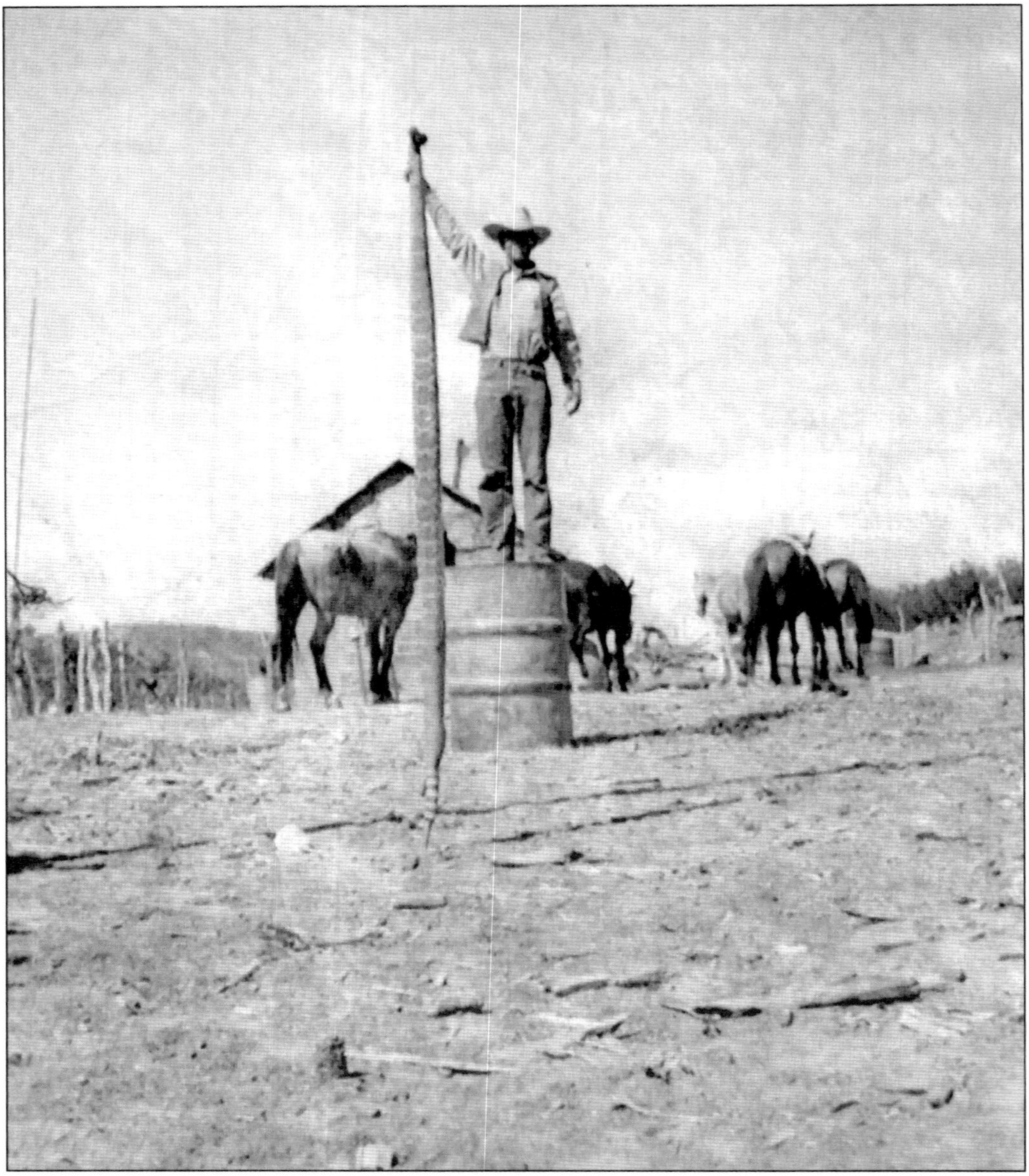

This 1930s photograph of a Salero Ranch hand with an impossibly long western diamondback rattlesnake hangs on the wall at Abe's Tumacácori Bar. A close examination of the shadows shows that the man "holding" the snake is several feet behind it, and the snake is suspended from an off-camera pole or wire. Since the snake appears to be headless, the thin wire required for the spoof possibly acted as a garrote. (Abraham Trujillo family.)

Four

Artistic Tubac

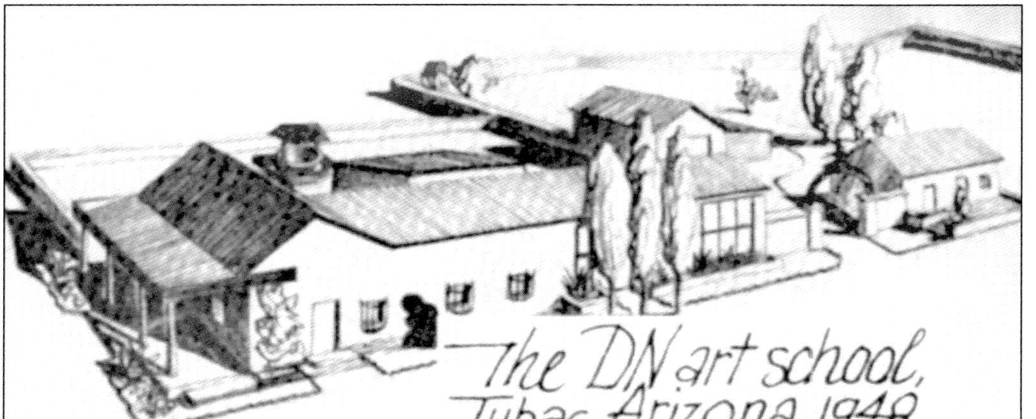

This sketch of Dale Nichols's art school marks Tubac's birth as an art colony. Nichols, Nebraska-born, Art Institute of Chicago-trained, came to Tubac in 1945 to establish an art school modeled on his friend Frank Lloyd Wright's Taliesin West in Scottsdale. Nichols's wife, Lucille, was against the idea, and it was only after a divorce that he moved his Tucson art school to Tubac. Nichols bought five adobe buildings near St. Ann's church and took in a group of students, including a number of ex-soldiers who were more interested in chatting up the nude models they hoped would be provided than in learning art. His students' exploits discouraged Nichols, and he closed the school in 1949, afterwards only making occasional painting trips here. After an artistic career lived in the United States and Guatemala, Nichols returned to Tubac in 1989 at the age of 89.

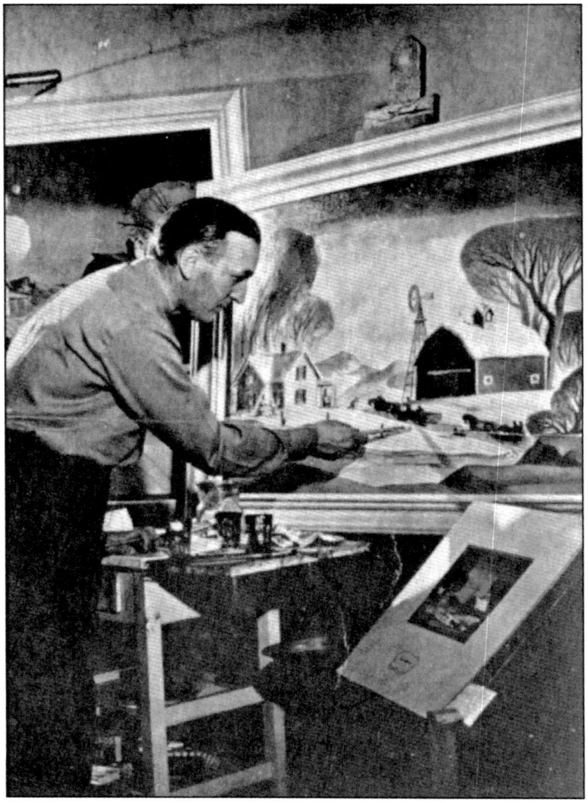

This photograph of Dale Nichols at his easel was owned by Marjorie Tolkin Nichols, a former student and Dale's fourth wife. She left Tubac at the same time but returned in 1959 and managed the Low Ruins Gallery for Collier Rogers. The gallery was in the old Pennington house, which had been the main building of Dale's school. It was also leased by the Santa Cruz Valley Art Association from 1965 to 1972 for their meetings and annual exhibitions.

Working with Collier Rogers, Marjorie Nichols arranged for a national juried art show in 1964 that brought national attention to Tubac. The peaked-roof structure shown here was built in 1857 and served as Marjorie Nichols's home and studio for more than 25 years. As one of Tubac's oldest buildings, U.S. Army records show it was used to house military officers in the 1860s, and Border Patrol officers lived here in the 1920s. (Santa Cruz Valley Art Association.)

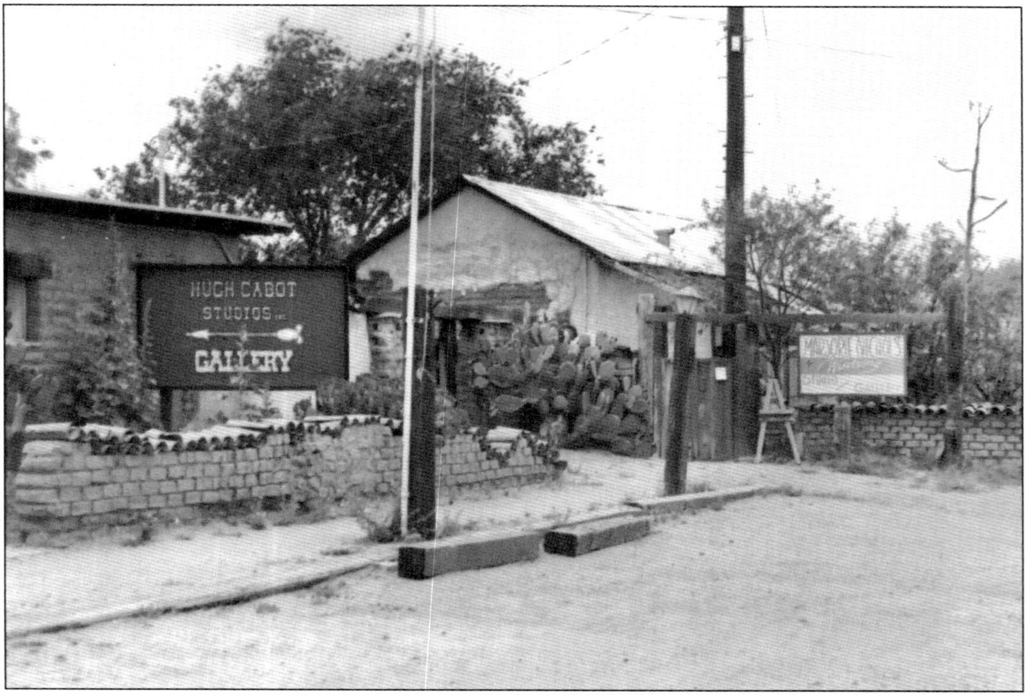

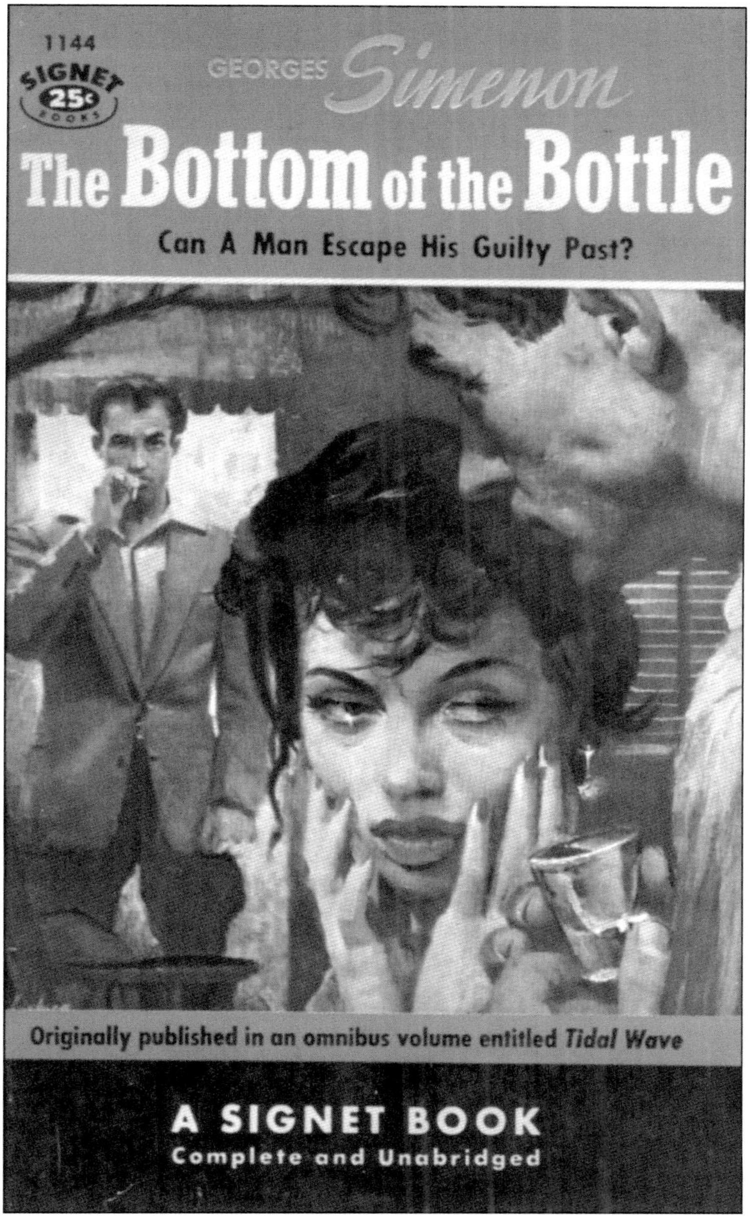

In 1948, Georges Simenon, the Belgian-born author of the Inspector Maigret mysteries, lived in the house on the southeast corner of Santa Gertrudis Lane and the Frontage Road. The house was once the Calabasas School, later the home of Charles C. Day, and is currently home to Day's daughter, Bunny Hanson. Here Simenon wrote *The Bottom of the Bottle* based on his observations of some of the characters living in what was then called "the Santa Booze Valley." The book came out in France in 1949 and in 1954 in the United States. It was made into a movie starring Van Johnson and Joseph Cotten in 1956. Judy England recalls meeting Simenon during his stay in Tumacácori and encountered him at Tucson Medical Center. Judy was there for the birth of her daughter Jeanie and shared the maternity ward with Simenon's mistress, Denyse Ouimet. (Shaw Kinsley.)

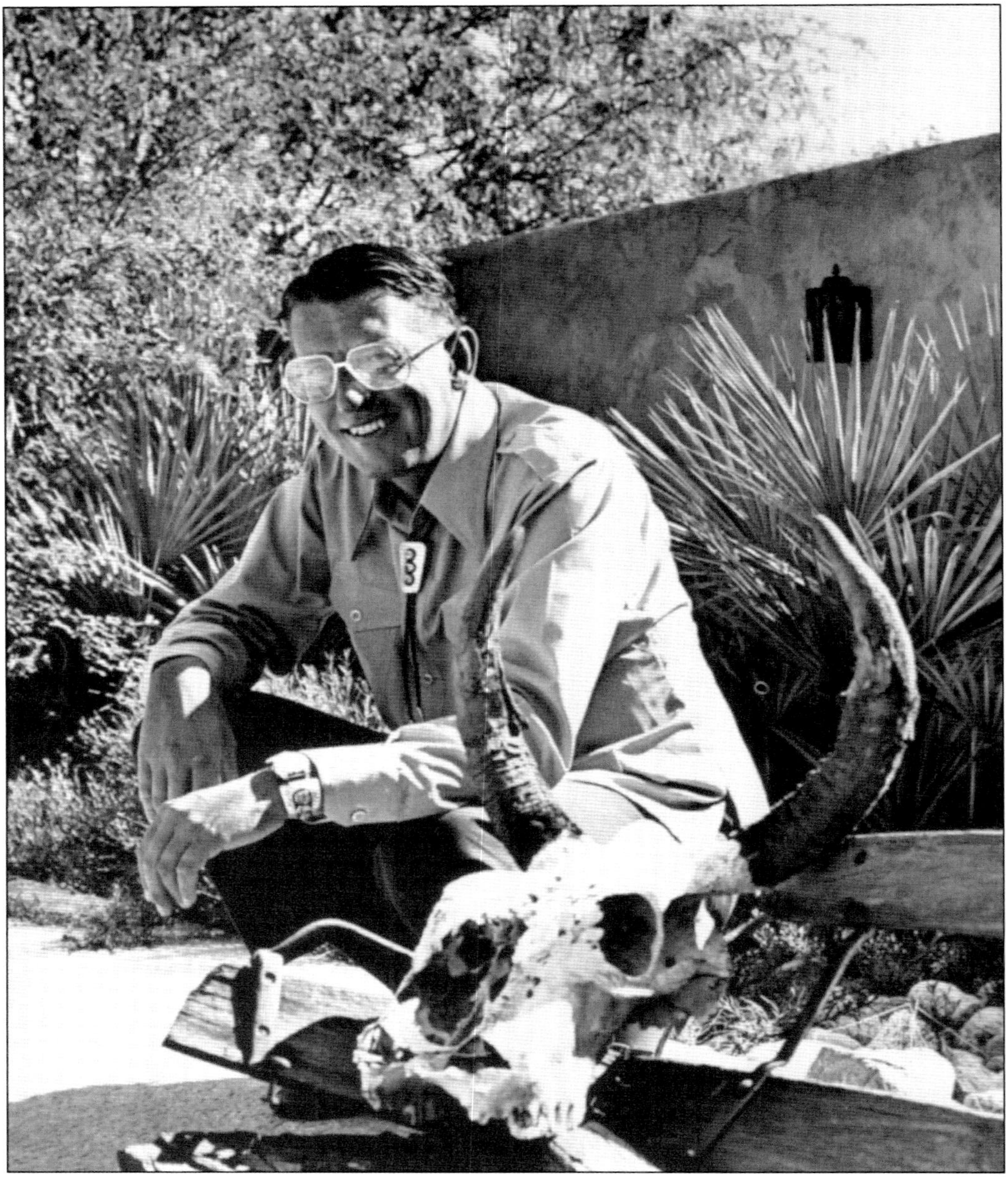

While Dale Nichols may have established the dream of Tubac as an art colony, his old friend and fellow artist Ross Stefan brought the dream to reality. Stefan came to Tubac in 1955 and rented Nichols's studio and gallery. Stefan was a great promoter and used some of his Tucson contacts to get newspaper articles published on Tubac. One of the people who dropped in on Stefan was William C. Morrow, the Father of Modern Tubac (see page 96), who gave him a check for $1,200 and said, "Buy me something, kid. I'll be back in six months." Stefan purchased the Lowe house for $1,095 and set Morrow on a Tubac acquisitions binge that would remake the town. (Jarvis Harriman.)

Sid Cedargreen (photographed here in 1969) arrived in Tubac from Wickenburg in 1957, just after Ross Stefan purchased 100 acres of land on the west side of the highway in the Diablito foothills. Cedargreen became enamored by Tubac and not only bought 20 acres of Stefan's property but worked out a partnership with Ross to build a studio and gallery. Cedargreen was active in the development of Morrow's Tubac Plaza and a founding member of the Santa Cruz Valley Art Association. (Santa Cruz Valley Art Association.)

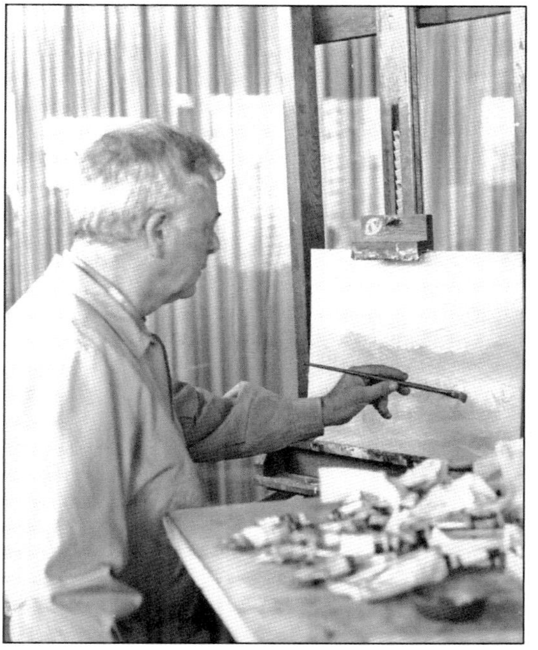

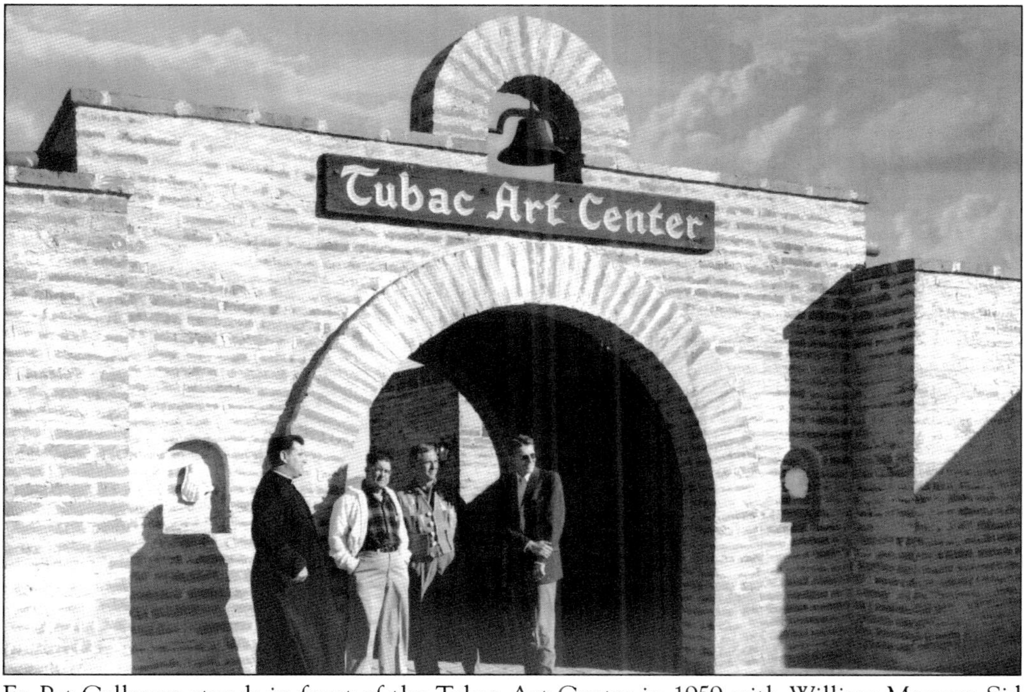

Fr. Pat Callanan stands in front of the Tubac Art Center in 1959 with William Morrow, Sid Cedargreen, and Ross Stefan. As the largest building in Tubac, it was difficult to light, so the partners Stefan and Cedargreen called on experienced Tucson gallery owner Ivan Rosequist for help. While solving the lighting problem, Rosequist perceived Stefan's talent and provided the financial security he needed to devote himself to painting with no more worries of promoting Tubac, teaching art, or selling real estate. (Tubac Presidio State Historic Park.)

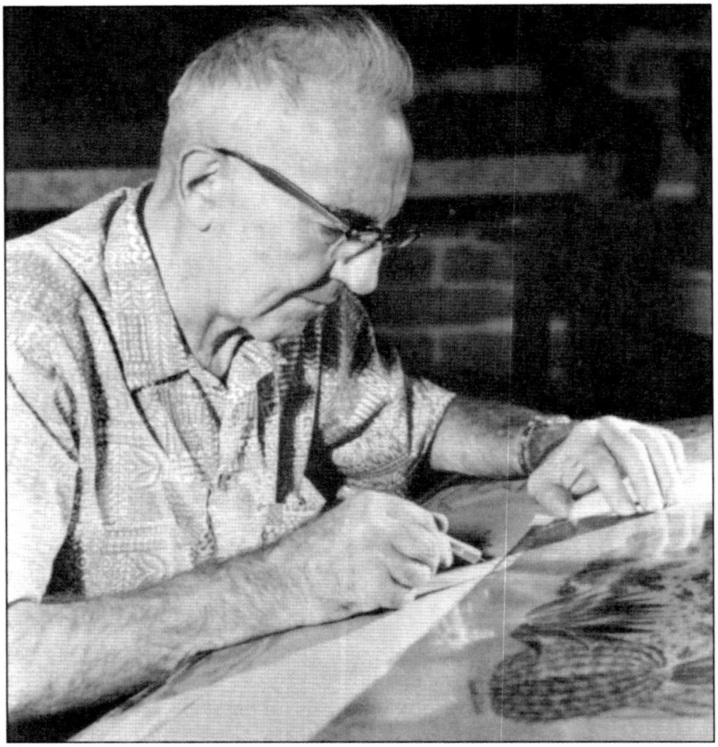

Harwood and Sophie Steiger came to Tubac in 1956 via Alamos, Sonora, and set up a silkscreen fabric shop on Tubac Road in 1958. Harwood is seen in this photograph working on a stencil for one of his bold fabric designs that incorporated plants, animals, and motifs of the Southwest. Earlier, he had been a commercial artist in New York City and had taught painting on Martha's Vineyard. The Steigers were among the founders of the Santa Cruz Valley Art Association. After their death, niece Wanda Halbwachs kept their shop going until 2006.

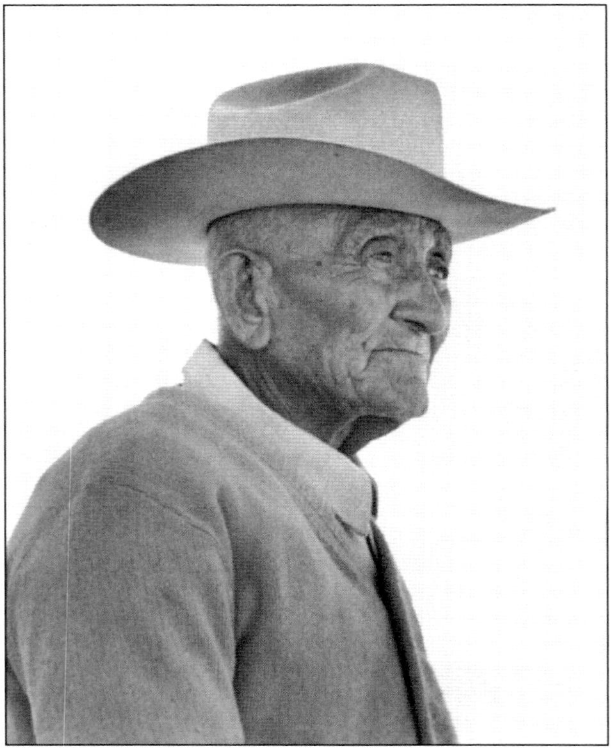

Tubac resident Jose Guaydacan represents an important part of the village's multicultural heritage. He worked as a cowboy for Tubac rancher Jim Garrett for most of his life and lived to age 94, passing away on Christmas Day 1982. Ross Stefan wrote in his memoir, "If during those years I was to meet no other person than Jose Guaydacan, an ancient Yaqui Indian who still lives in the adobe mill house on the Santa Cruz River, it would have been worthwhile."

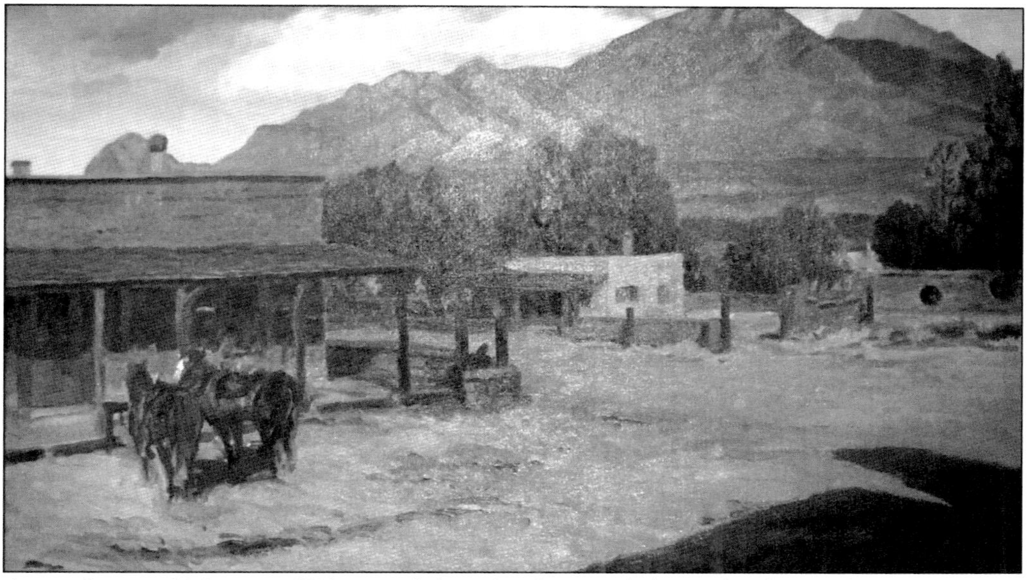

Artists Jean and Mortimer Wilson and their daughter settled in Tubac by accident in 1957. On their way to Mexico, they stayed the night at Rancho Santa Cruz and just decided to stay. They rented three small buildings of Josephine Bailey's Tumacácori ranch and lived there for years. Jean, an exceptional designer and painter, is noted for her trompe l'oeil creations, the light fixtures at the Arizona Inn, the design of the official seal of Santa Cruz County, and paintings of Tubac, like this one accurately depicting Tubac in the 1950s and 1960s. (Trudi Fletcher.)

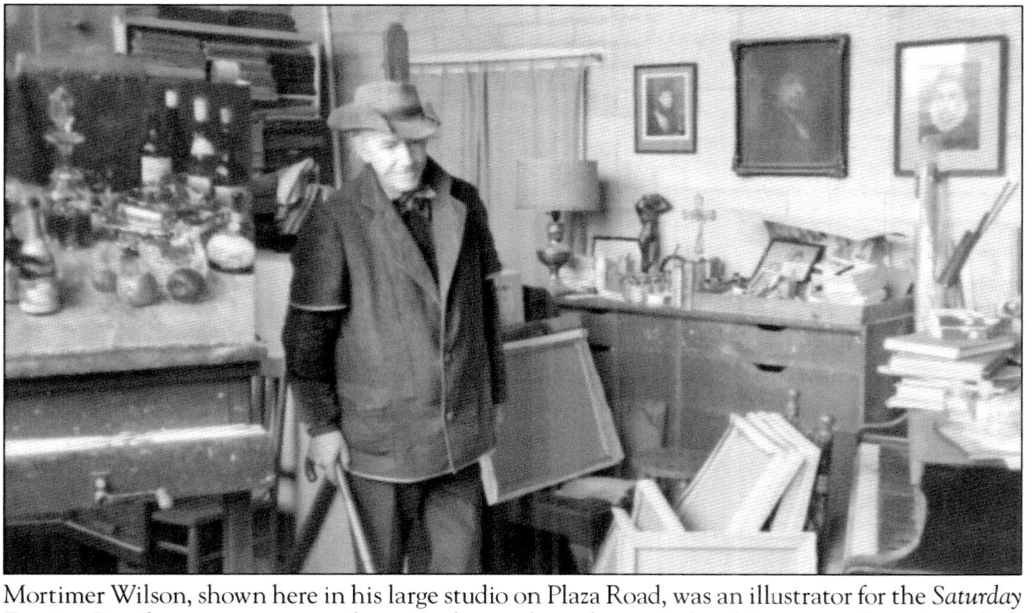

Mortimer Wilson, shown here in his large studio on Plaza Road, was an illustrator for the *Saturday Evening Post* for many years until an eye disease brought an end to his career. Once in Tubac, Wilson was an early president of the Santa Cruz Valley Art Association. When his vision was restored by what he calls "a gift from the Almighty," he again began to paint. His still life paintings frequently depict pieces of silver and crystal and are highly prized. The sculptor Lee Blackwell later took over Wilson's studio. (Lorraine Mitchell Halvorsen.)

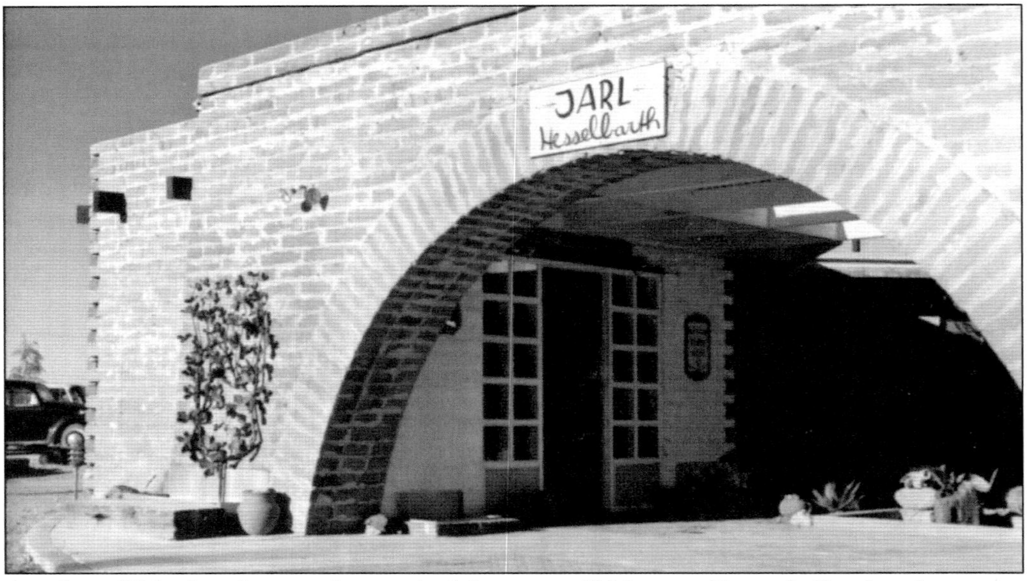

Another of Tubac's early art studios was built by painter El Meyer and his wife, Hazel, and mosaicist Lou Smith and his wife, Lora. Both men were active in Tubac's civic affairs, El serving as the first president of the Tubac Chamber of Commerce and Lou as chairman of its Architectural Committee. Meyer drew the renderings for the development of the Tubac Valley Country Club Estates. Later in the 1960s, when this photograph was taken, the gallery was bought by Jarl and Suzi Hesselbarth. Still later, master silversmith John Ford bought it. (Santa Cruz Valley Art Association.)

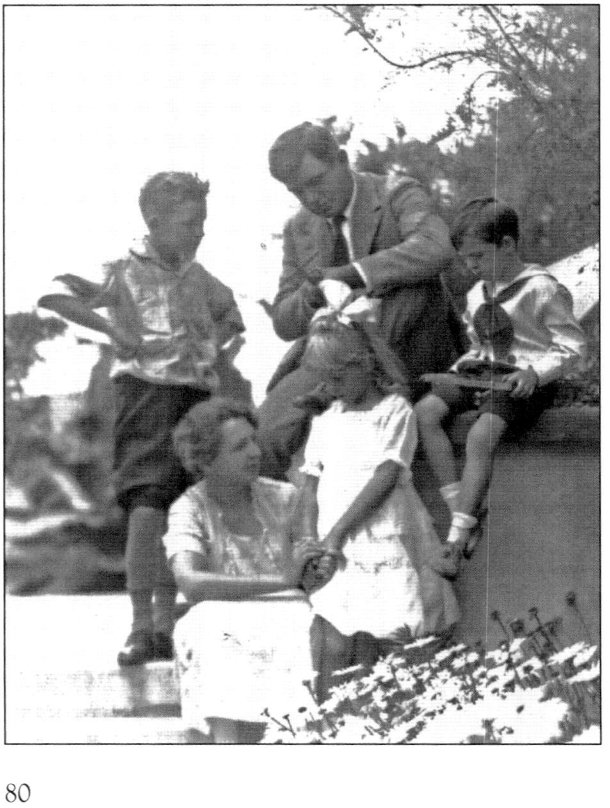

This image of famous humorist-journalist-movie star Will Rogers shows him fussing with an erector set with his children: Will Jr. (left), daughter Amelia (center), and James (right) while Betty Rogers holds Amelia's hands. Will Jr. and his wife, Collier, found Tubac on a Western car trip in 1955 and became its leading citizens. Will Jr. served in the U.S. Congress from California, resigned to enlist in the army, serving as a tank commander under Patton. Having met and talked with Ross Stefan, they bought the Garretts' two-story house, where they lived for many years. They also purchased the old Pennington house, which Collier restored and established as one of Tubac's first art galleries.

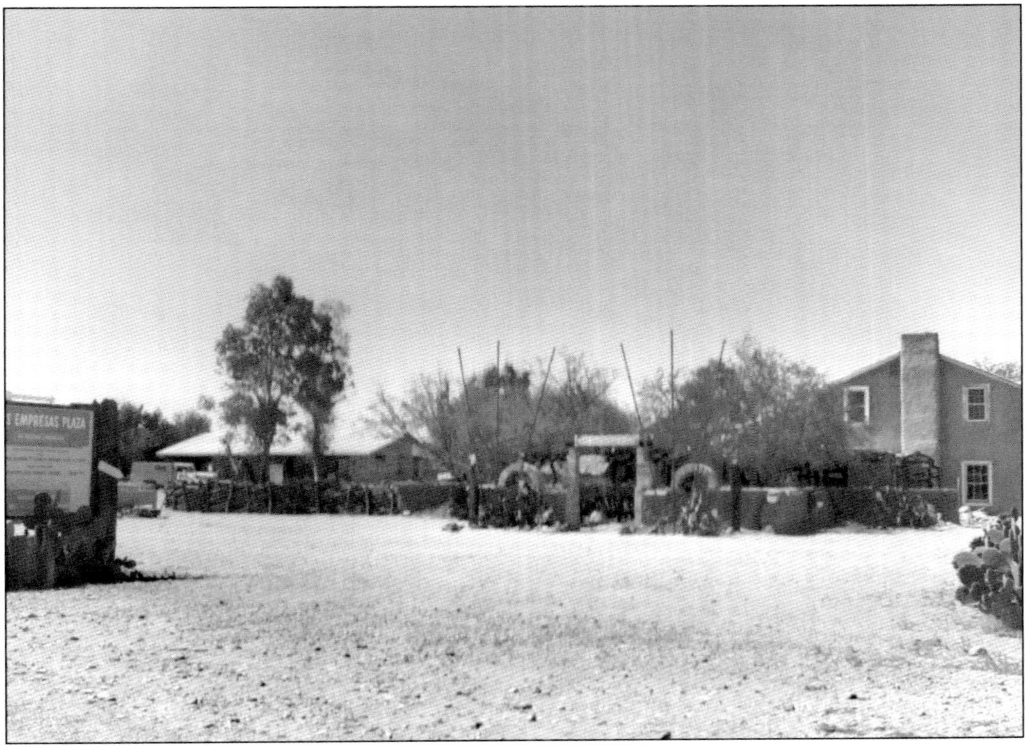

The two-story Garrett ranch house, built around 1913, is shown here when it was the home of Collier and Will Rogers Jr. The area beyond the gate at center is today the Country Shop. At left is the tienda where Alfonso and Tiburcia Flores sold mesquite carvings and other merchandise from Oaxaca, Mexico.

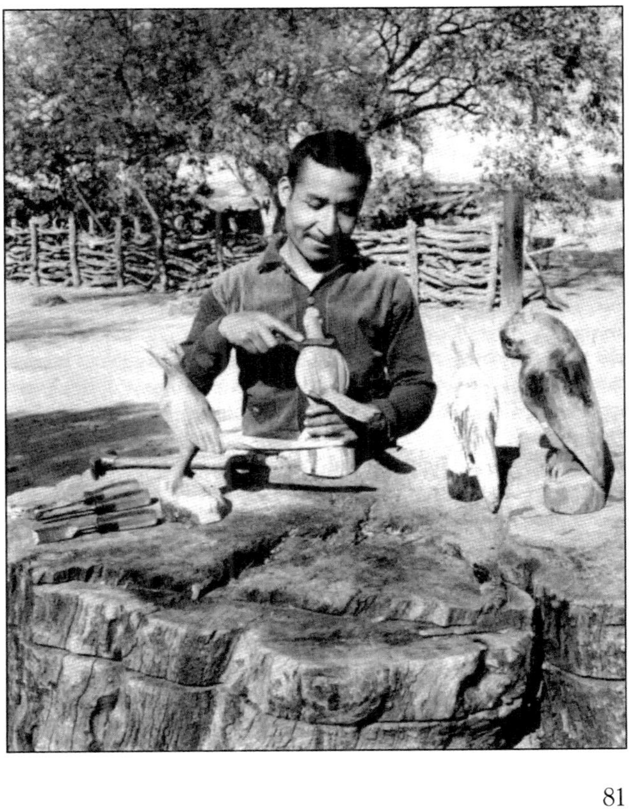

Alfonso Flores and his wife, Tiburcia, came from their native Oaxaca to work for Bill and Collier Rogers, Tiburcia as cook and Alfonso as gardener. Tiburcia enkindled in the Rogers a love of Mexican cuisine, and Collier was so impressed with Alfonso's ability as a wood carver that she helped to promote him and start his own shop. Flores also became a skilled silk screener and worked with Harwood Steiger for many years.

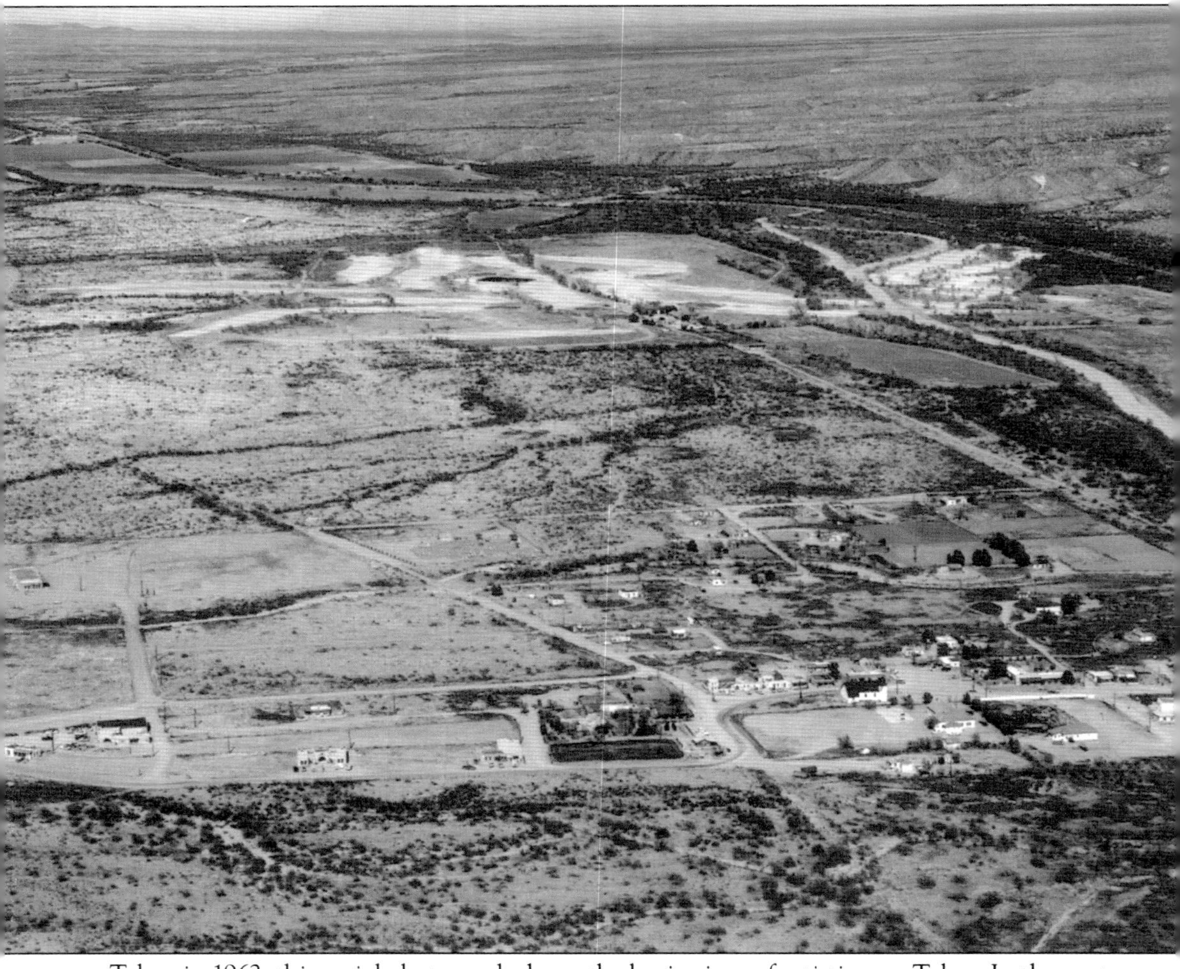

Taken in 1962, this aerial photograph shows the beginnings of artistic new Tubac. In the center is the old Garrett Ranch house where Will Rogers Jr. and his wife, Collier, now lived, and to the left is the Steiger Studio, then the Tubac Art Center built by Sid Cedargreen and Ross Stefan, and to the left, built by artists El Meyer and Lou Smith, the building that housed the Hesselbarths and later John Ford. The building in the foreground first held the office of Bill Morrow and later Louise Trees's real estate business. Above is St. Ann's Parish Hall. To the right of Garrett's plot, the old state highway is coming in on an angle past the cemetery and Trailer Tether to Frank and Gay Griffin's El Presidito; to the right of it are the Pennington House, St. Ann's, and the state park before the museum was built. The Tubac golf course is being built in the distance, and the old Otero Ranch houses are visible in a copse of trees. The Santa Cruz River runs within steep banks 100 yards west of its present course.

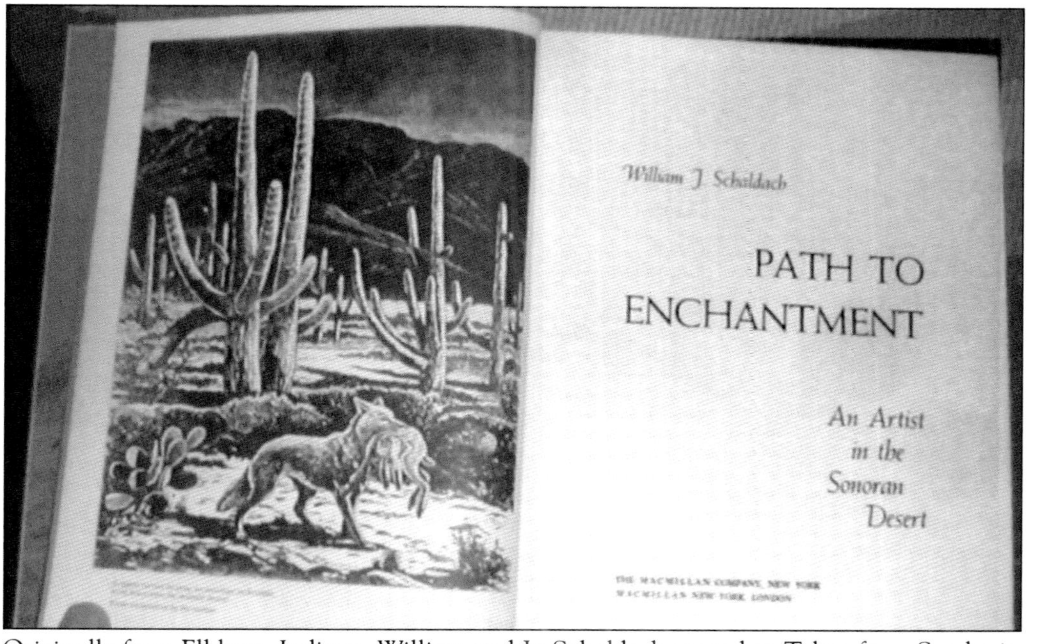

Originally from Elkhart, Indiana, William and Jo Schaldach moved to Tubac from Sasabe in 1958. William learned the skills of drypoint, etching, and aquatint in New York and put these skills to use in Tubac where he wrote and illustrated his famous 1963 *Path to Enchantment: An Artist in the Sonoran Desert*, reflecting his knowledge and love of the flora and fauna of the area. (Shaw Kinsley.)

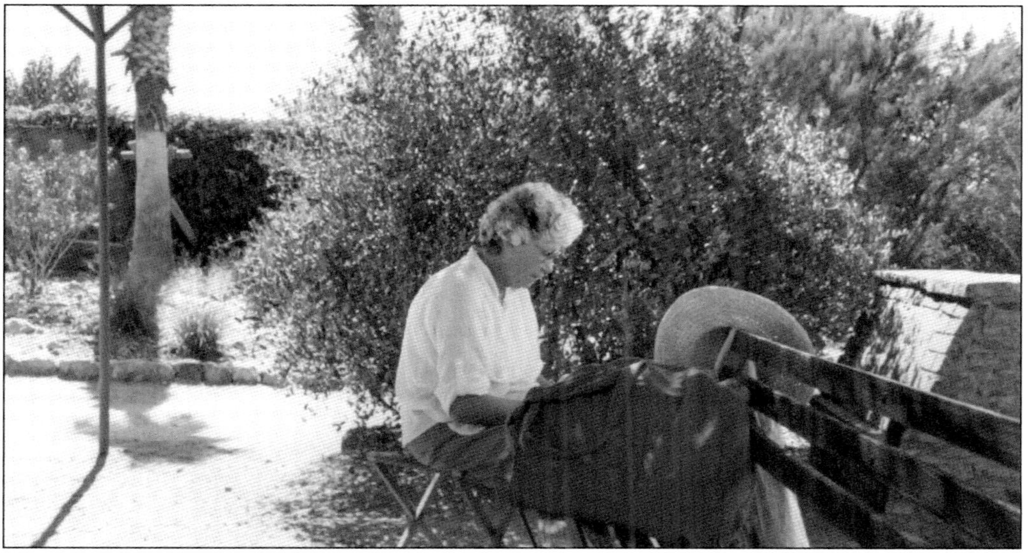
Encouraged by New York City friends the Steigers, Jarl and Suzi Hesselbarth moved to Tubac and bought the gallery built by El Meyer and Lou Smith in 1964. Jarl was a Norwegian biologist and sailing master who created metal and ceramic sculptures he dubbed "People-watchers." One critic said of Suzi, shown in this undated photograph, she "brings all the joy in the world to her watercolors." Many of Tubac's street signs feature her paintings on ceramic tiles. (Santa Cruz Valley Art Association.)

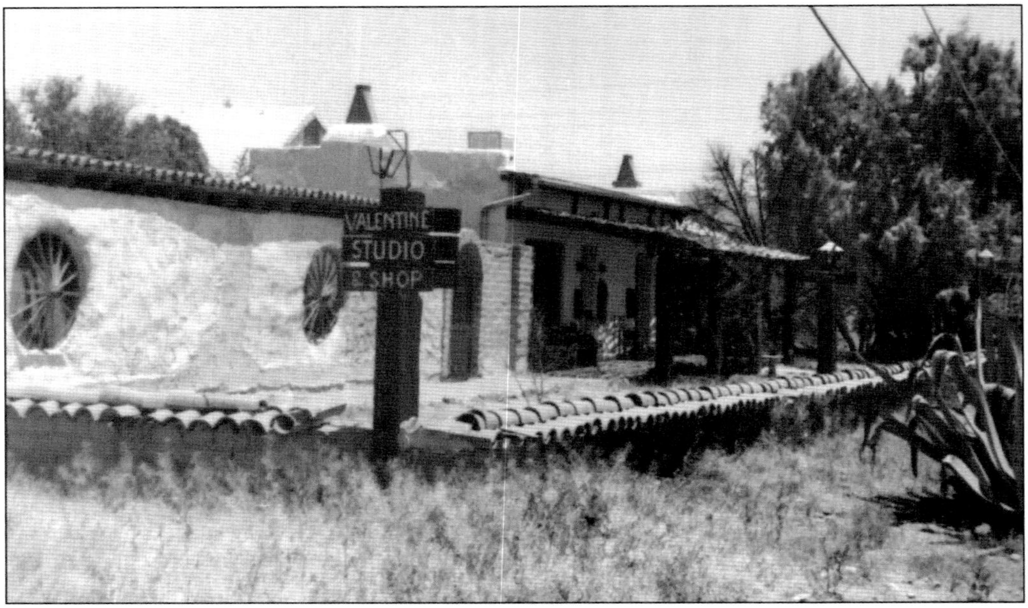

From 1904 to 1940, this series of three buildings was owned by the Lowe family. The central part was the center of village life as it was the post office with William Lowe as postmaster. Ross Stefan bought the property for $1,095 in 1958 for William Morrow, who lived there while he dreamed of Tubac's future. Collier Rogers had the wagon wheels set in the adobe wall around the time the Valentines bought the property and combined the three buildings as their home, gallery, and studio. (Santa Cruz Valley Art Association.)

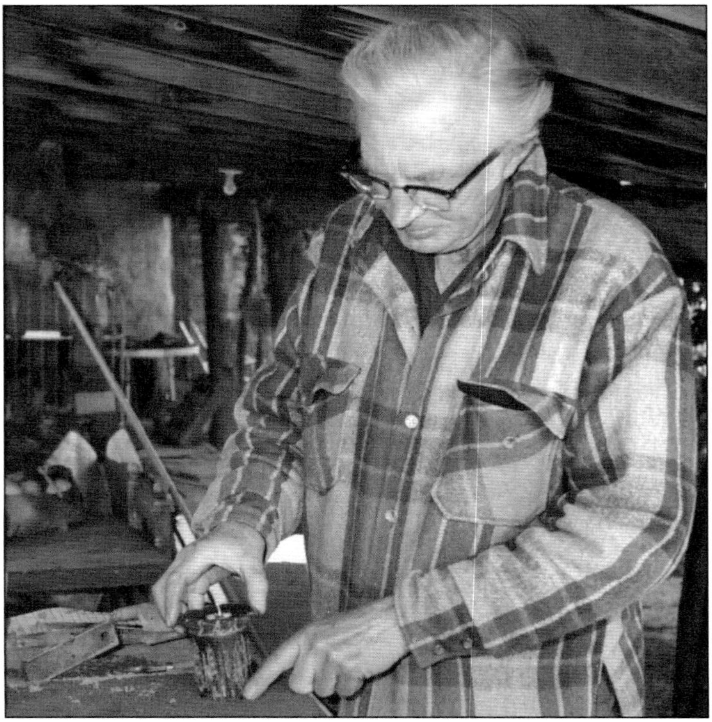

Hans and Marion Valentine came to Arizona from Wisconsin for Marion's health. They first lived in Tucson before buying the Lowe House from Bill Morrow. Hans made sand-cast wax cactus candles for years before the demands of running the gallery and selling Marion's paintings forced him to give it up. Hans was an early treasurer of the Tubac Historical Society, member of the Tubac Fire Department, and not only one of the first graduates of that organization's EMT training but also its oldest volunteer in the state. (Santa Cruz Valley Art Association.)

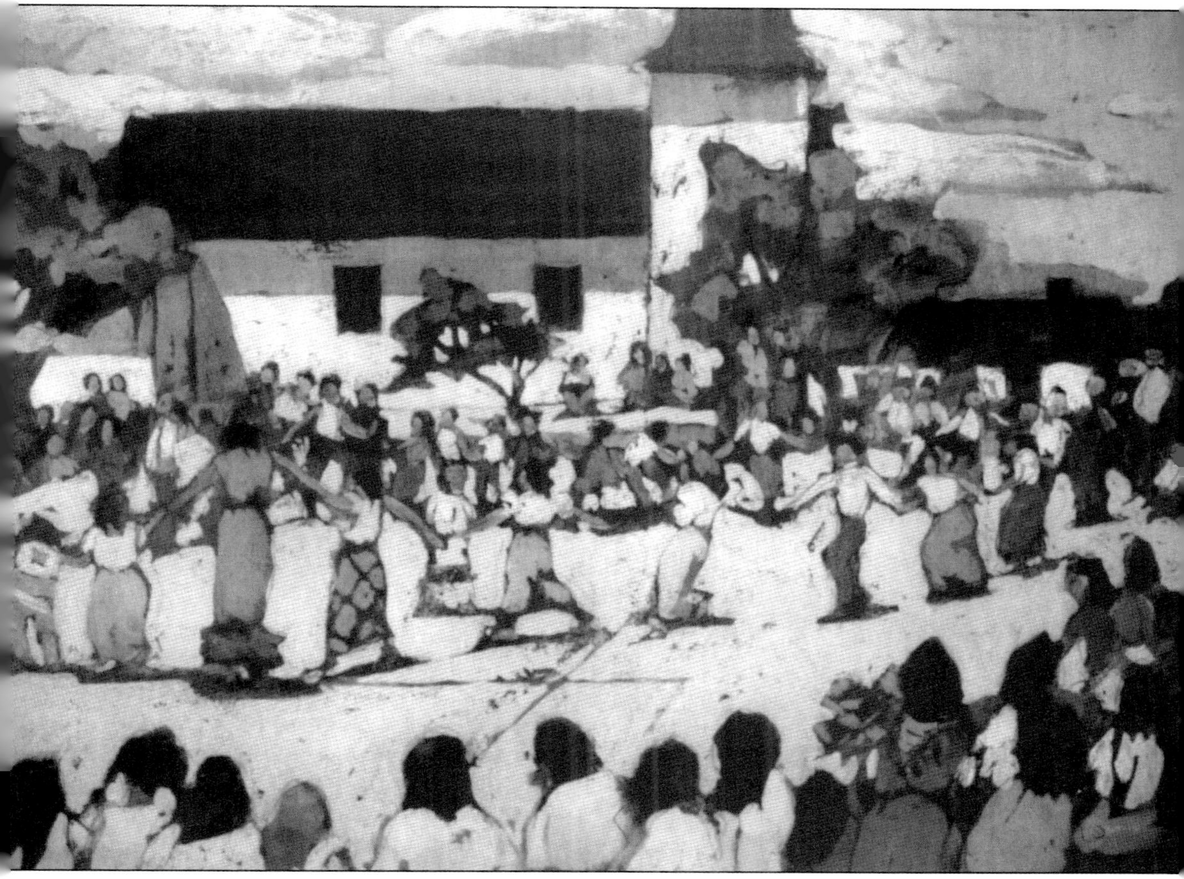

During the Anza Days festival in 1976, the local elementary schoolchildren held a pageant based on the book *How Far Felipe?*, about a little boy and his burro and their experiences on the trek from Tubac to San Francisco. Marion Valentine saw the pageant, went home, and created this painting in her own technique of wax-resist watercolor. It was hung in a members' show at the Tubac Center of the Arts when a group of second graders came with their teacher and were enchanted by it. They wanted to buy Marion's painting for their school and began to raise the funds by holding cookie sales and newspaper drives. The art center helped by taking donations, and the children were successful. The painting hung in the school art collection for many years, but its whereabouts is currently a mystery.

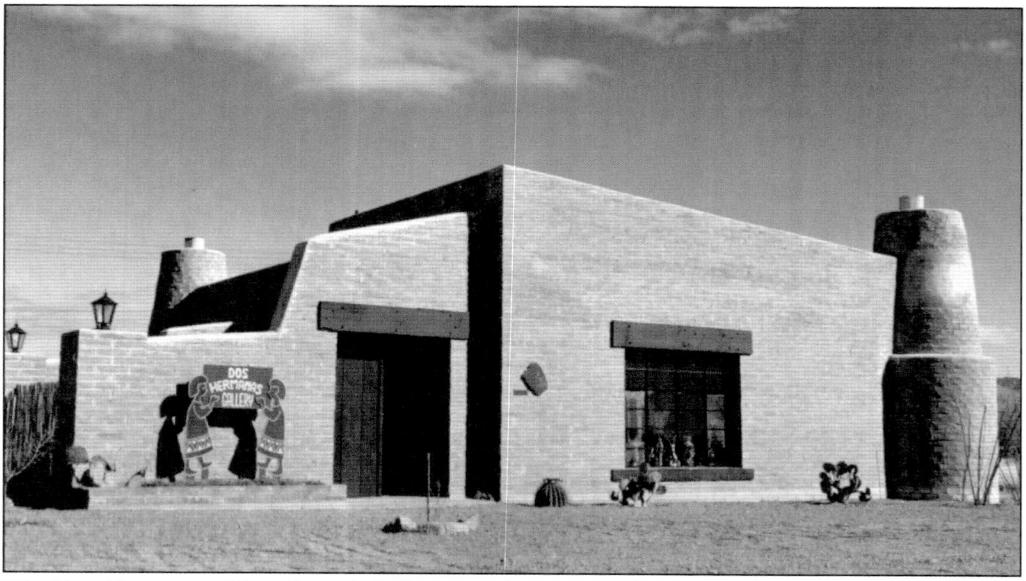

The Dos Hermanas (Two Sisters) Gallery, on the corner of Hesselbarth Lane and Tubac Road, was designed by noted Nogales architect Benny Gonzales and constructed by Tubac builders Ed Maizel and Gil Tesso. It is a fine example of blending local southwestern adobe building methods with contemporary Mexican architectural design and the individual tastes of its owners. The gallery was named for artist/owners and siblings Trudi Fletcher and Kay Davis and dedicated in an elaborate ceremony on December 8, 1968. (Santa Cruz Valley Art Association.)

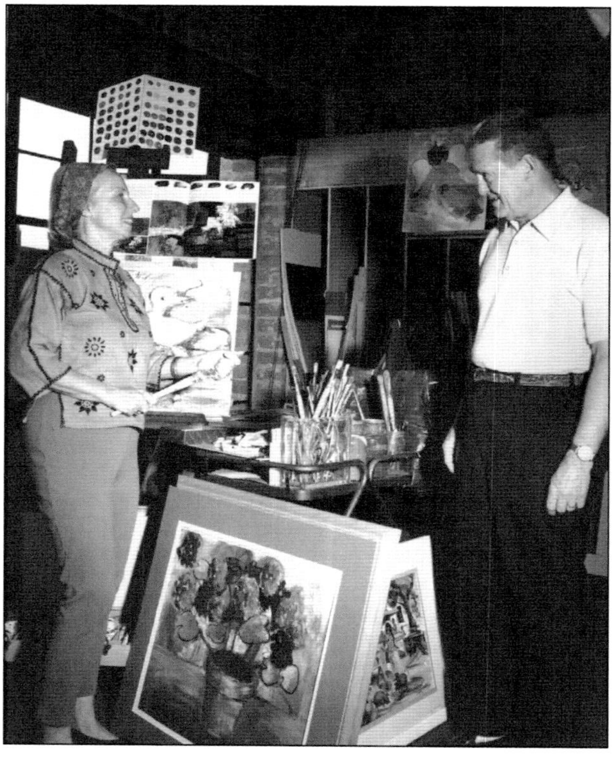

Albert and Trudi Fletcher stand inside Dos Hermanas Gallery shortly after the opening. When Albie retired from AT&T and suggested moving to Naples, Florida, Trudi said she knew a better place. She and her first husband, Robert Whitacre, had visited Arizona in 1949 when Dale Nichols's art school was running, and Trudi never forgot Tubac. The Fletchers bought a house they called Miniwhim on the west side of the highway in 1967. (Santa Cruz Valley Art Association.)

Trudi Fletcher, shown here with Pablo, is a superb artist and an art teacher capable of instructing almost any age or skill level. She taught art in California and studied with Don Kingman, Millard Sheets, and Jerry Brommer, and she has traveled extensively in Mexico, Asia, and Africa. Trudi works in many artistic media, while the other *hermana*, Kay Davis, preferred large mosaics and fine embroideries.

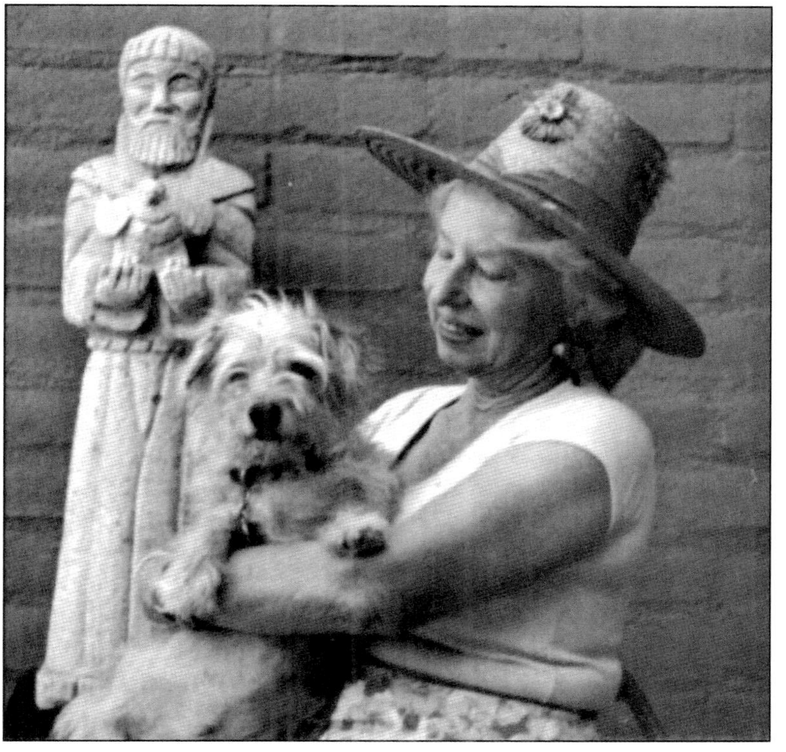

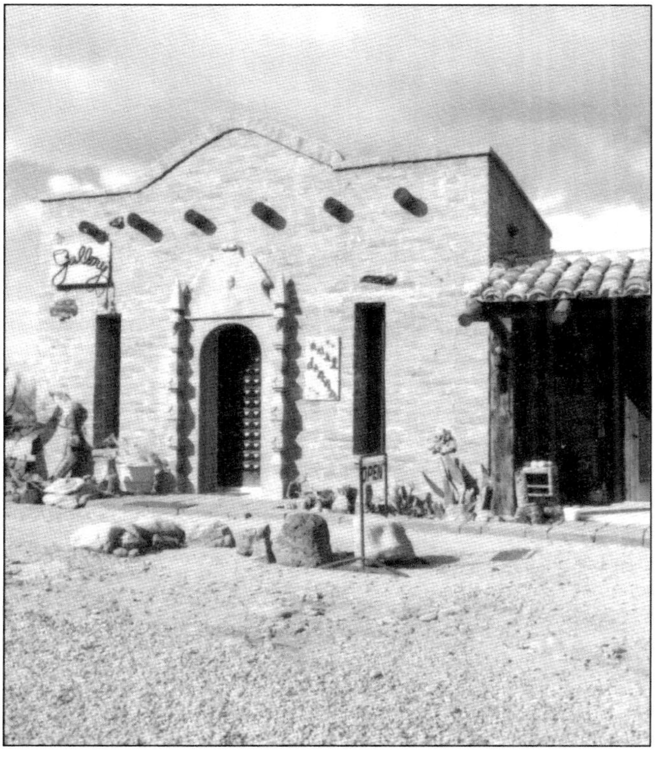

Thanks to Marjorie Nichols, Earl and Faye Dravis came to Tubac from Indiana in the late 1950s. Their gallery and home, shown here shortly after its completion in 1969, is one of Tubac's more unusual adobe buildings. The stone archway was cast in Italy and originally graced the entrance to Tucson's El Conquistador Hotel, which also supplied the interior beams and massive mahogany door. Several of the windows were salvaged from Tucson's San Augustín Cathedral. The Dravis Gallery sold Earl's paintings and fine North American Indian artifacts and housed Faye's historically significant doll collection. It has been a restaurant almost continuously since the Dravises left. (Santa Cruz Valley Art Association.)

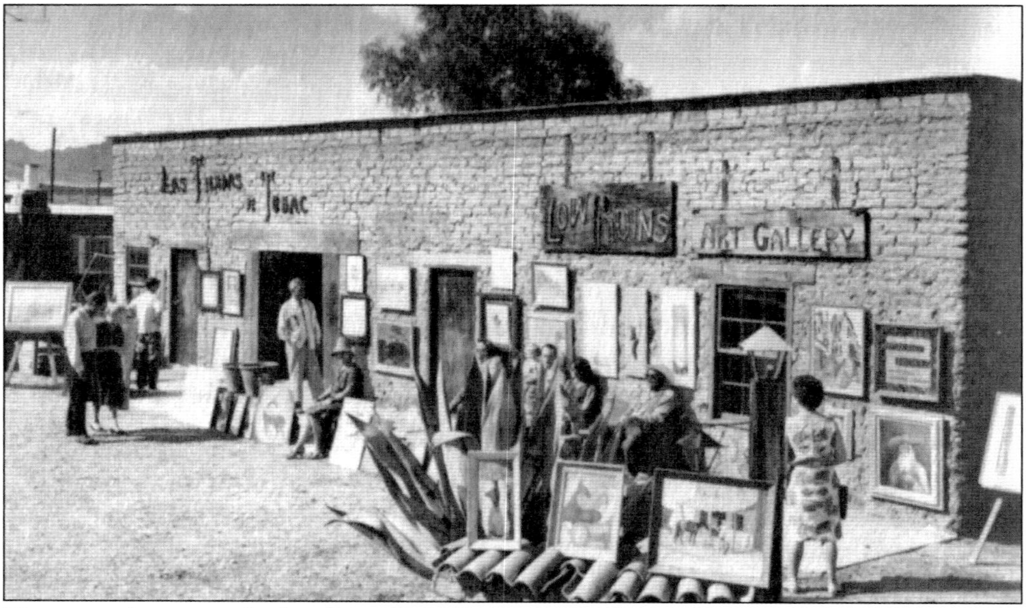

This view of paintings displayed outside the Low Ruins Gallery in the north end of the Pennington house was taken during the June 1964 national art show arranged by Collier Rogers and Marjorie Nichols. The exhibition attracted a large number of visitors and played a significant role in establishing Tubac as an arts community, but it was controversial at the time for not showing the work of any local artists.

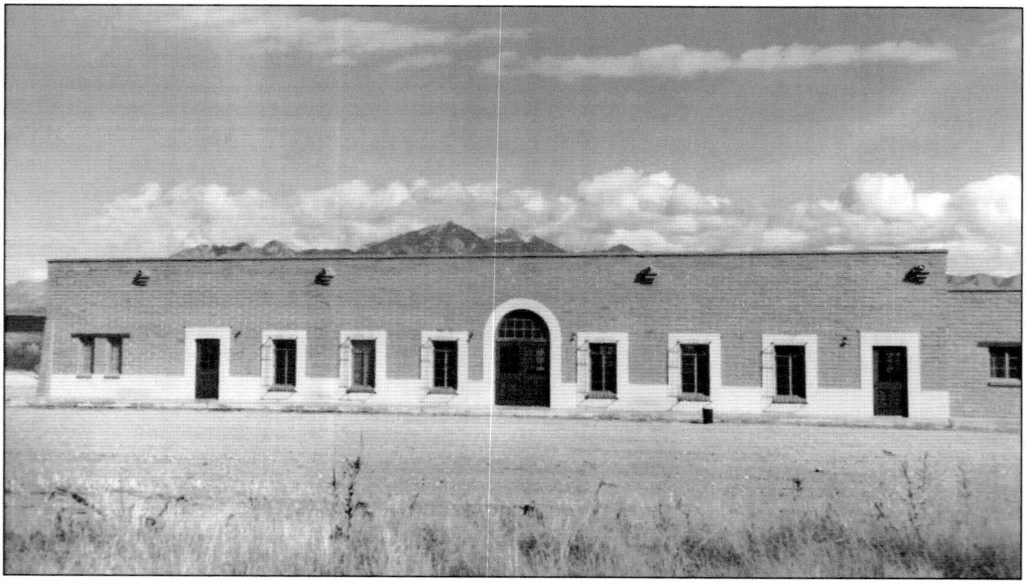

In 1958, William Morrow gave 13 acres immediately north of the village to the Catholic Diocese of Tucson for a parochial school, but sufficient teachers were not available. Morrow then gave the land for a community center, and there was community-wide involvement in raising the funds to build what is now St. Ann's Hall. It has been used for Festival of the Arts exhibits, civic meetings, school events, parties, and bazaars. Since 1999 it has been the home of Montessori de Santa Cruz Charter School. (Santa Cruz Valley Art Association.)

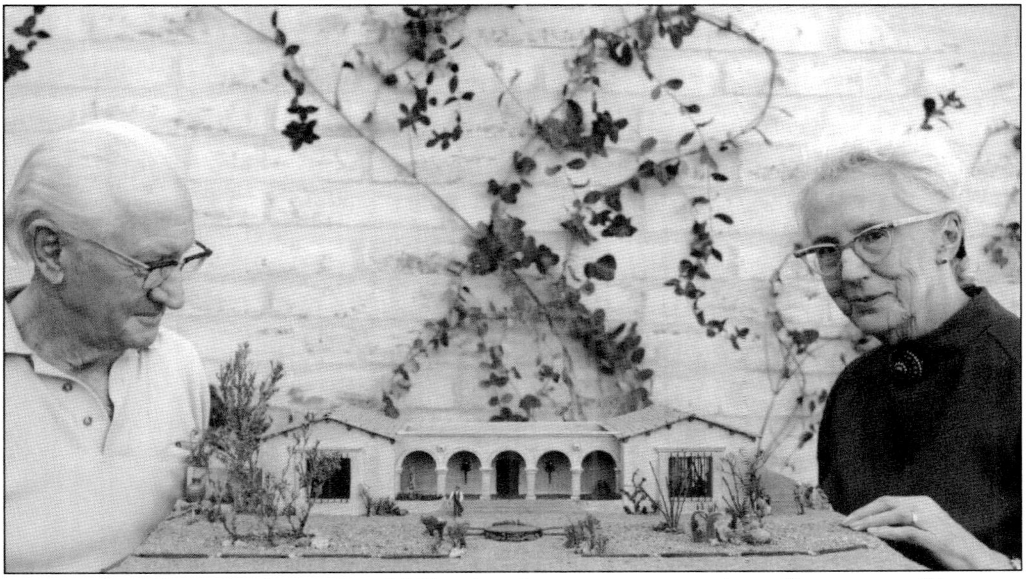

From its founding, the Santa Cruz Valley Art Association wanted a gallery space of its own. William Morrow gave one lot on the plaza in 1963 and Carney Matheson contributed three others five years later, but it was not until Theodora McCurdy (right) was elected president in 1971 that desire became reality. Harold Wilson (left), a new resident and noted California architect, offered a design and submitted the model shown here. Wilson is also remembered today as a fine animal sculptor whose work can still be seen at Disneyland in Anaheim, California. (Santa Cruz Valley Art Association.)

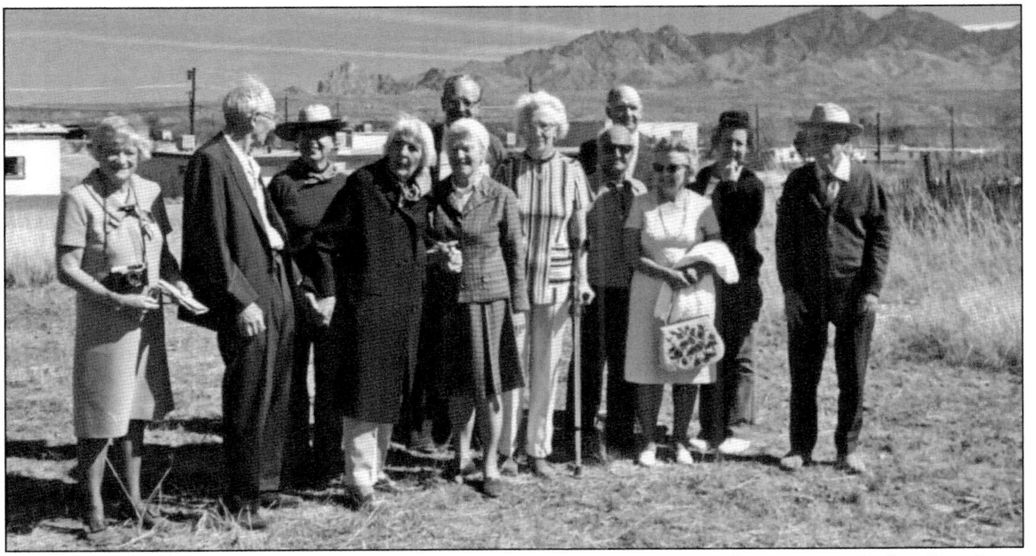

The good and the great of the Santa Cruz Valley Art Association gather in 1971 before breaking ground for the Tubac Center of the Arts. From left to right are Elizabeth Brownell, Harwood Steiger, Jean Wilson, Sophie Steiger, Eldon Holmquist, Jo Schaldach, Theodora "Teddy" McCurdy, Carney Matheson, Ariel Nielsen, Connie Rand, Henrietta Itule, and William Schaldach. The structure visible behind the group at left is the home of architect Harold Wilson; at right is Mortimer Wilson's studio. (Santa Cruz Valley Art Association.)

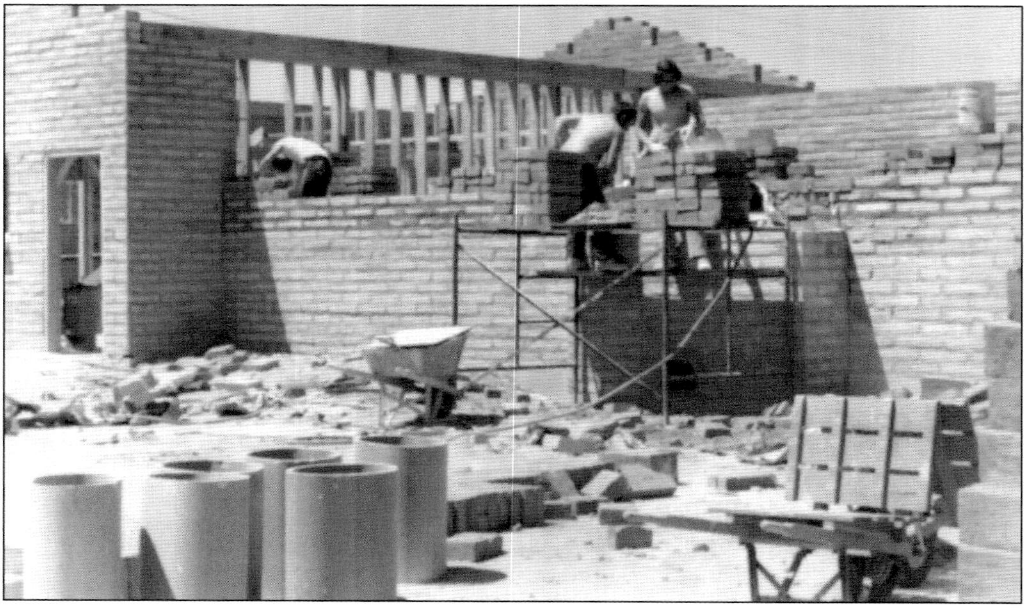

Tubac's art community was still small at the time, and there were arguments pro and con over the wisdom of the art association having its own gallery. During construction, architect Harold Wilson watched over every step, always on the lookout for economical and long-lasting materials. The building was completed within the budget of $50,000 because of strong local support. (Santa Cruz Valley Art Association.)

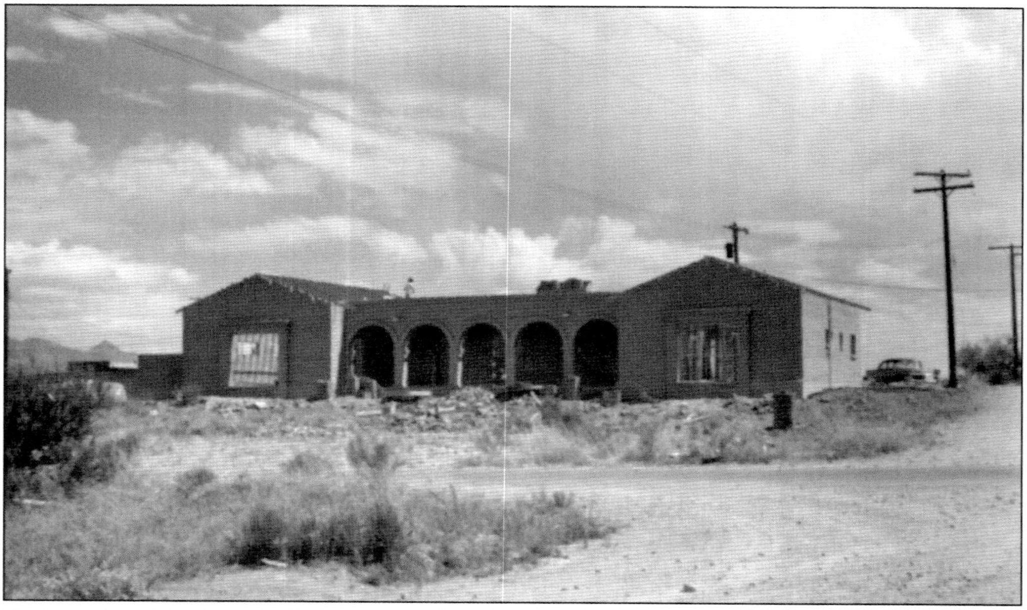

Dedicated on October 21, 1972, two months after this photograph was taken, the Tubac Center of the Arts provided a physical space to fulfill its stated purpose: "encourage and promote friendship and good fellowship among those engaged in the Arts." The exhibits, classes, seminars, and performances over the years have stimulated an interest in the regional arts and crafts of the Santa Cruz Valley and burnished Tubac's reputation. (Santa Cruz Valley Art Association.)

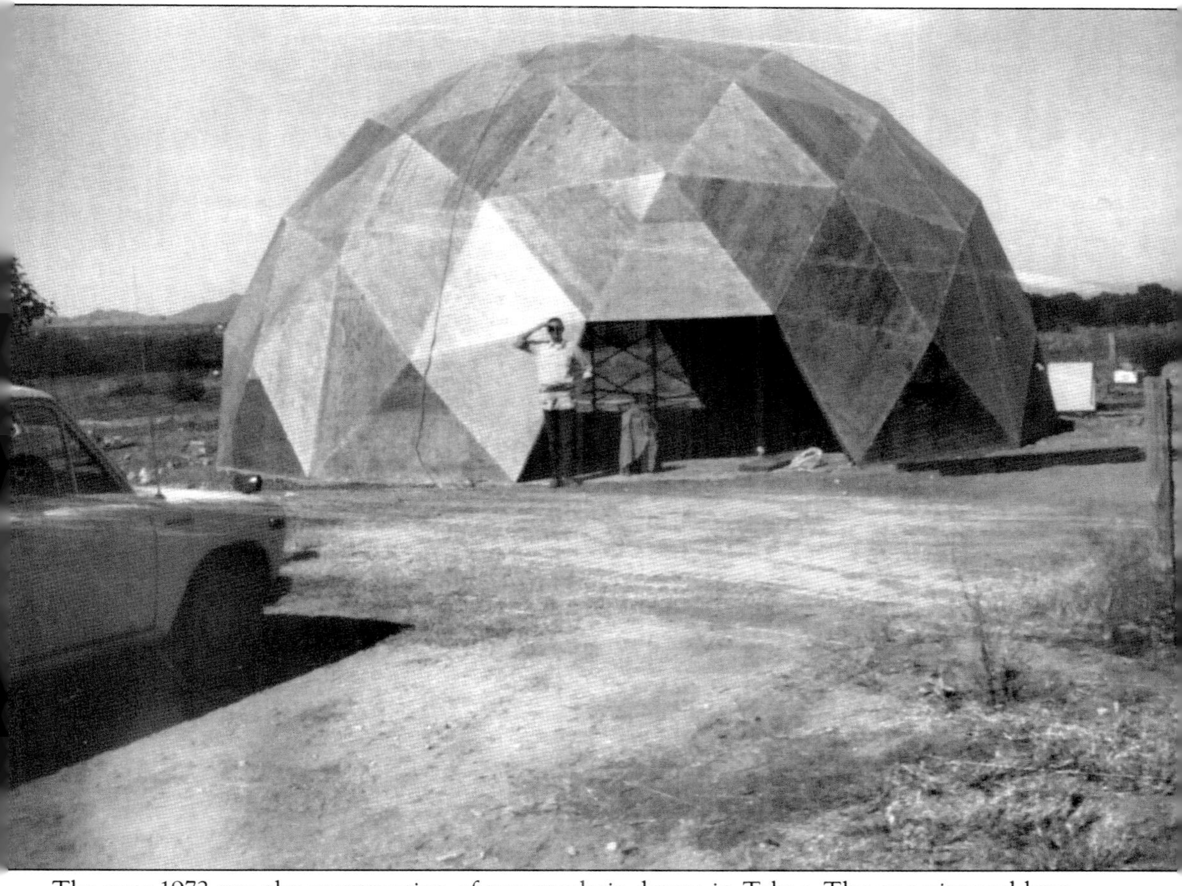

The year 1972 saw the construction of two geodesic domes in Tubac. The one pictured here was built for Chuck Tougas, manager of the Smithsonian Observatory on Mount Hopkins, on the east side of the Santa Cruz River. The other dome, on Calle Baca in the village, was built for Edgar and Cindy Loucks by Clyde Morse of Duck Island, New York. In 1976, the dome was taken over by Peter Holmes, who established Origins Press there, the only stone lithographic operation in Arizona. Holmes was a master in the art of lithographic printing, and Origins had two 500-pound slabs of Bavarian limestone and 10 of Italian marble, making it one of the best lithographic studios in the country. Origins brought R. C. Gorman to Tubac and printed works by such other well-known artists as Jon Lightfoot, Earl Biss, and Jacquelin Rochester. Gorman did a one-man show of his lithographs at the Tubac Center of the Arts in 1977, and it drew over 450 people, the largest show there to date. Gorman owned the lot next to the Art Center for several years but never moved here. (Jennifer Tougas.)

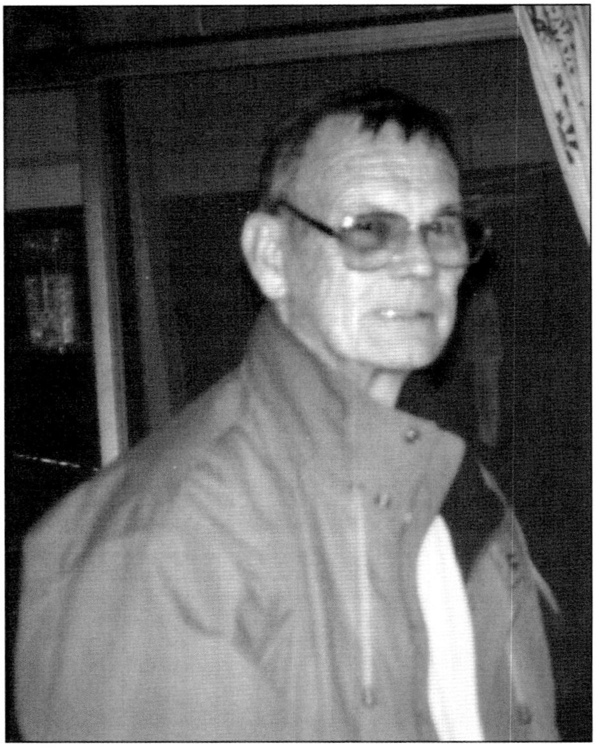

John Montgomery, a native Arizonan and oil painter of desert scenes and student of Hal Empie, designed and built the Artes Alegres Gallery on Camino Otero in the early 1970s with his partner Curley Heiss. They represented a stable of western artists and sold high-end Native American artifacts. Artes Alegres was a frequent meeting place for locals, and the garden tended by Curley was a true oasis. (Jennifer Tougas.)

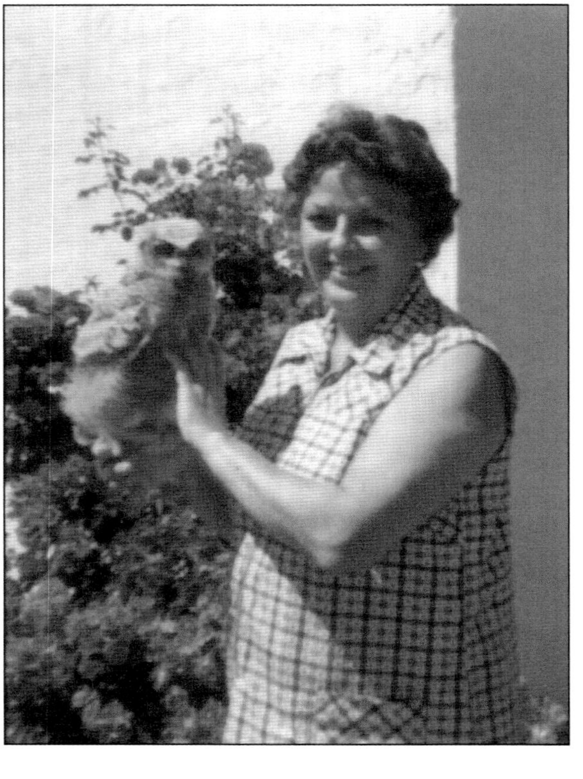

Maxine Guy first visited Tubac in 1965 at the suggestion of the wife of the commanding general at Fort Huachuca and was charmed by its artist-craftsmen making and selling their own work. A brilliant potter, she moved here in 1972 and built a studio called the Potted Owl. She was also a skilled wildlife rehabilitator and is shown here with a baby great-horned owl, one of hundreds of animals she saved. (Nancy Bohman.)

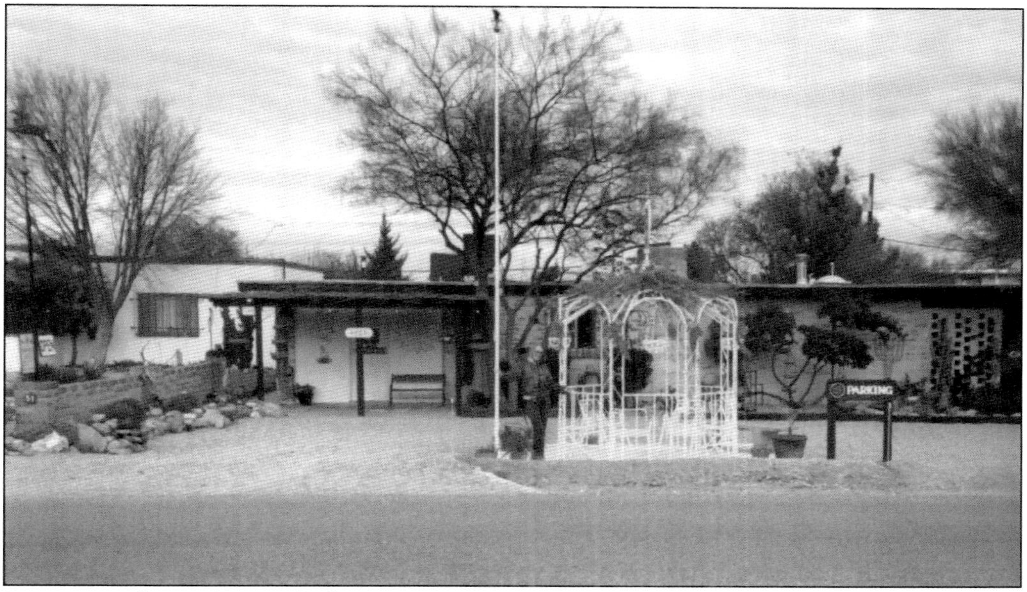

Lorraine and "Mitch" Mitchell came to Tubac in 1973, and after starting a building on Calle Baca, they purchased Harold Wilson's house and established Tubac Iron Works there. Mitch made large bakers' racks, candelabra, bells, and other ornamental pieces in addition to doing custom ironwork for homes and businesses. The shop also sold Lorraine's copper enamels and watercolors (she was a student of Trudi Fletcher's). (Lorraine Mitchell Halvorsen.)

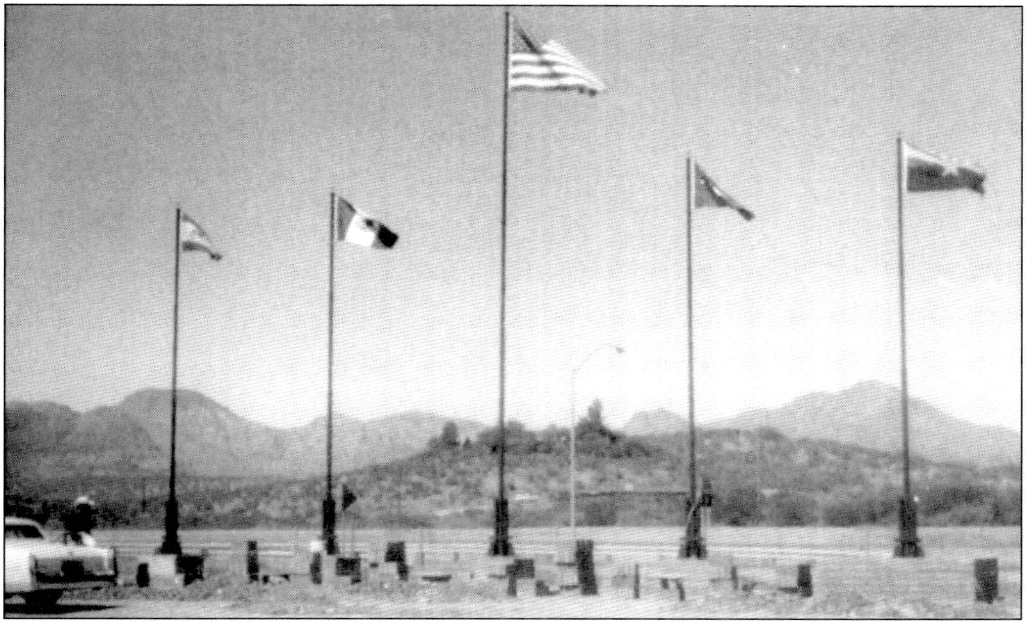

The five flags at Tubac's entrance were dedicated in 1980. The poles and bases were made by "Mitch" Mitchell, and Paul McDonald (lower left) donated the flags. The Spanish flag (left) ruled from 1691 to 1820, the Mexican flag (second from left) from 1821 to 1853, and the Stars and Stripes (center) since 1853. The Confederate Stars and Bars (second from right) flew for a short period in 1862. The Arizona state flag has flown since February 14, 1912.

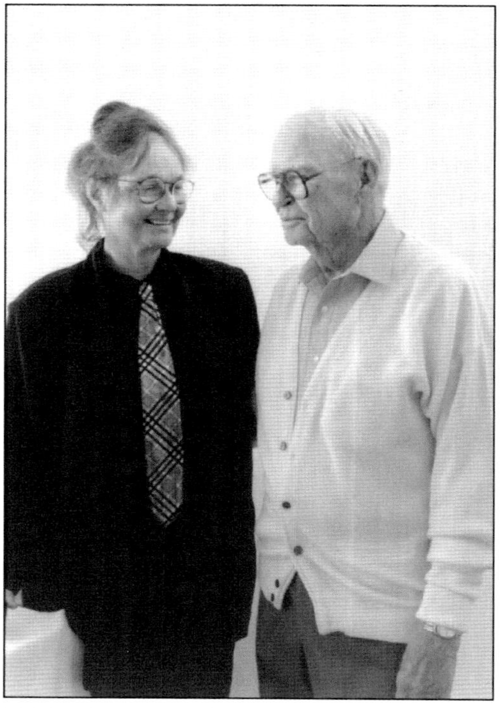

Virginia Hall (left) bought land in Tubac in 1974 and moved here from Michigan in 1979. She designed and built her studio that summer, inspired by the white-walled restoration of the Poston Block by Doug and Frances Luger. Hal Empie (right), celebrated as the dean of Arizona artists for his pivotal role in fostering Arizona art by Arizona artists, moved to Tubac in 1986.

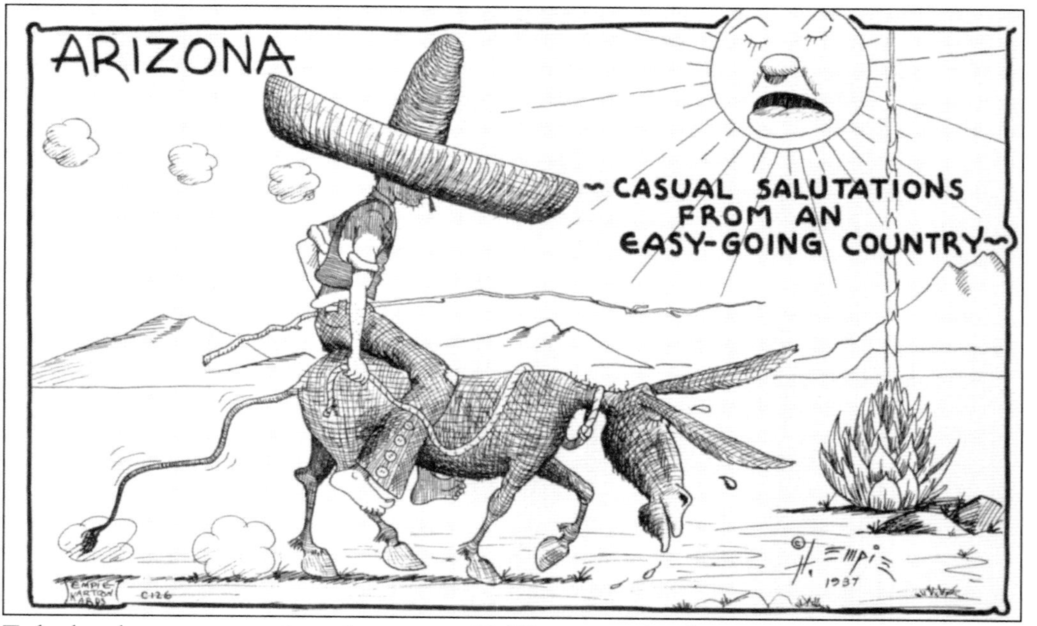

Today best known as an artist and cartoonist, Hal Empie was also the youngest licensed pharmacist in Arizona and ran the Duncan (Arizona) Drug Store from 1934 until it was destroyed by a catastrophic flood in the late 1980s. Hal didn't create any cartoons specifically about Tubac, but this sombrero-wearing fellow looks like he is from around here. The original artwork for Empie's postcards is preserved in the archives of the Smithsonian National Museum of American History. (Hal Empie Gallery.)

The Tubac Historical Society was incorporated late in 1966, continuing the work begun by Frank Griffin's Tubac Restoration Foundation. In 1976, over 200 books, maps, and photographs collected by Kenyon Ranch and its guests were given to the society, forming the basis of their library. Hugh Cabot provided the bookplate shown here as a testament of his appreciation of Tubac's history and the society's role in its preservation.

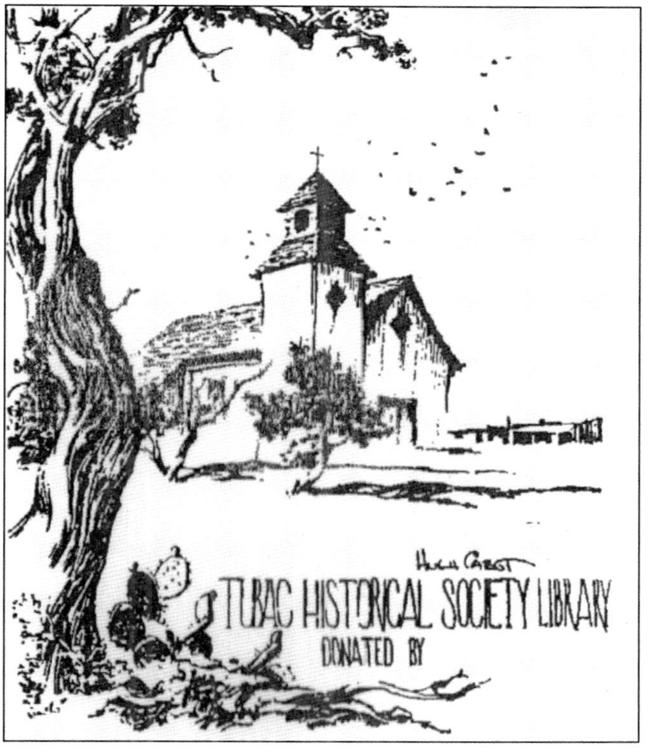

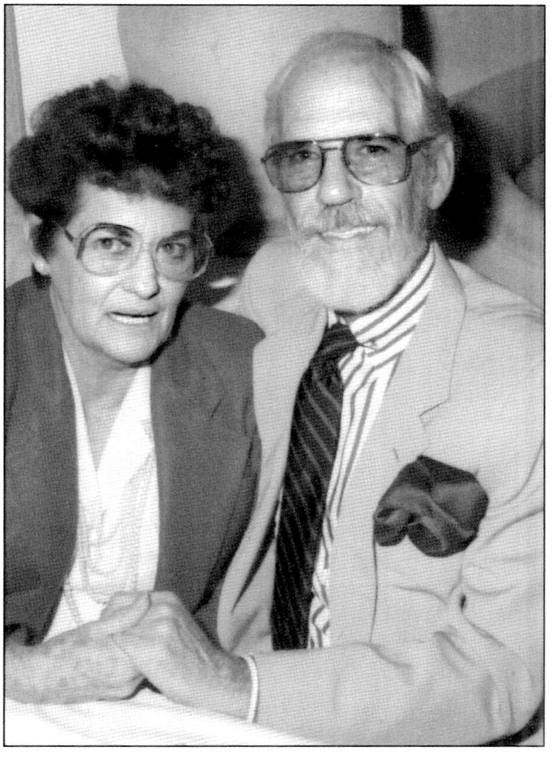

Olivia Cabot met her husband, Hugh, at her Sedona gallery, the first one there. Named an American master painter in 2005, Hugh Cabot worked in all artistic media except acrylic, and his works have been shown in the old Pennington house for more than three decades. Hugh credited Olivia as a major force in his success for her effort in managing the gallery, which left him free to paint. (Olivia Cabot.)

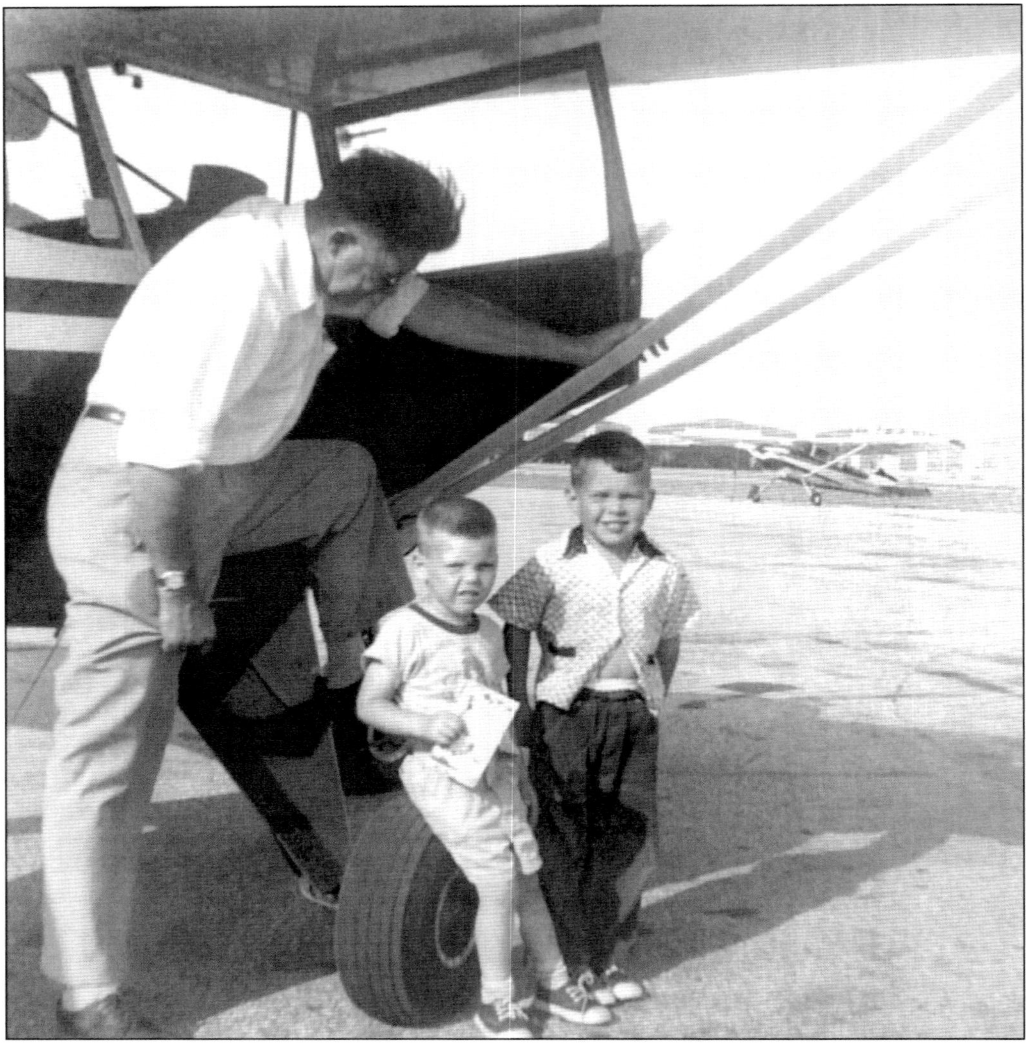

William Morrow's daughter Pat drove through Tubac in 1958 and immediately knew her father would love it. She wrote to him, and he flew out from Swarthmore, Pennsylvania, in his Piper Tri-pacer, dropping in on Ross Stefan and asking him "to buy me something." When he returned, Morrow spent some money fixing up the Lowe house and moved in. Over the following four years, he began to acquire Tubac land both on his own and in partnerships. On the east side of the highway, he owned all of what is now the Tubac Vistas, the Tubac Golf Resort, and most of Tubac west of Burruel Street, which he called Tubac Plaza. Across the highway, he had Tubac Heights No. 1 and No. 2, Tubac Terrace, and Piedra Drive. In all of these subdivisions and developments, Morrow arranged things so structures and landscaping would conform to Spanish Colonial styles, that businesses would be excluded from residential areas, and that buildings would be approved by himself or his designated architects. William C. Morrow, shown here with grandson Truly "Bill" Nolen and son Jimmy Morrow (right), is the father of modern Tubac. (Pat Morrow.)

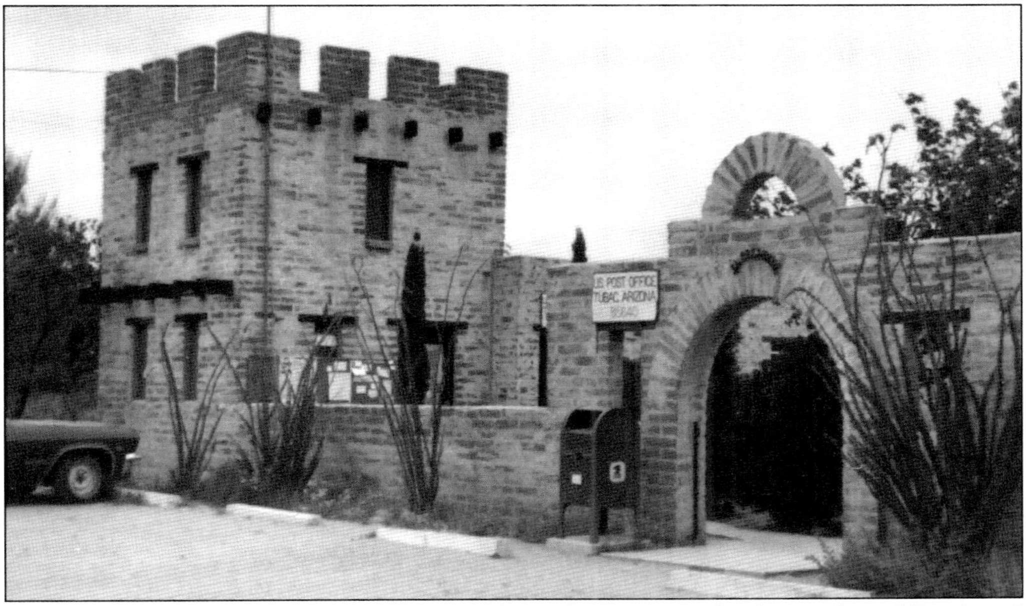

Another family name that figures prominently in the creation of Tubac is that of Frank and Gay Griffin, who arrived here from Indiana in 1956. They constructed this complex of buildings known as the Presidito in 1957 and poured themselves into the cultural and physical restoration of Tubac. Frank Griffin died suddenly in 1960, and Tubac was deprived of his vision and energy. (Santa Cruz Valley Art Association.)

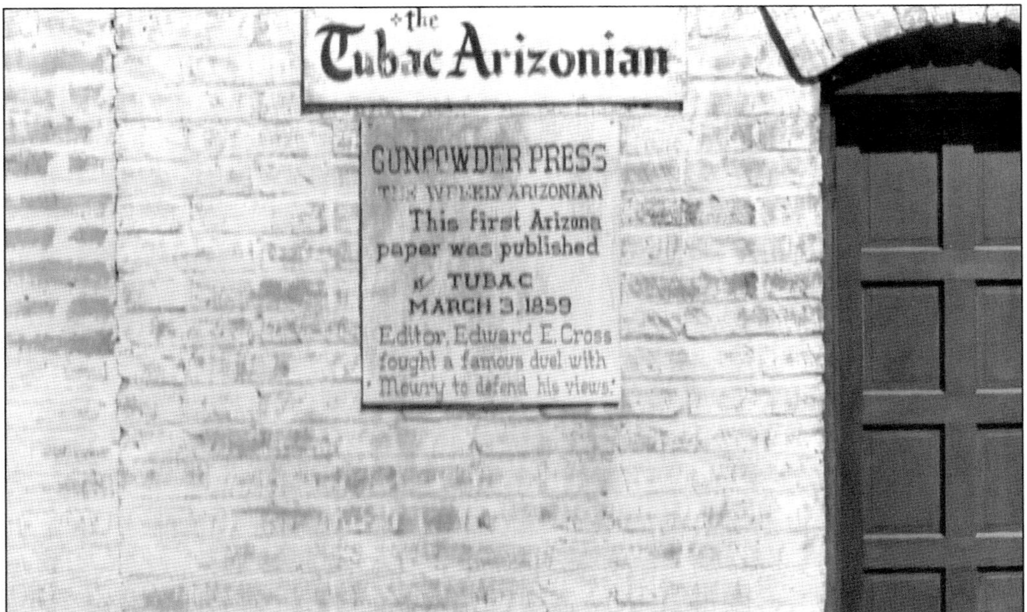

Gay Griffin, a former editor and reporter, was a member of the Arizona Press Women's Association. She and her husband were intrigued by the importance of Tubac's location as the site of the state's first newspaper in 1859, so together they revived the *Weekly Arizonian*. It was printed at their own Gunpowder Press, where a street-side sign celebrated the *Arizonian* and the Cross-Mowry duel.

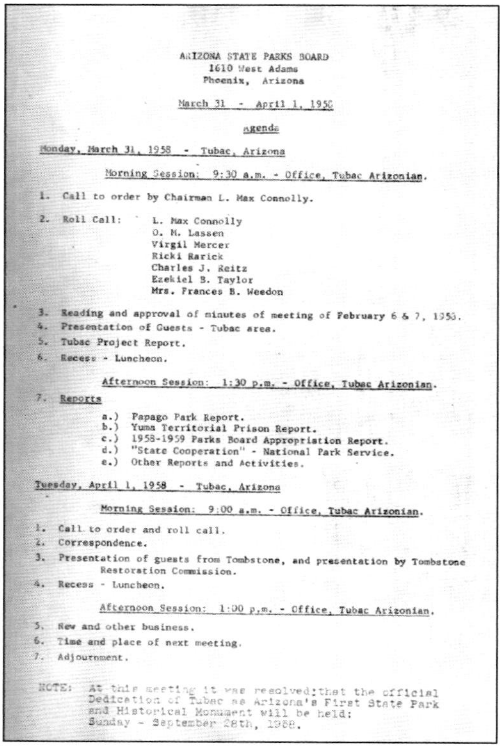

ARIZONA STATE PARKS BOARD
1610 West Adams
Phoenix, Arizona

March 31 - April 1, 1958

Agenda

Monday, March 31, 1958 - Tubac, Arizona

Morning Session: 9:30 a.m. - Office, Tubac Arizonian.

1. Call to order by Chairman L. Max Connolly.
2. Roll Call: L. Max Connolly
   O. M. Lassen
   Virgil Mercer
   Ricki Rarick
   Charles J. Reitz
   Ezekiel B. Taylor
   Mrs. Frances B. Weedon
3. Reading and approval of minutes of meeting of February 6 & 7, 1958.
4. Presentation of Guests - Tubac area.
5. Tubac Project Report.
6. Recess - Luncheon.

Afternoon Session: 1:30 p.m. - Office, Tubac Arizonian.

7. Reports
   a.) Papago Park Report.
   b.) Yuma Territorial Prison Report.
   c.) 1958-1959 Parks Board Appropriation Report.
   d.) "State Cooperation" - National Park Service.
   e.) Other Reports and Activities.

Tuesday, April 1, 1958 - Tubac, Arizona

Morning Session: 9:00 a.m. - Office, Tubac Arizonian.

1. Call to order and roll call.
2. Correspondence.
3. Presentation of guests from Tombstone, and presentation by Tombstone Restoration Commission.
4. Recess - Luncheon.

Afternoon Session: 1:00 p.m. - Office, Tubac Arizonian.

5. New and other business.
6. Time and place of next meeting.
7. Adjournment.

NOTE: At this meeting it was resolved: that the official Dedication of Tubac as Arizona's First State Park and Historical Monument will be held: Sunday - September 28th, 1958.

The Griffins were tireless in their efforts to get county and state recognition of Tubac's historic assets and helped establish the Tubac Restoration Foundation in 1957. The incorporators included Frank Griffin, Ross Stefan, Douglas Luger, Mike Megariz, and Watkins Jackson, Tubac's lone black citizen. The recently formed Arizona State Parks Board met with this agenda at the Griffins' Tubac *Arizonian* office, and the state's first park came into being on January 24, 1958.

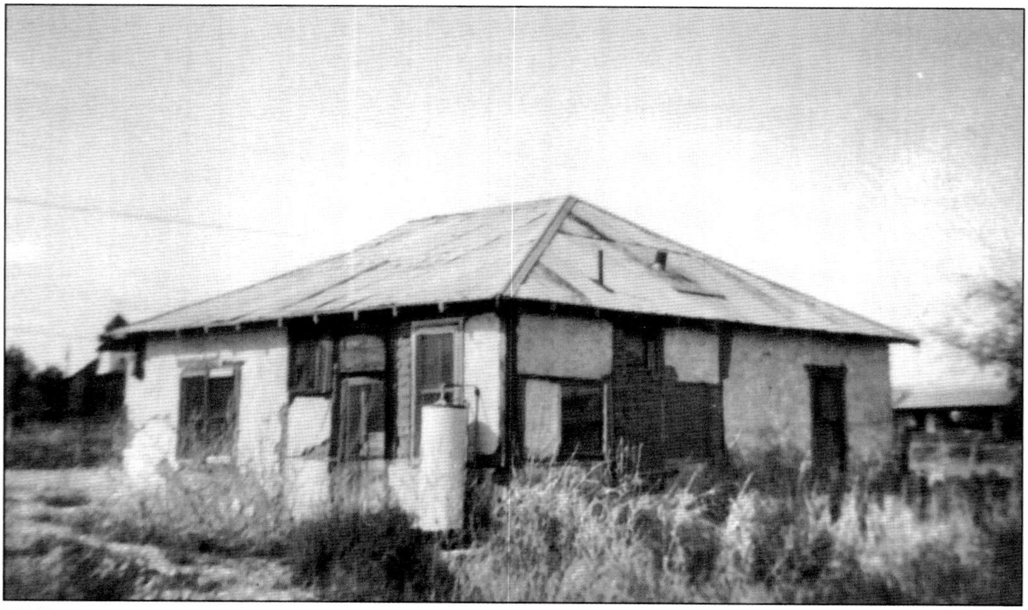

William Morrow presented lots 9, 10, and 13 in block 8 to the State Parks Board, complementing the Griffins' gift of lots 8, 9, and 18 in block 7. The building above was first used as a temporary museum, later as a residence for the park supervisor, and still later as museum office. The formal dedication took place on September 28, 1958, and 2,000 people assembled to hear a number of dignitaries speak, including Gov. Ernest McFarland. (Tubac Presidio State Historic Park.)

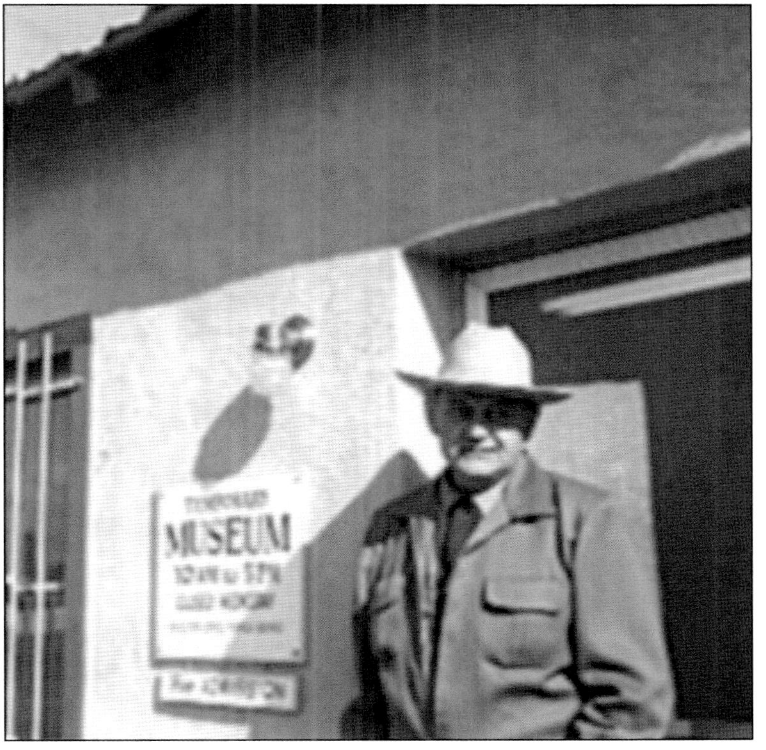

Paul Deno was the first manager of the Tubac Presidio State Historic Park. An architect, he was asked to draft a plan for the museum and headquarters building similar in design to the original presidial headquarters. His task was complicated by the fact that it was not until 1974 that the necessary archaeological excavations revealing the foundations were made. In spite of this, Deno's plan worked well, and the museum is one of Tubac's major cultural assets. (Tubac Presidio State Historic Park.)

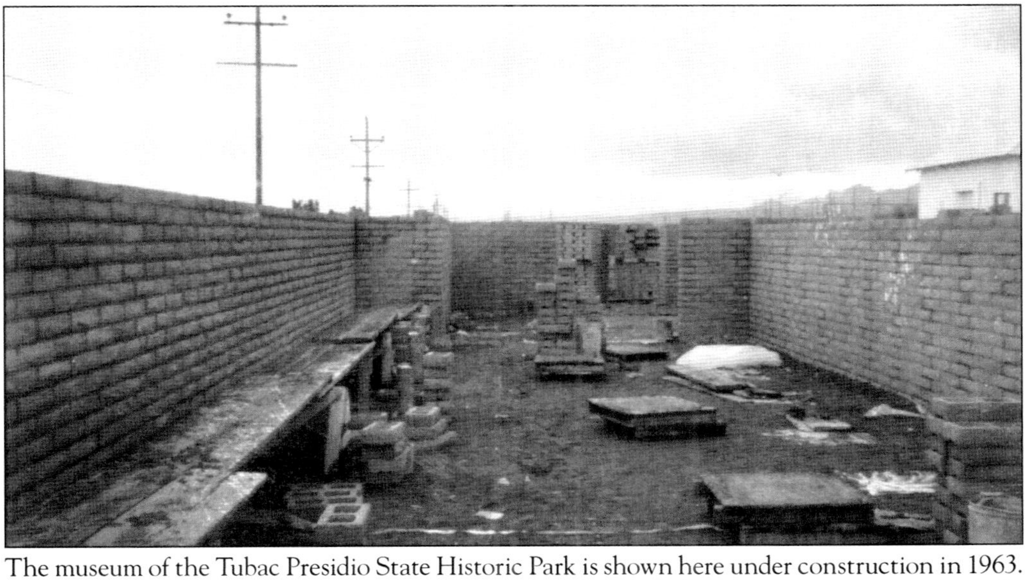

The museum of the Tubac Presidio State Historic Park is shown here under construction in 1963. The adobe brick structure, styled after 18th-century Spanish frontier architecture, is actually concrete and was completed by the Ed E. Pierson Construction Company of Nogales for $60,000. As a first step in the development of the new historic complex, Henry F. Dobyns was appointed to compile an accurate and complete history of Tubac. His *Tubac Through Four Centuries* covers Tubac's history to 1854 and is now available online through the University of Arizona Library's Web site. (Tubac Presidio State Historic Park.)

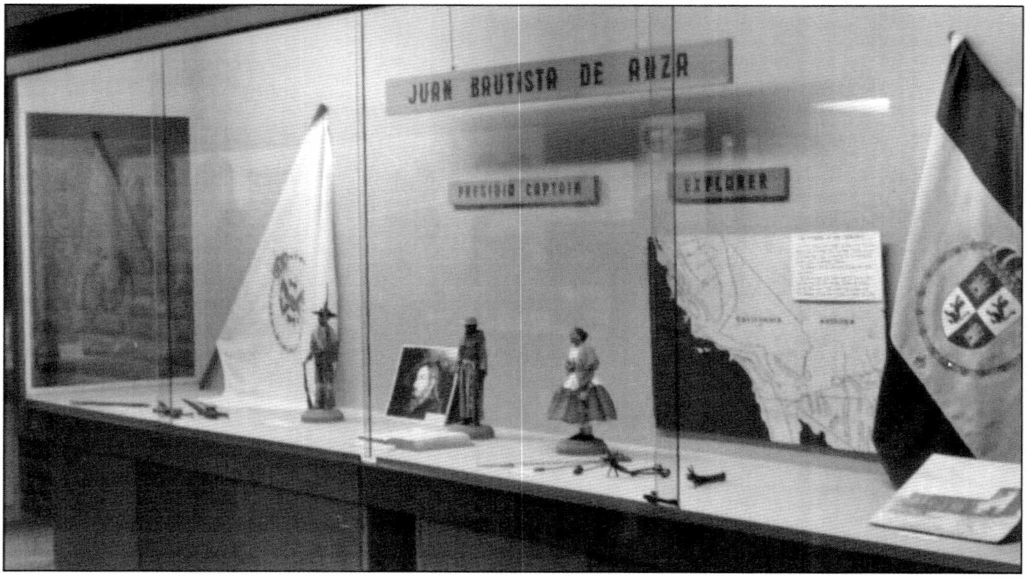

This 1964 photograph of one of the first museum displays shows the likely flags used by Juan Bautista de Anza, as well as swords and spurs of the period. Arthur Woodward, a former curator at the Los Angeles County Museum, was commissioned to search out and purchase appropriate artifacts for the museum. The objects he found are today complemented by additional artifacts from archaeological excavations on the park grounds and in the Tubac area. (Tubac Presidio State Historic Park.)

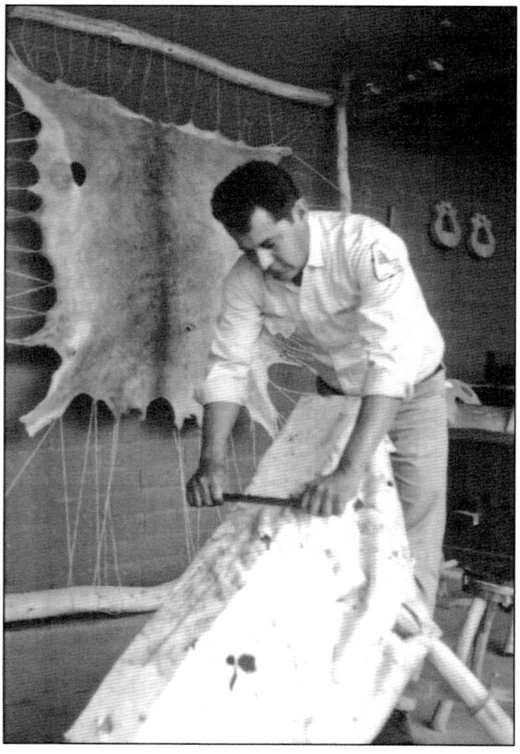

Luis Martinez, with his knowledge of ancient crafts, was a living exhibit at the museum. Here he is shown preparing animal hides using a scraper. Martinez worked as a ranch hand before joining the park service and helped Will Rogers Jr. restore parts of the old Garrett Ranch house. He served in the park continuously from its opening in 1958 until 1992, when he retired. His son Joe is now park manager. (Tubac Presidio State Historic Park.)

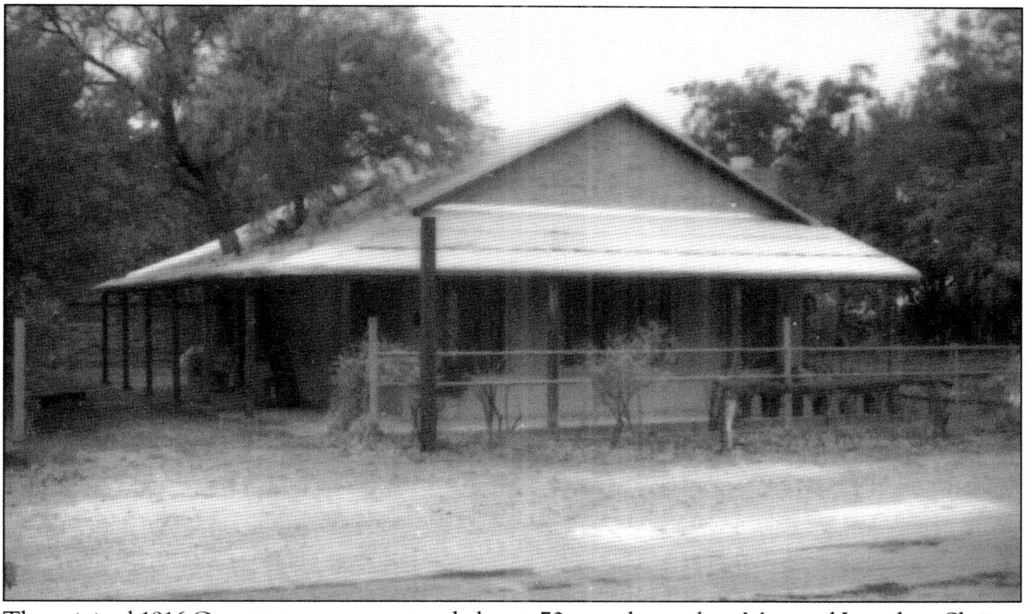

The original 1916 Garrett store was restored almost 70 years later when Max and Jonathan Shriver created the Folk Art Plus gallery in 1985, winning an award from Tubac's Historic Zone Advisory Board. All the work, repair of the original adobes and windows and adding brick patios beneath the porch roofs, was done by Tubac-area craftspeople, including Manuel, Robert, Joe, and Steven Solares, Frank Figeroa, and Henry and John Kane. (*Green Valley News*.)

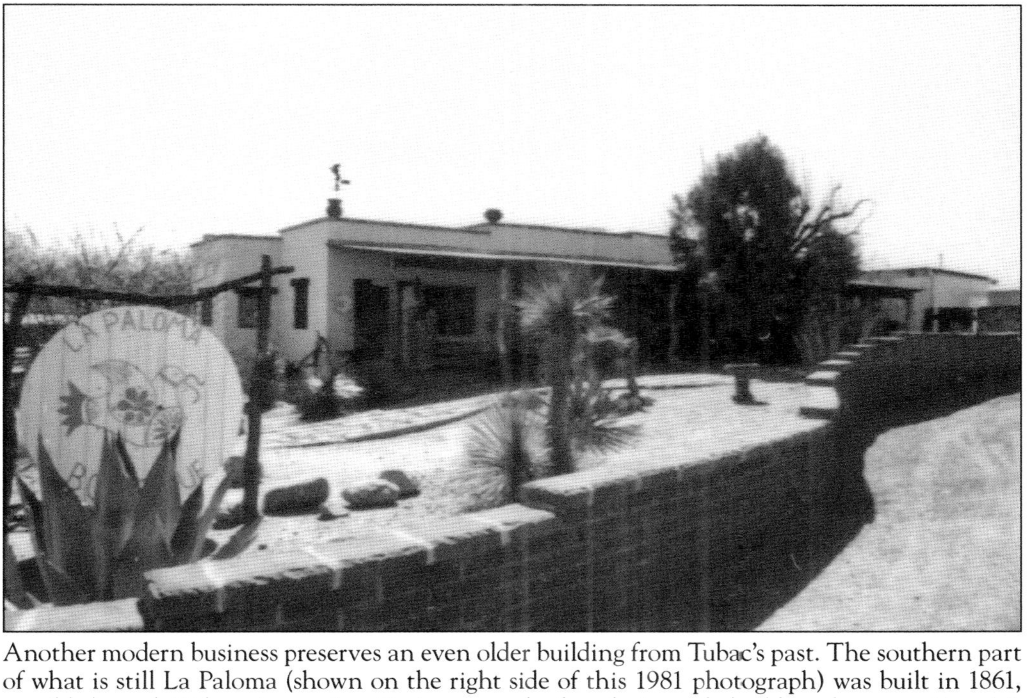

Another modern business preserves an even older building from Tubac's past. The southern part of what is still La Paloma (shown on the right side of this 1981 photograph) was built in 1861, possibly by early Tubac pioneer Inez Espinoza, on the foundations of a building shown on Urrutia's 1767 map (see page 18). (*Green Valley News*.)

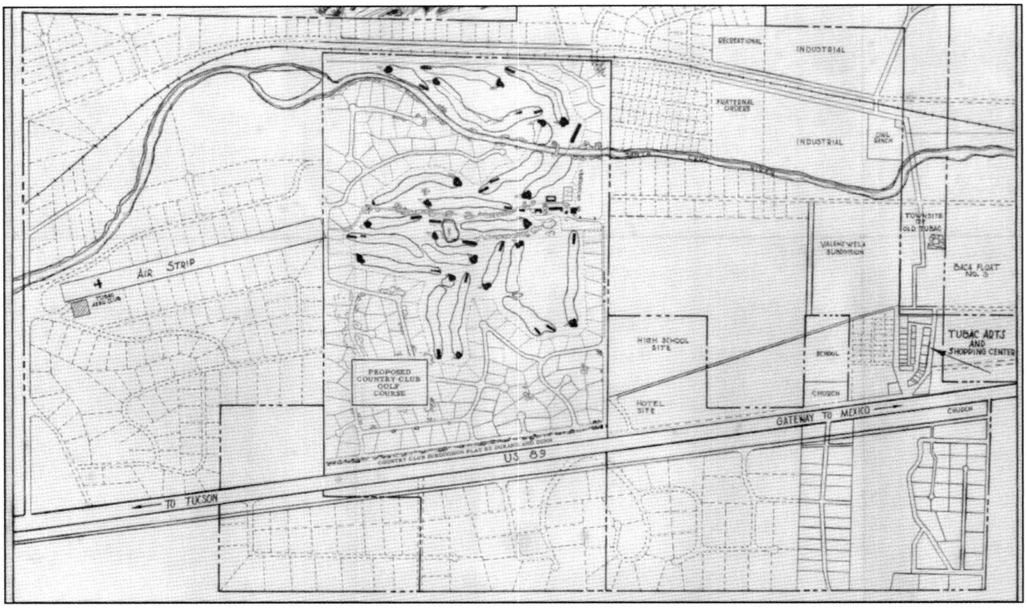

While the village was focused on creating the state park, Morrow's plans for Greater Tubac were coming together. This rendering of his proposal probably dates from 1959 and shows a different layout than exists today. The Baca Float boundary defines Tubac's southern edge, and land is provided for industry, two schools, fraternal orders, and an "aero club" in addition to plenty of house lots on both sides of the highway and adjacent to a river that was never known to flood.

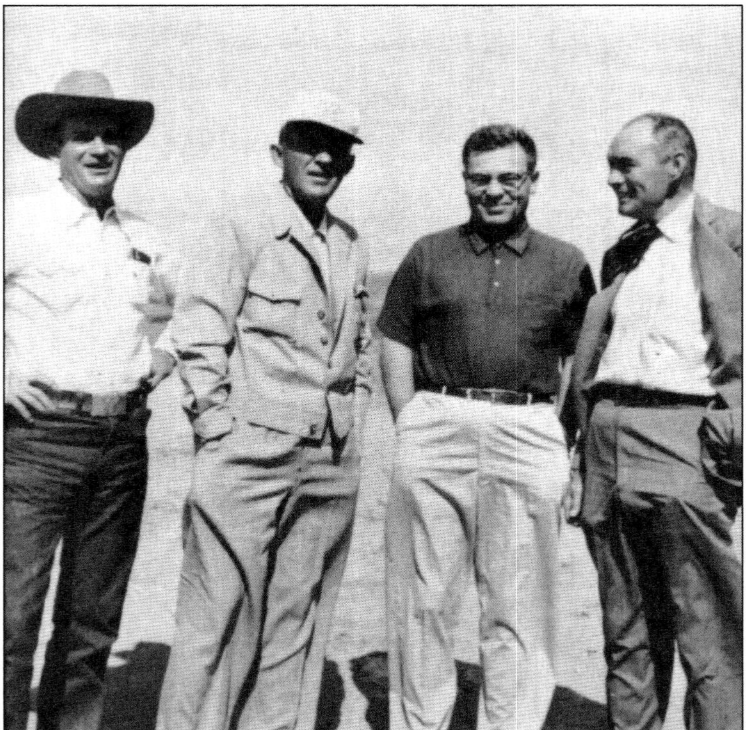

Morrow sold his interest in the prospective country club to Howard Cursey, Richard Baker, Charles Crary, and William C. Scott. These men and a dozen others formed the Tubac Valley Country Club and elected Bing Crosby chairman of the board of directors. While sightings of Crosby in the area were few, this 1960 photograph of, from left to right, Al Jensen, Crosby, and Dick Ensign and Howard Cursey, the new club treasurer and vice president respectively, seems to prove he was indeed here. (Wendy and Jeff Williams.)

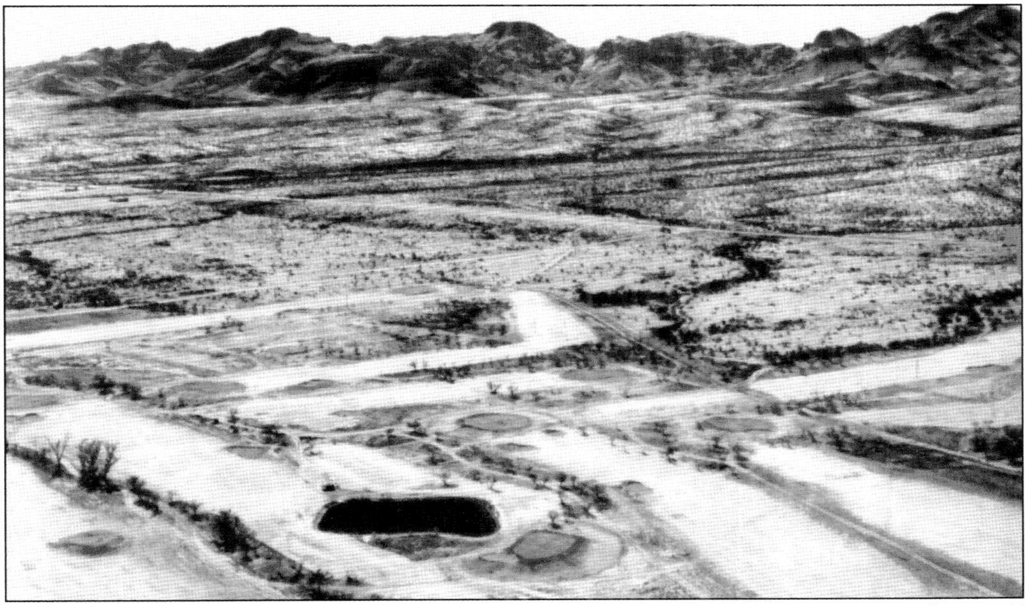

This aerial view looking west toward the Tumacácori Mountains shows progress on Tubac's golf course. No homes are visible, but the arch is there along the highway. The rectangular pond in the foreground was one of several Otero wells and still exists on what is today the eighth hole on the Otero course. St. Ann's Parish Hall and the gas station at the entrance to the village are visible at the upper left.

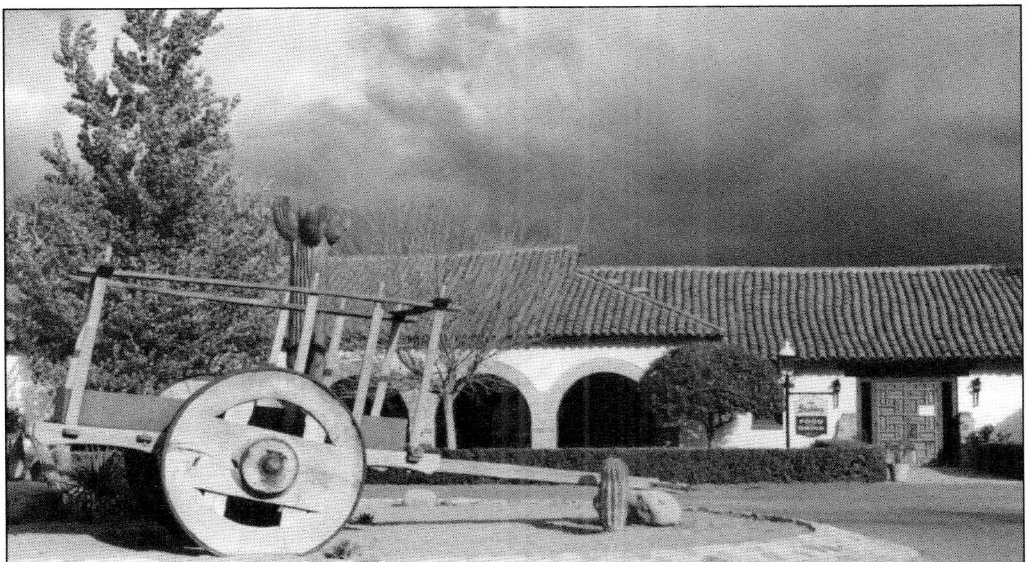

What was the barn on the Otero Ranch became Stables Restaurant at the Tubac Country Club. When Addison Pelletier bought the Otero Ranch in 1937, she contracted with Jim Garrett to manage it for her for three years. In what is now part of the dining room, he kept his stud horse Guinea Pig in the stalls, and later former Tubac postmaster William Lowe used the building for his dairy operation, which saw Arizona's first use of electric milking machines. (Santa Cruz Valley Art Association.)

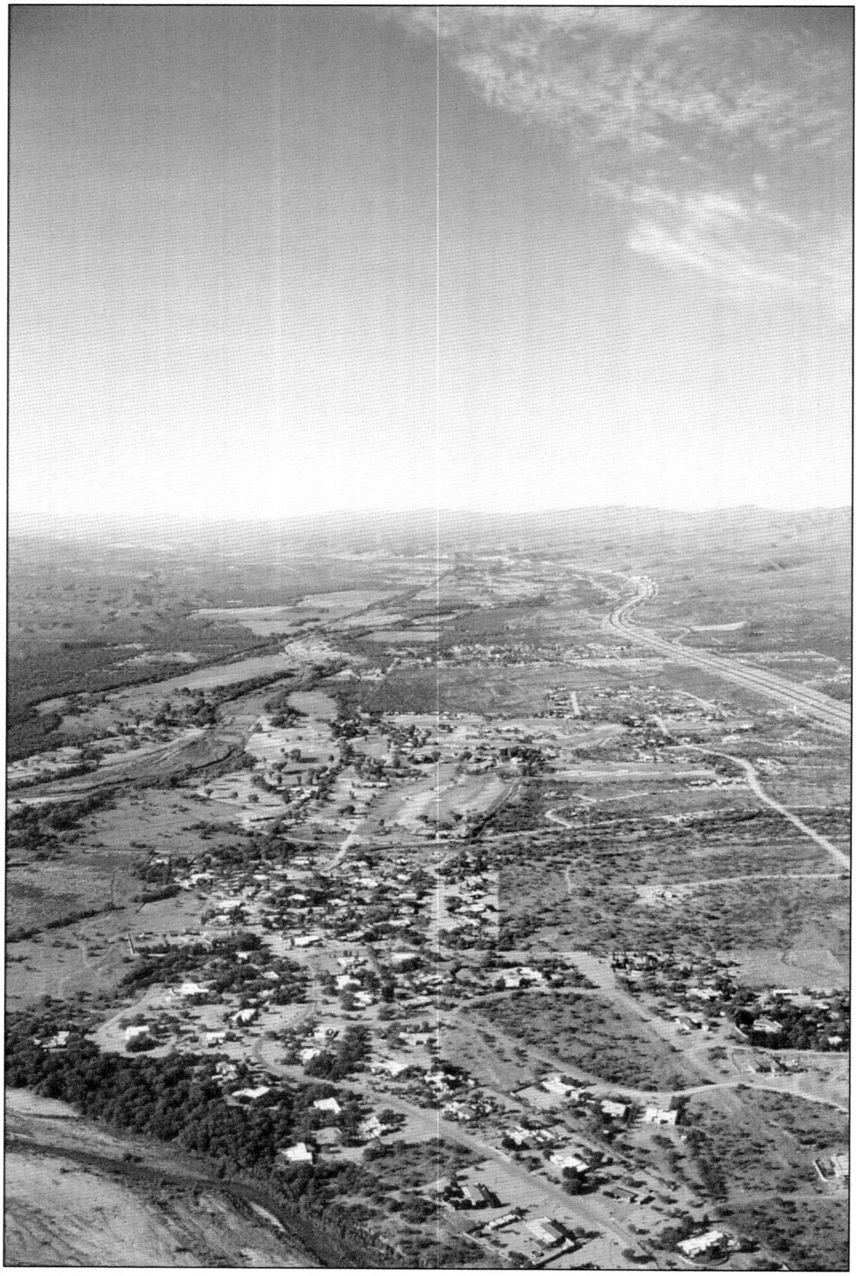

The Tubac Valley Vistas shown in this 1987 aerial view was developed by A. C. Ray between 1965 and 1972. Before purchasing 85 acres from the Tubac Valley Country Club at the north end of their holdings, A. C. had worked in Houston, Texas, and with the Maxons in Green Valley. A. C. laid out the Vistas in 1-acre lots and offered six different models priced from $12,500 to $17,500. An airstrip, hangar, and house formerly owned by Col. Charles Van Sicklen and his wife, Fritzie, bordered the western edge of the Vistas, and consideration was given for a short time to letting residents with private planes use the airstrip, but the idea was dropped as impractical. (Jennifer Tougas.)

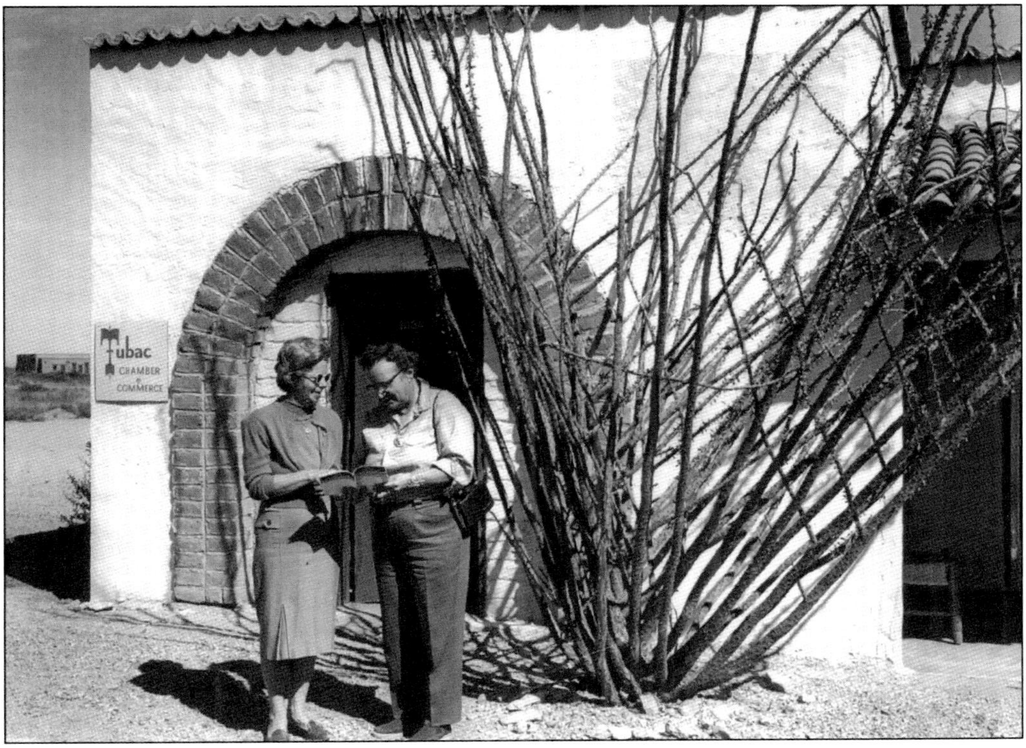

Lou Trees was called "the realtor of Tubac" in the 1960s. She is shown here (right) in front of her Arizona-Tubac Realty with assistant Helen Erickson. The building was put up by William Morrow in the late 1950s, perhaps the fifth building of modern Tubac. Trees was the moving spirit behind the Tubac Chamber of Commerce and was one of the incorporators of the Tubac Historical Society. She also served several years as Tubac's postmaster.

FOR YOUR CONVENIENCE

★

TUBAC TELEPHONE DIRECTORY

Arizona - Tubac Realty	Tubac 8
Austin, C. LeRoy	Tubac 12
Crebbs, Chester M.	Tubac 6
Davis, Carl E.	Tubac 7
Garrett, J. T.	Tubac 4
Green, John R.	Tubac 16
Hanna, Joseph	Tubac 2
Keating, Edward L.	Tubac 15
Kenyon Ranch	Tubac 3
Lofton, Dale Aubrey	Tubac 24
Maizel, Edward	Tubac 21
Museum Presidio & Park Site	Tubac 10
Rogers, Bill	Tubac 8
Shea, James B.	Tubac 17
Steiger, Harwood	Tubac 25
Stephens, Neville R.	Tubac 9
Taylor, J. A.	Tubac 1
Trees, E. Louise	Tubac 8
Tubac Cafe & Gift Shop	Tubac 5
Tubac Country Club	Tubac 13
Tubac Industries	Tubac 21
Tubac Inn	Tubac 11
Tubac Realty	Tubac 14
Tubac Valley Water Co.	Tubac 13
Tubac Village Hotel and Restaurant	Tubac 20
Wolff, John F.	Tubac 23

★

Furnished By

ARIZONA - TUBAC REALTY

Tubac 8

This c. 1960 phone card furnished by Louise Trees's Arizona-Tubac Realty lists 26 numbers, including the hoped-for Museum Presidio and Park Site and the early residents who wanted phones. Dale Lofton ran the gas station at the village entrance, Chester Crebbs bought the old Shankle place, the Garretts were since 1935 on the west side of the highway, and Harwood Steiger is the only artist with a listed phone.

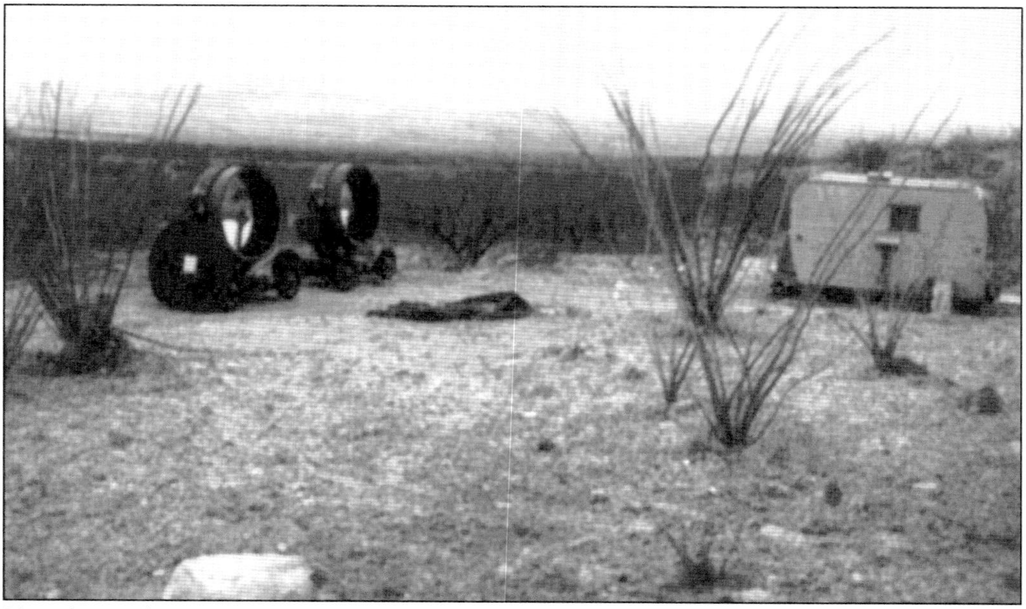

Plans for an observatory on Mount Hopkins began in 1966 as a multiple-use facility with a satellite tracking station, equipment for gamma-ray astronomy, and optical telescopes to study stars and galaxies. The mirrors in these World War II searchlights were used by Trevor Weekes for gamma-ray collection tests near Amado. The travel trailer at right was later airlifted via helicopter to a saddle near the summit. (Fred Lawrence Whipple Observatory.)

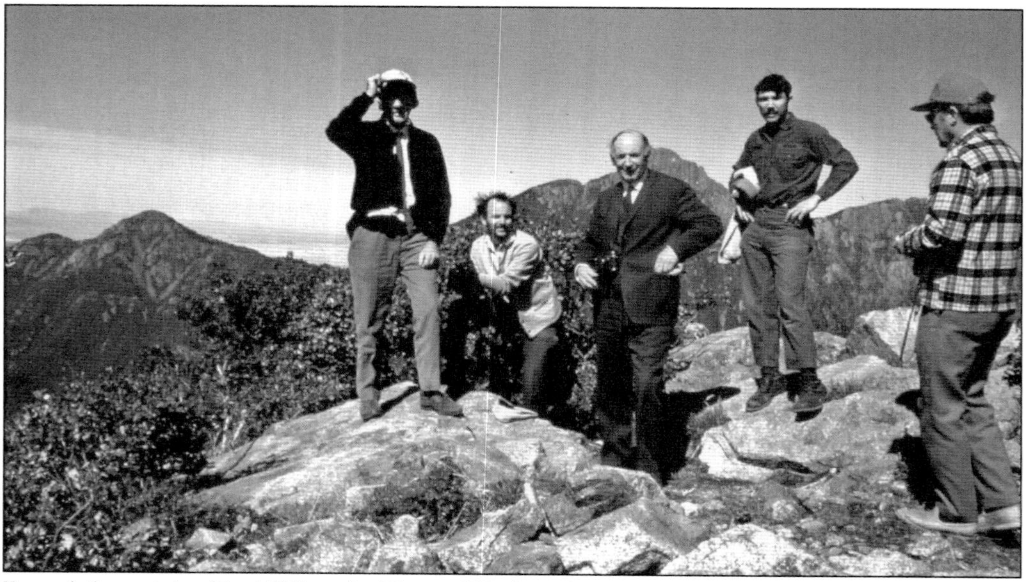

From left to right, Fred Whipple, Trevor Weekes, Sir Bernard Lovell, Fred Chaffee, and an unidentified administrator pose on Mount Hopkins with Mount Wrightson in the background around 1973. The Mount Hopkins Observatory was renamed in honor of Whipple in 1982, Weekes and Chaffee still conduct scientific research there, and Sir Bernard, a famous British radio astronomer, was shown the site during a meeting in Tucson of the American Astronomical Society. (Fred Lawrence Whipple Observatory.)

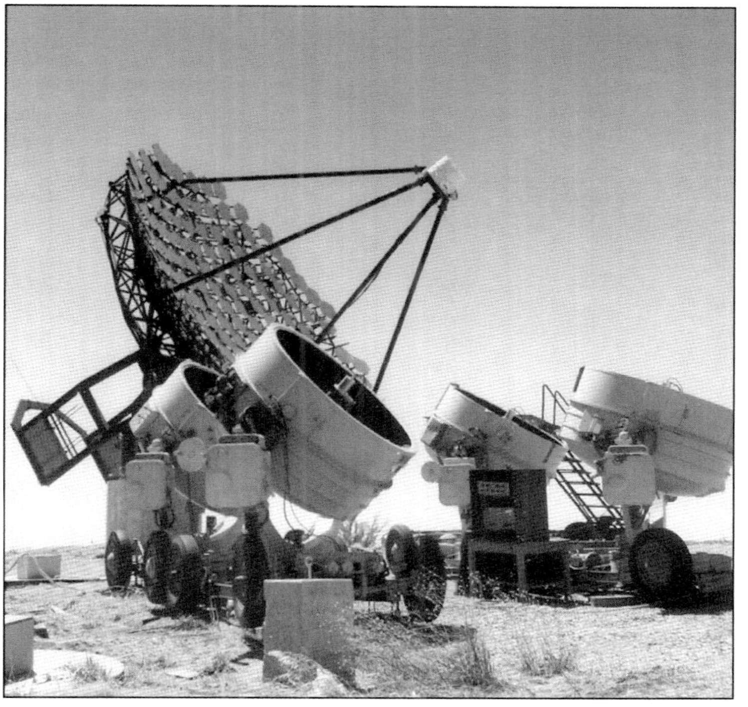

This 10-meter dish with 248 small hexagonal mirrors is used in gamma-ray astronomy, the branch of astronomy dealing with the origin and nature of extraterrestrial emissions in the gamma-ray range of electromagnetic radiation rather than in the visible range. It was the first instrument installed at the observatory and was dedicated in 1968 in a ceremony led by Morris Udall and Tucson mayor James Corbett. (Fred Lawrence Whipple Observatory.)

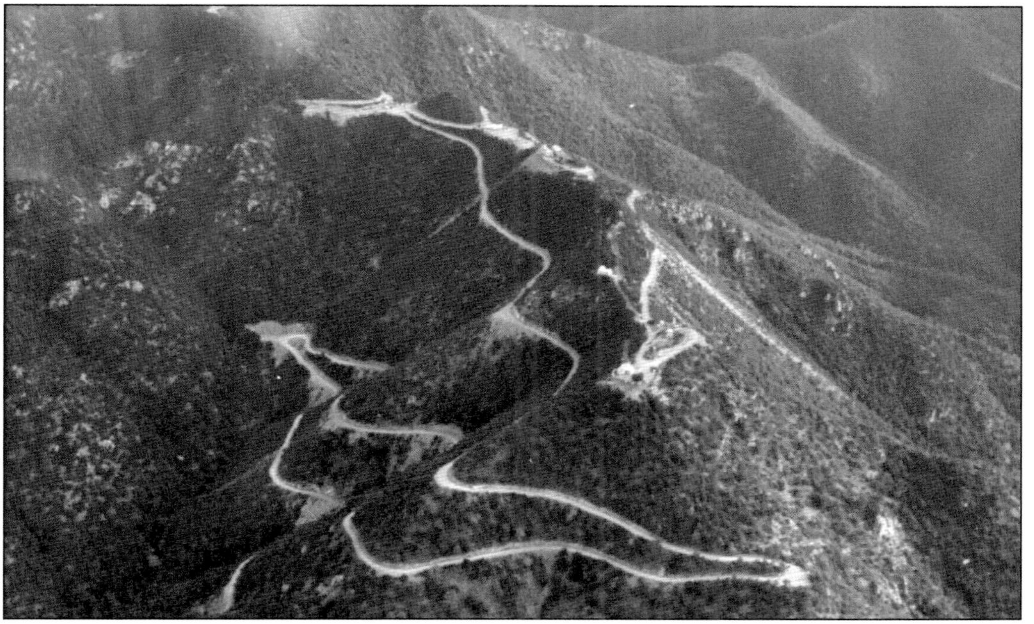

This aerial view of the road to the ridge on Mount Hopkins shows how it was designed as a firebreak from the prevailing southwest winds. The in-sloped road, designed by Sanford Evans and built in 1967 by Sierrita Mining and Ranching (SMR), was maintained for many years by Tubac resident Myron Clark. At the time, the observatory's office was located in Carmen, and their official mailing and shipping address was "Third house south of the Carmen Store, Carmen, Arizona." (Fred Lawrence Whipple Observatory.)

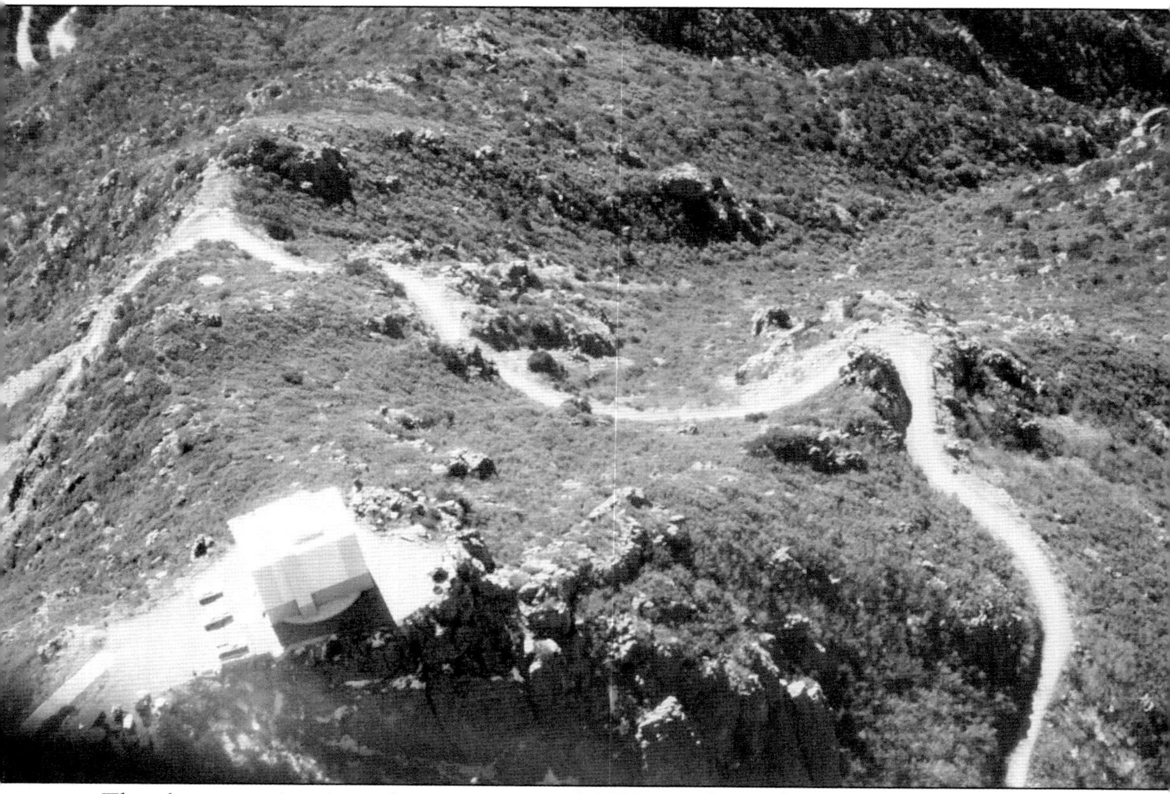

The observatory's principal instrument until 1998 was the Multiple-Mirror Telescope (MMT), operated jointly by the Smithsonian Astrophysical Observatory and the University of Arizona. The instrument employed six identical 1.8-meter mirrors. The combined light-gathering power of the MMT was comparable to that of a single-mirror 4.5-meter reflector. It was located not on the ridge with the other instruments, but on the summit, which had to be lowered by 35 feet in 1976 to provide a suitable base for the telescope. This photograph was taken in 1987 and shows part of the final stretch of road that is heated to mitigate the effects of ice and snow. In 1998, the six mirrors were replaced with the current, single 6.5-meter mirror. Former Tubac resident Chuck Tougas was the original on-site manager assigned to develop the Mount Hopkins Observatory; present Tubac resident Tom Hoffman was the observatory's chief engineer from the early 1960s until his retirement in 1986, and Myron Clark has assisted the observatory in countless ways from construction to maintenance. (Jennifer Tougas.)

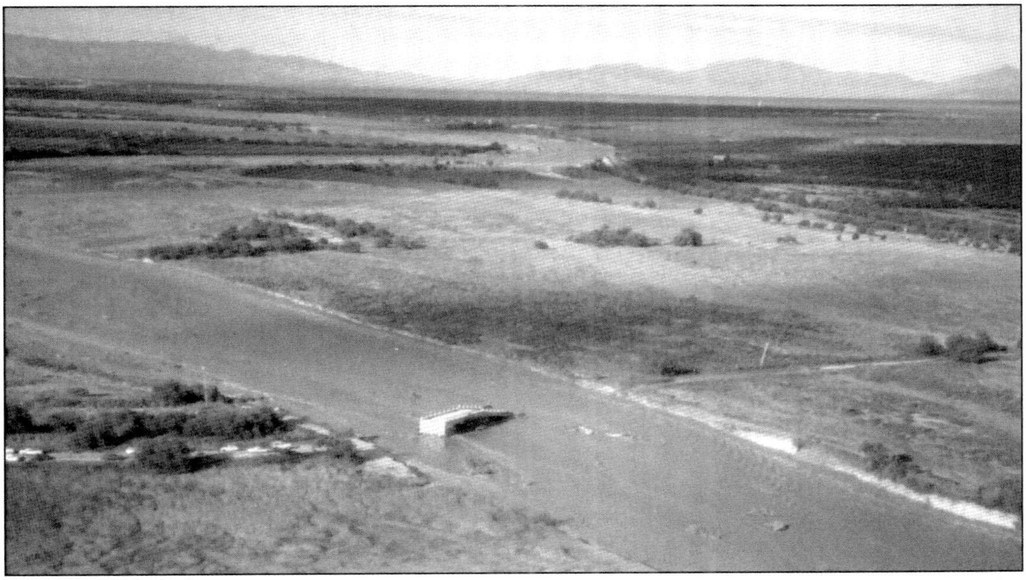

In the 1970s, the observatory's office moved from Carmen to the old schoolhouse in Amado, currently the home of Barbara and Dick Blake, located on the west side of the Santa Cruz River. Travel between the office and the observatory was interrupted by a massive October 1977 flood, which washed away the Observatory Road Bridge, a 60-foot single-lane structure similar to a railroad trestle. Staff members were lifted across the river by a navy-type highline. (Fred Lawrence Whipple Observatory.)

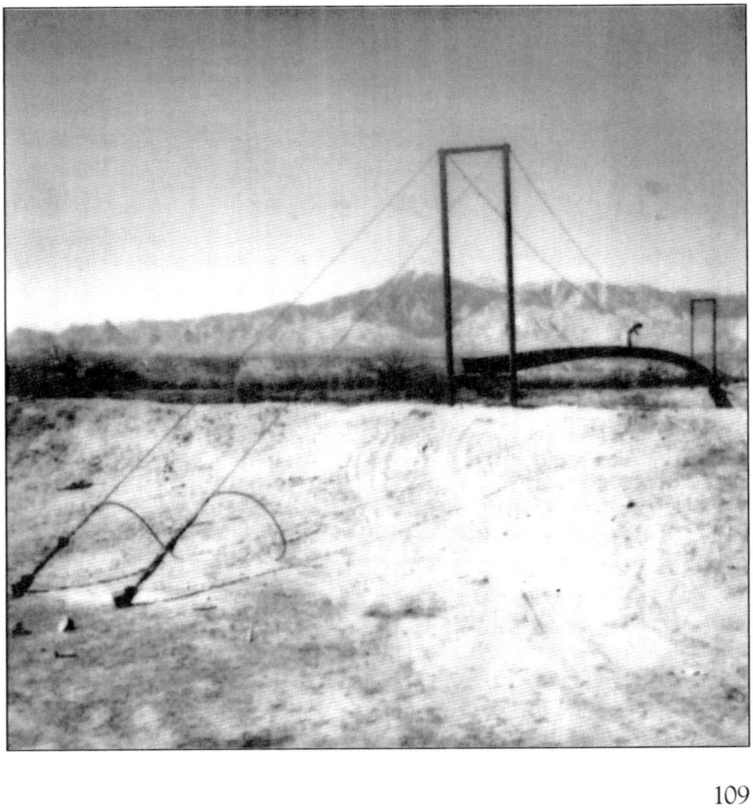

Before a 130-foot replacement bridge was built, the Smithsonian created this footbridge, dubbed the "Amado Golden Gate." It was used for the first time on February 28, 1979. The bridge spanned 200 feet over a river whose depth was 2 feet, 9 inches. It was designed by John Harris and built in three weeks by Sierrita Mining and Ranching at a cost of $9,000. (Fred Lawrence Whipple Observatory.)

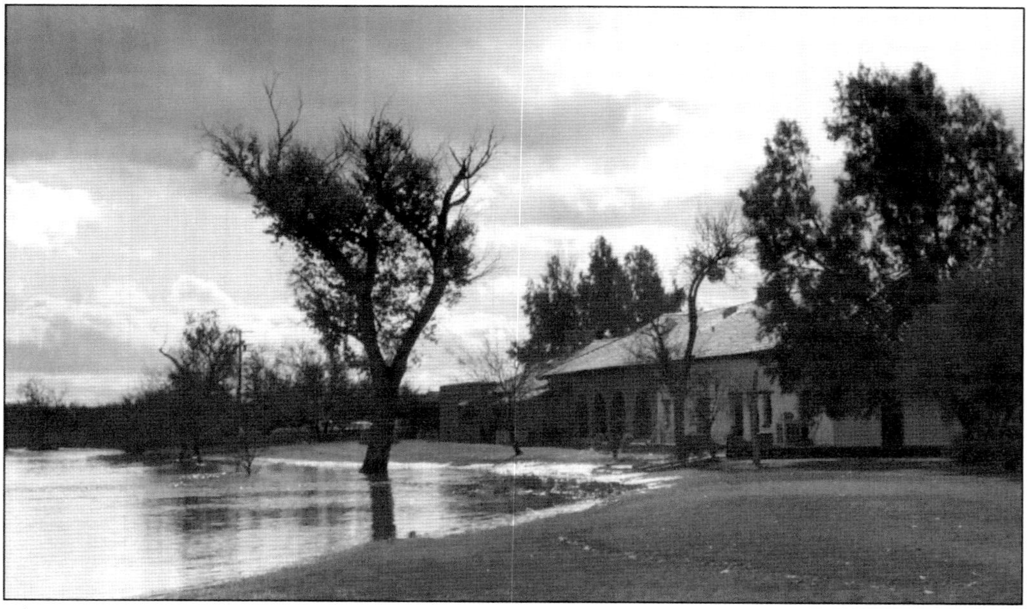

There were three 100-year floods between 1967 and 1983. The flood of December 1967 came after a storm left 15-foot snowdrifts on Mount Hopkins, the worst recorded storm since 1914. The runoff was particularly devastating for the Tubac Valley Country Club. This image shows the water within feet of the east side of Stables Restaurant, and six golf holes on the east side of the river, numbers 13 to 18, were completely washed out.

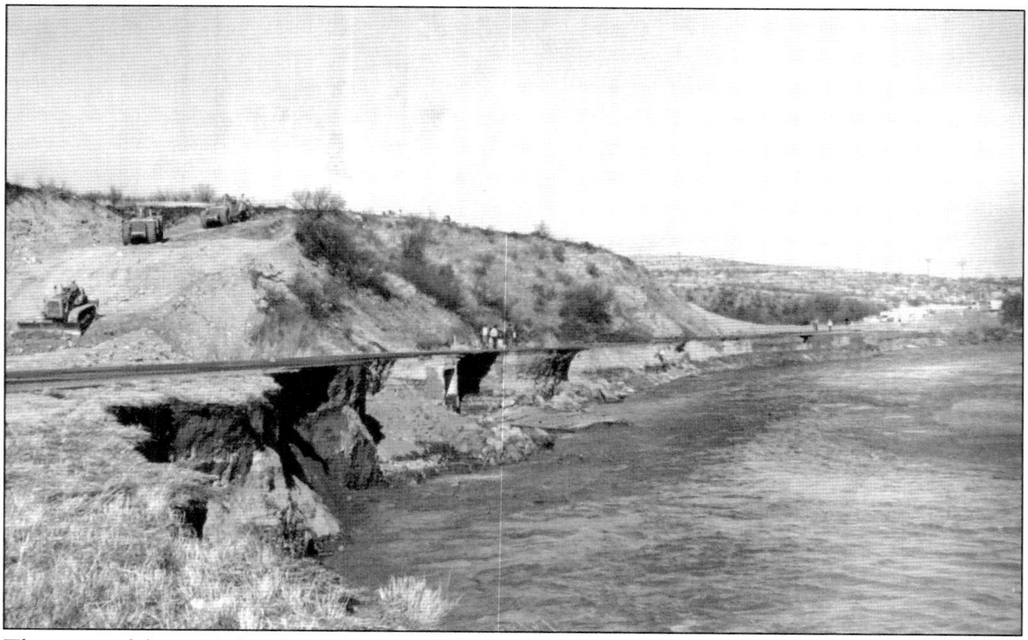

This view of the 1967 flood on old Highway 89 just above the modern interstate exit at Tumacácori shows 300 feet missing. Residents in the area had no water or electricity for a week and no access to Tucson or Nogales for several days. Gene England sold the state a strip of land, part of which was bulldozed into the river and part provided a new roadbed to the west. (Peggy Vanderventer.)

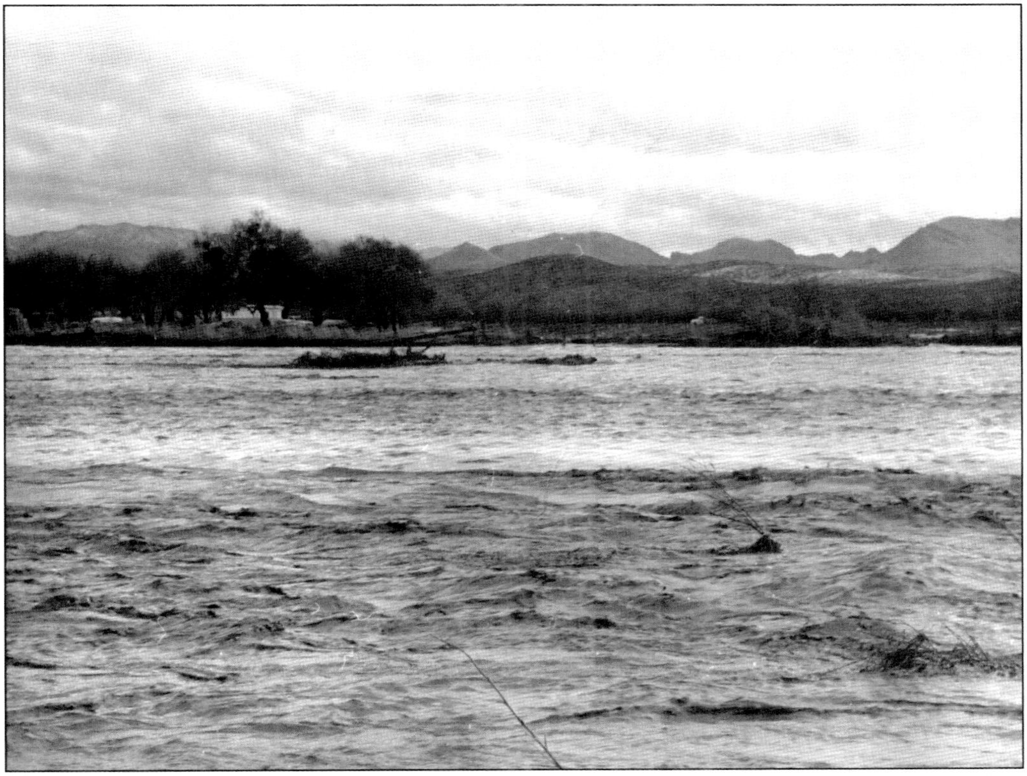

This view looking west at the Carmen Crossing dramatically shows the effect of six straight days of rain and snow. Seven people in Nogales, Sonora, died, and 40 people in Amado and Tubac were rescued from their rooftops by helicopters from Davis-Monthan airbase. Two washouts of the Southern Pacific's rail line were reported, and floodwaters reached the foothills of the Santa Rita Mountains east of Tubac. (Peggy Vanderventer.)

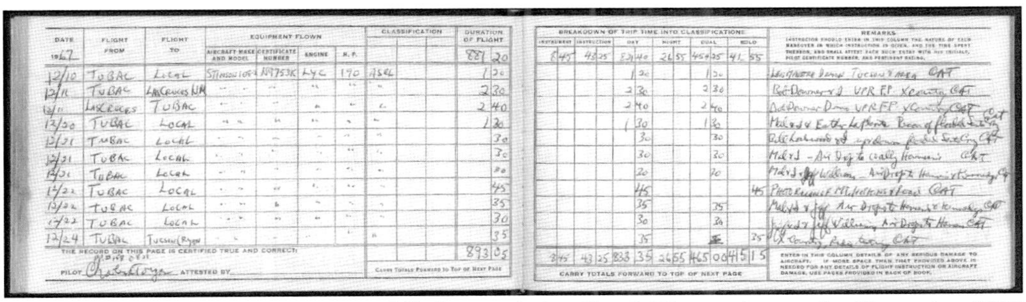

Date 1967	Flight From	Flight To	Aircraft Make and Model	Certificate Number	Engine	H.P.	Classification	Duration of Flight	Instrument	Instruction	Day	Night	Dual	Solo	Remarks
								881 20	8 45	43 25	831 40	26 55	454 25	41 55	
12/10	TUBAC	LOCAL	Stinson 108	N9753K	LYC	190	ASEL	1 20			1 20		1 20		[illegible] Tucson [illegible] CAT
12/11	TUBAC	Las Cruces NM	"	"	"	"	"	2 30			2 30		2 30		[illegible] VFR F.P. X country CAT
12/11	Las Cruces	TUBAC	"	"	"	"	"	2 40			2 40		2 40		[illegible] VFR F.P. X country CAT
12/20	TUBAC	LOCAL	"	"	"	"	"	1 30			1 30		1 30		[illegible] CAT
12/21	TUBAC	LOCAL	"	"	"	"	"	30			30		30		[illegible] CAT
12/21	TUBAC	LOCAL	"	"	"	"	"	30			30		30		Mal & J – Air Drop to [illegible] CAT
12/21	TUBAC	LOCAL	"	"	"	"	"	20			20		20		Mal & Jeff Williams – Air Drop to [illegible] CAT
12/22	TUBAC	LOCAL	"	"	"	"	"	45			45			45	Photo [illegible] CAT
12/22	TUBAC	LOCAL	"	"	"	"	"	35			35		35		Mal & Jeff Air Drop to [illegible] CAT
12/22	TUBAC	LOCAL	"	"	"	"	"	30			30		30		[illegible] Jeff Williams Air Drop to [illegible] CAT
12/24	TUBAC	Tucson (Ryan)	"	"	"	"	"	35			35		[illegible]	35	X Country [illegible] CAT
								893 05	8 45	43 25	833 35	26 55	465 00	415 15	

THE RECORD ON THIS PAGE IS CERTIFIED TRUE AND CORRECT:
PILOT [signature] ATTESTED BY
CARRY TOTALS FORWARD TO TOP OF NEXT PAGE

This flight log documents a series of flights made by Chuck Tougas during the December 1967 flood. Ann Kennedy Huntoon kept a journal called "Great Christmas Flood." She writes, "On the way home [from the Hansons] we watched the air-lift with a small plane. Mal and Chuck Tougas dropped mail and groceries first at the Hansons and then at our stable. They flew about ten feet off the ground, opened the door, and tossed the bundles out." (Jennifer Tougas.)

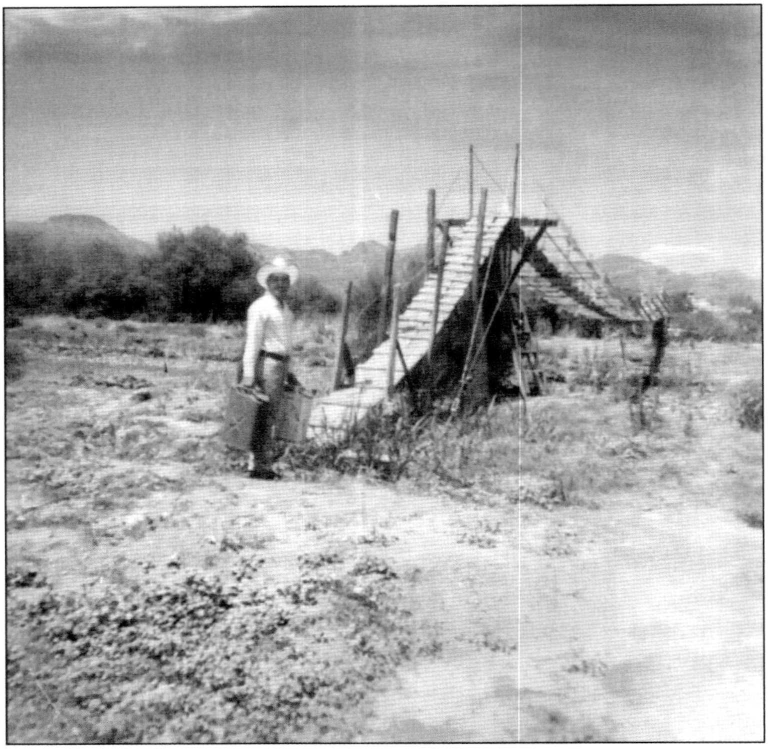

Prior to the 1967 flood, people in Tubac could cross the Santa Cruz River using this footbridge. It is the second of at least three footbridges here. The crossings at Clarke's Crossing as well as Santa Gertrudis Lane also had footbridges. Here Alex Megariz prepares to cross from the east side to the west with two 5-gallon containers. This bridge was built by Alex's father and brother, Mike Megariz Sr. and Jr., and Myron Clark. (Alex Megariz.)

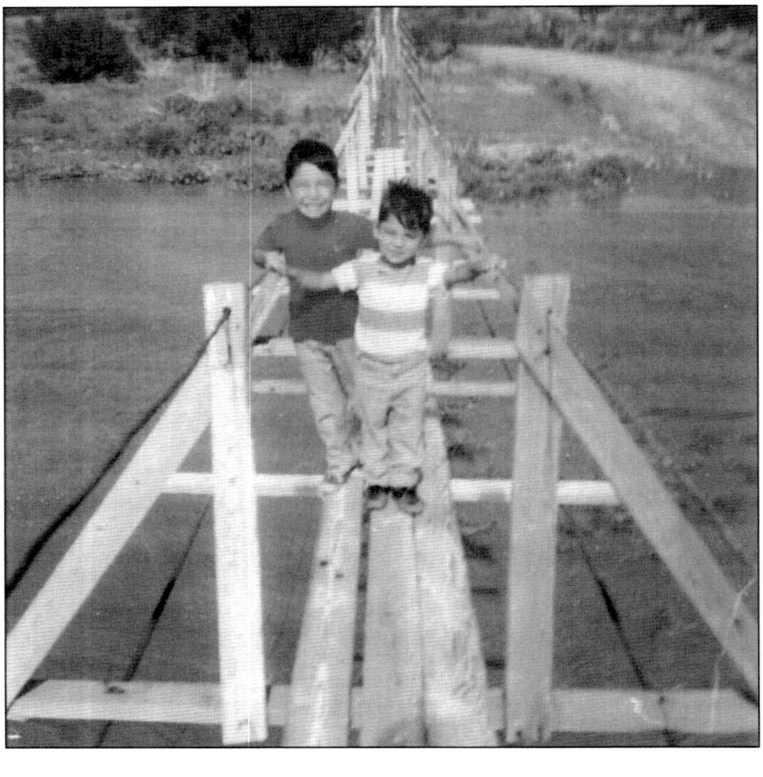

Six-year-old Wayne Megariz (left) and brother Adam pose with the confidence of youth on the Tubac footbridge above the swollen Santa Cruz. At the time of this photograph, the river flowed 100 yards west of its present course. The Megariz house was swept away when the Santa Cruz carved its new channel in 1983. (Alex Megariz.)

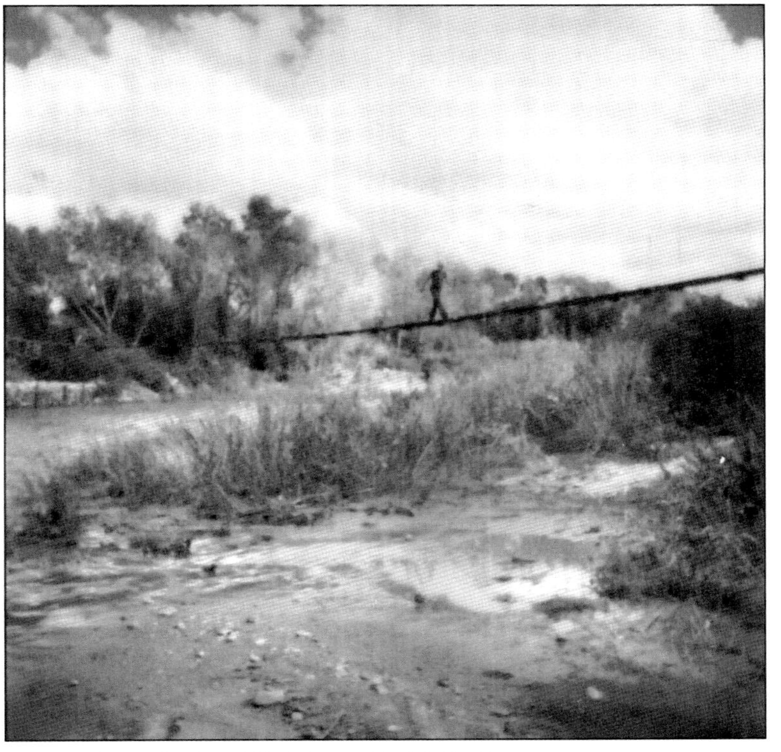

The bridge shown here in 1978 replaced the earlier bridge sometime after the 1967 flood. Residents who used it described its use as "thrilling," as it swayed considerably and the wire cable handrails drooped ever lower toward the center of the channel. The vegetation indicates a period of calm in the river's flow. (Irene Deaton.)

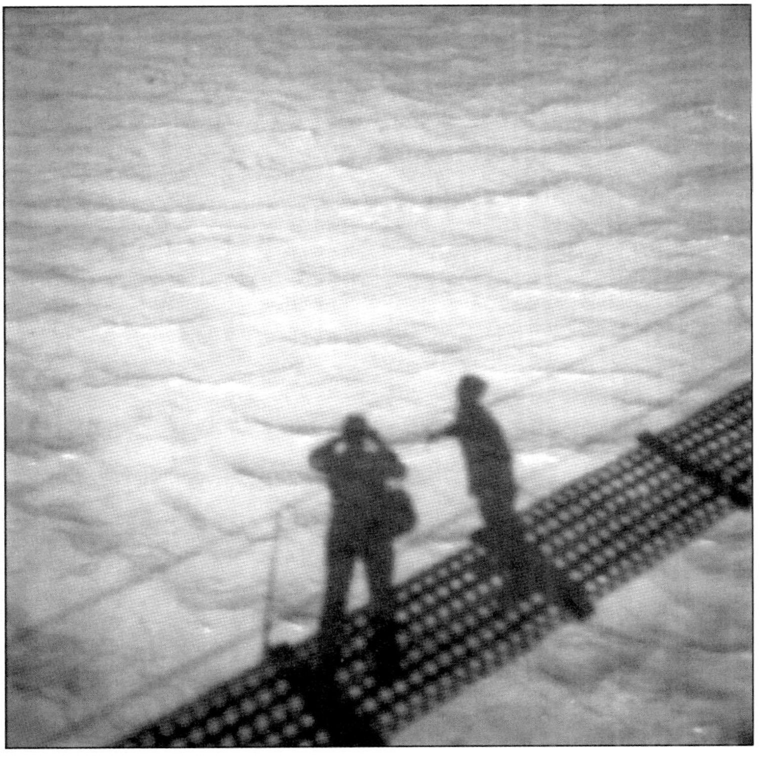

This image of the shadow cast by two adventurous souls crossing the Santa Cruz in 1978 shows the bridge's construction of portable steel landing mats used during World War II to create runways. They were also used for the border fence in the 1970s. The see-through nature of the bridge added to the excitement and made it difficult for ladies on the east side to cross in fancy heels to events on the west side. (Irene Deaton.)

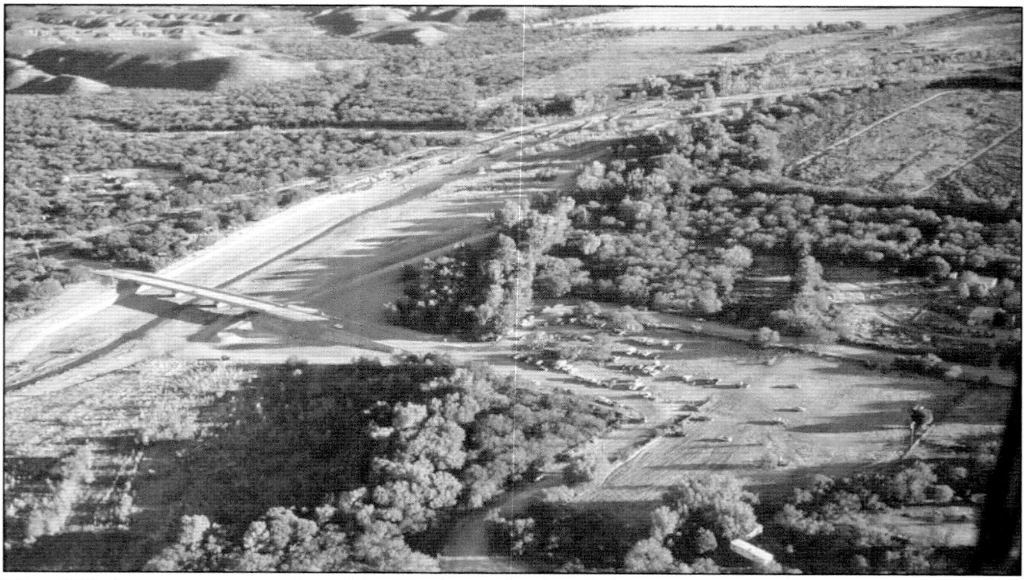

This 350-foot concrete and steel bridge has solved Tubac's river crossing problems since 1987, when it was officially dedicated as the Ralph Wingfield Tubac Crossing Bridge. Wingfield helped fund the bridge and owned the Guevavi Ranch, encompassing the 18th-century mission and other property as well. The ceremonies began solemnly with a procession of Tubac Girl Scouts carrying Tubac's five flags and a formal blessing of the bridge by Fr. Jan Lundgren of St. Ann's. (Jennifer Tougas.)

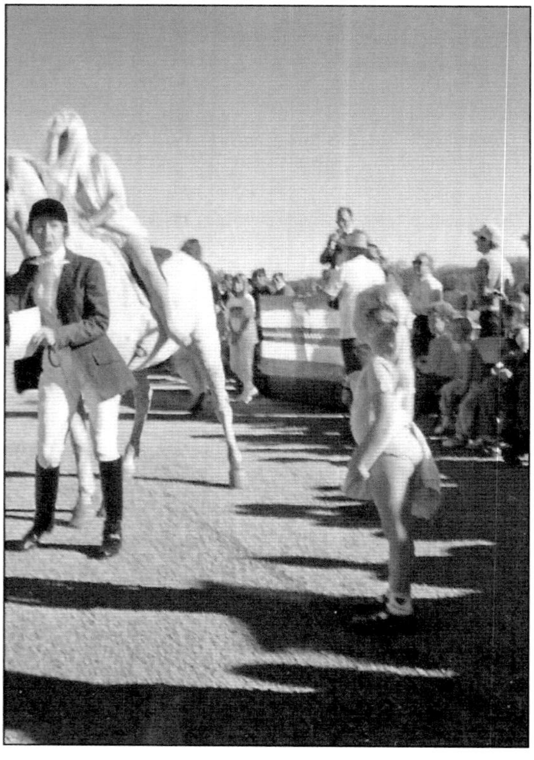

Leila Pearsall chaired the fund-raising committee that issued "First Across the Bridge" certificates in numerous categories—first sketch on the bridge, first bottle of wine opened, first to play tennis, and so on. This photograph shows Annie Wyer as Lady Godiva on Pete Alegria's horse. She is led by her aunt Arlene Taylor, Robin Peck is the little blonde in the foreground, and event emcee Arthur Loew is seen with the microphone in the distance. (Nancy Valentine.)

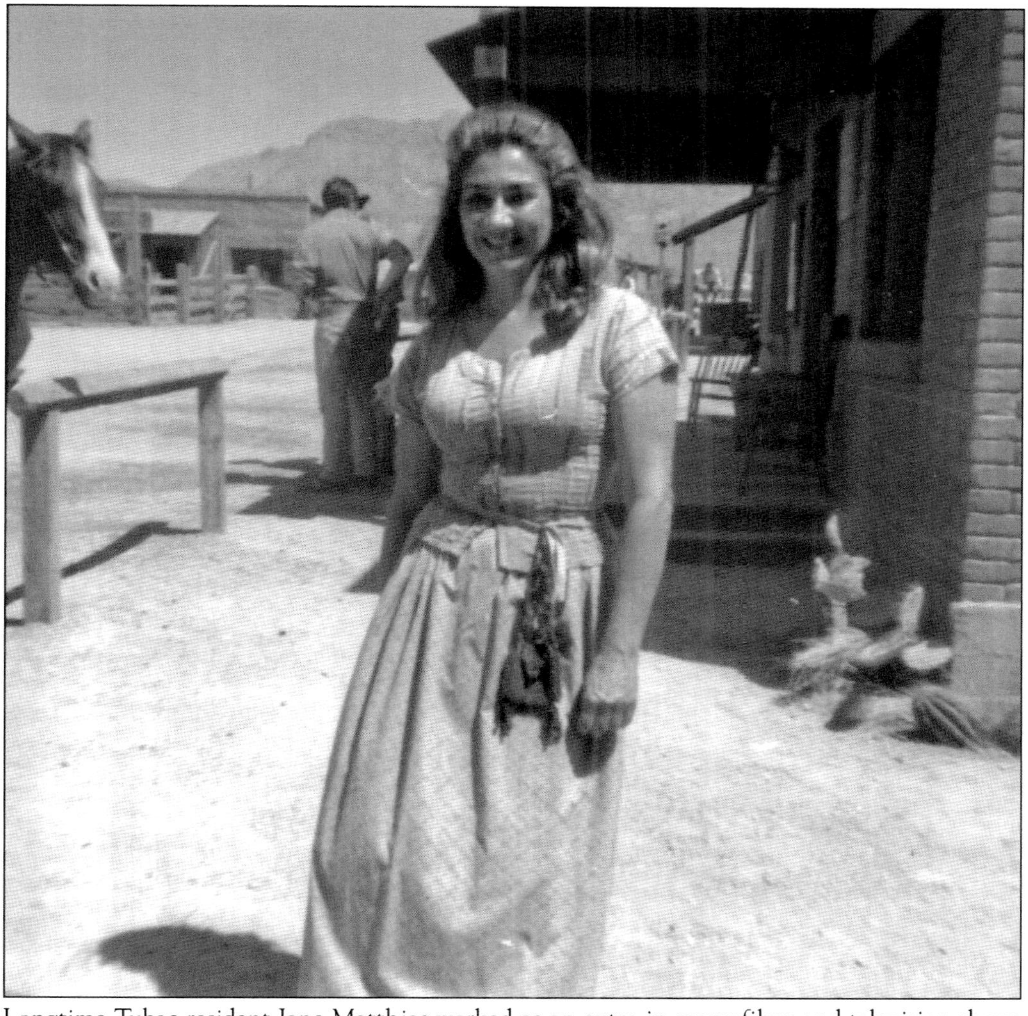

Longtime Tubac resident Jane Matthias worked as an extra in many films and television shows created in southern Arizona. Here she is on the set of *Rio Lobo* (1970), which starred John Wayne and Jennifer O'Neill and used the Tumacácori Mission in several scenes. She appeared as a Spanish noblewoman in *The Life and Times of Judge Roy Bean* (1972). Another John Wayne film, *Red River*, was made near here in 1947, and Elephant Head Butte is plainly visible beyond a vast herd of longhorn cattle supplied to the film by Ralph Wingfield, who became a close personal friend of Wayne's afterward. Many scenes in *Tin Cup* (1996) with Kevin Costner were filmed at the Tubac Golf Resort. Local resident Jane Loew is the granddaughter of the founders of both Paramount and MGM and helped start Old Tucson with her former husband Bob Shelton. (Nancy Bohman.)

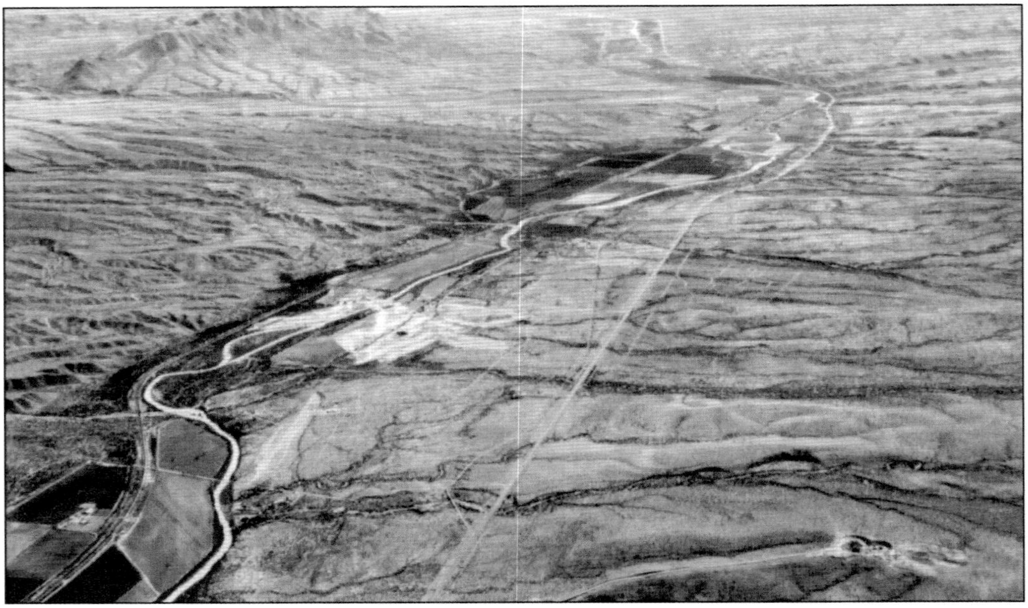

Looking south along the Santa Cruz River to San Cayetano Mountain (upper left), this 1962 view shows Chester Crebbs's cultivated fields (lower left) and (in the area between the railroad and the river) the location of the old Shankle airfield. Construction work on the golf course fairways is visible (left center), Tubac beyond, and the agricultural fields of Carmen and Tumacácori beyond that. Right of old U.S. Highway 89 the site of Tubac's Titan missile silo is seen (lower right).

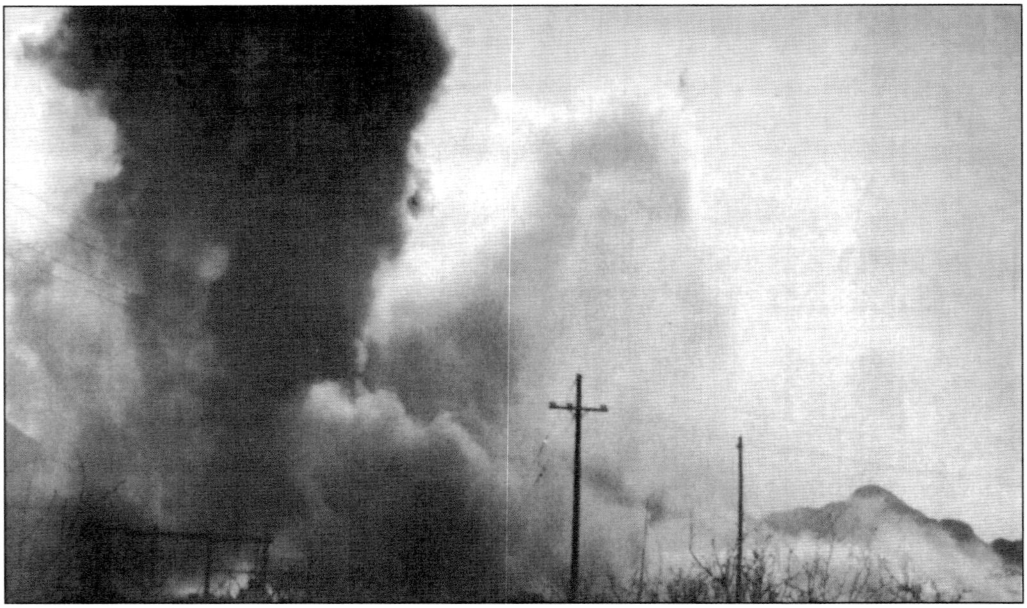

Deactivated in 1982, Tubac's missile site was one of 18 in the Tucson area. This super-hardened steel and concrete structure held a 114-foot Titan-2 missile programmed for three possible targets. After the highly combustible propellant was transferred to tanks and taken to Davis Monthan Air Base, the missile itself was removed (possibly for use as a rocket booster for NASA) with other material. The underground complex was destroyed by 8,000 pounds of dynamite in February 1984.

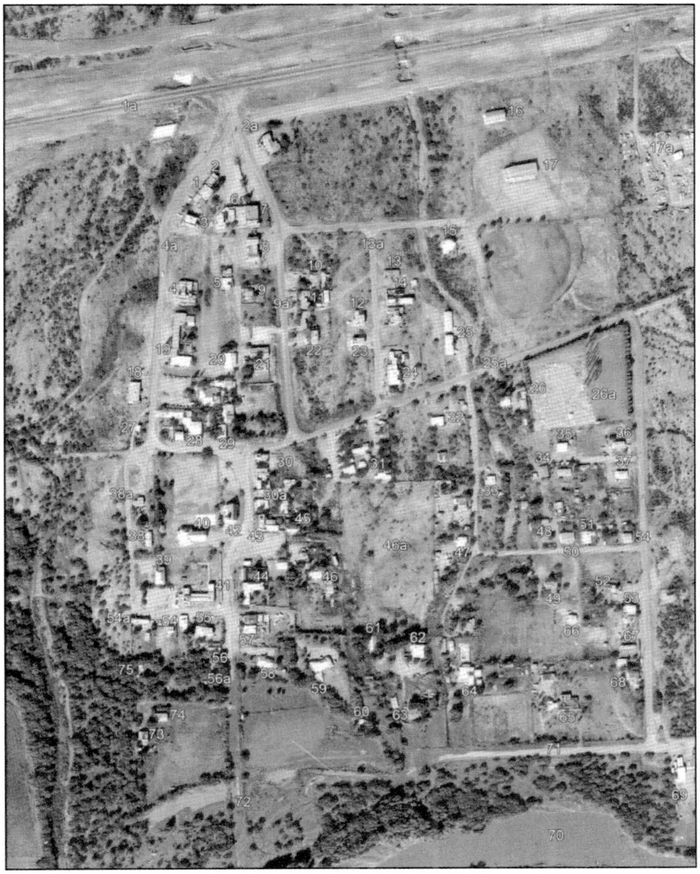

This 1977 aerial view of the village stops time. Listed on a fire department map of the same date are the following: 1. Bailey Realty; 1a. I-19 under construction; 2. Century 21; 2a. Palmer/Frostic Studio; 3. Fletcher's Dos Hermanas; 4a. Tubac Road; 4. Valley National Bank and Ciruli; 5. Geoffrey Jenkinson, 6. Hesselbarth/Leone; 7. Tubac Inn; 8. Tubac Center of the Arts; 9. St. Ann's Rectory; 9a. Plaza Road; 10. Maxine Guy's Potted Owl; 11. Mitchell's Tubac Iron Works; 12. R. Chapman "Something Special"; 13. Ray Rodriguez; 13a. Camino Otero; 14. Fancher's "Designs in Pine" (top), Artes Alegres (center), El Sapo (bottom); 15. Holmes/Rush (dome); 16. Tubac-Tumacácori Volunteer Fire Department; 17. St. Ann's Parish Hall; 17a. I-19 construction work yard; 18. Stowell/vacant; 19. Steiger Studio; 20. Alfonso Flores; 21. Will Rogers Jr.; 22. Mortimer Wilson; 23. Mountain Bell phone building; 24. Dravis; 25. Tubac Apartments; 25a. Burruel Street; 26. Ed Maizel; 26a. Tubac Cemetery (land given by Pat Ybarra); 27. Mamer; 28. Munger (Country Shop); 29. Crawford; 30. El Presidito; 30a. John Duncklee (west), Julio Montoya (east); 31. Trailer Tether; 32. Voorhees; 33. Joe Solares; 34. Theo Ybarra; 35. Henry Jimenez; 36. Eddie Jimenez; 37. Vince Montoya; 38. Sabori; 38a. unidentified; 39. Otero Hall; 40. Old Schoolhouse and State Park headquarters; 41. Presidio museum; 42. St. Ann's Church; 43. Cabot gallery; 44. Valentine; 45. Marjorie Nichols; 46. Bertha Jackson; 46a. Jackson pasture; 47. Manny Solares; 48. Cecilia Ybarra; 49. Francisca Solares; 50. Irene Ybarra; 51. Pat Ybarra; 52. Figueroa; 53. Angelita Gortarez; 54. Hollis Cook; 54a. Luisa Yoas; 55. Ros Lee "El Sol Pottery"; 56. Brownell; 56a. Grunwald; 57. Luger; 58. Allen; 59. Nielsen; 60. Jose Guaydacan; 61. Constantino Megariz; 62. Freddie Alegria; 63. Eddie Megariz; 64. Beaugureau; 65. Baird; 66. Angie Solares; 67. Pete Alegria; 68. Manuel Salcido; 69. Tubac School (to the right); 70. Santa Cruz River (west of current location); 71. Bridge Road; 72. path leading to footbridge; 73. Guaydacan; 74. Valencia; and 75. Geren.

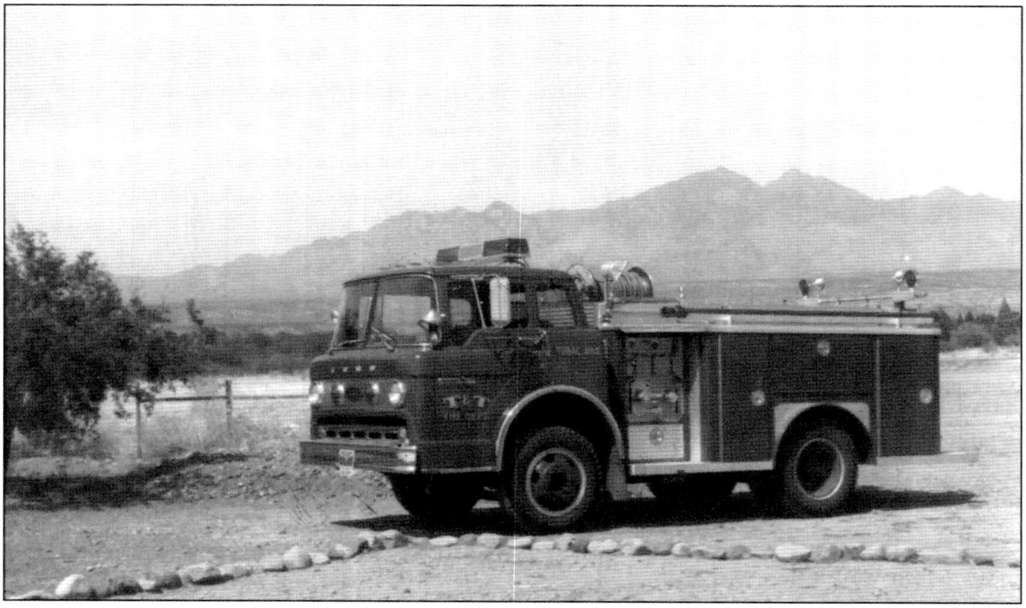

The Tubac-Tumacácori Volunteer Fire Department was started by Don Williams, Ed Maizel, and Judy England in 1960, and the first "fire engine" was a trailer with a 500-gallon tank pulled by a 1946 Willys CJ-2A Jeep. Gene Kellerman helped develop and get funding for Tubac's modern fire protection system. This engine, Old 721, arrived in 1978 and served the department for 25 years. (Tubac Fire District.)

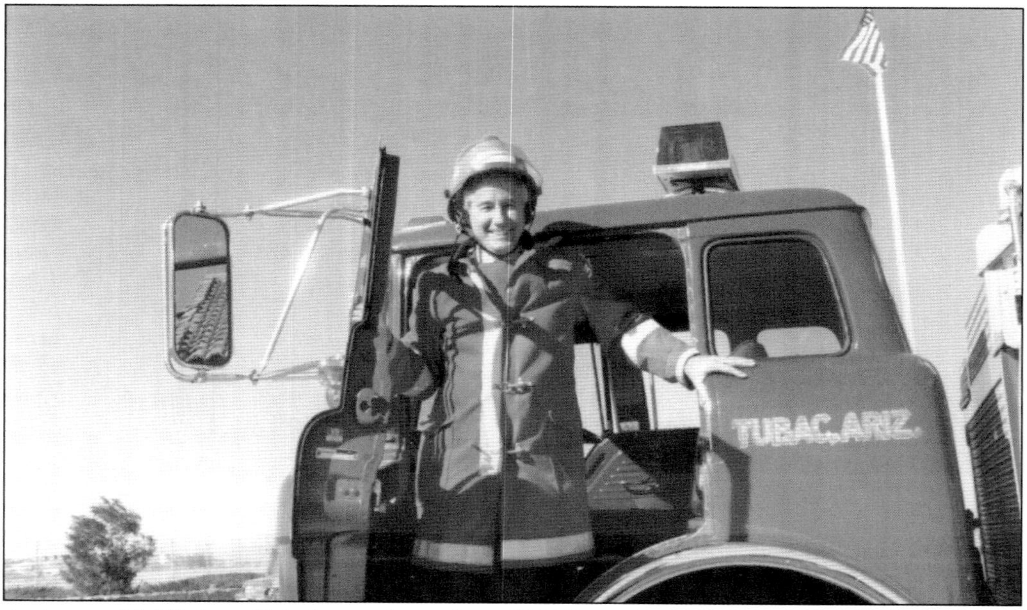

Assistant chief Delores Beitel steps down from Old 721 in this 1988 image. Delores volunteered with the Tubac-Tumacácori Volunteer Fire Department for many years (as did her husband, Tim), and they are just two in a long line of civic-minded citizens who helped make everybody's lives more comfortable by seeing to the essential chore of preserving life, health, and property in Tubac. (Tubac Fire District.)

Dr. Newton McCollough retired from an orthopedic surgery practice in Orlando, Florida, and moved to Tubac in 1967. In his retirement, he served Tubac's residents as a family practitioner, making innumerable house calls and showing a never-ending concern for the community. Among many honors, he was named Arizona's rural health practitioner in 1986. In this undated photograph, Doc and his wife, Donna, stand between their horses, from left to right, Sand, Charlie, and Sage. (Gillian Brooks.)

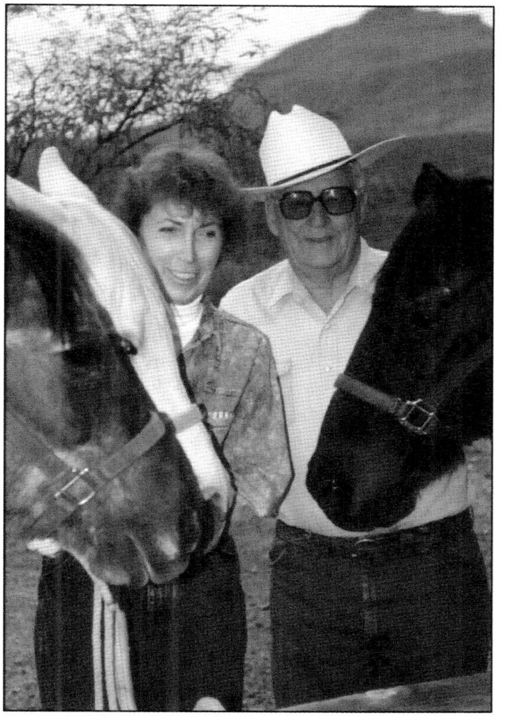

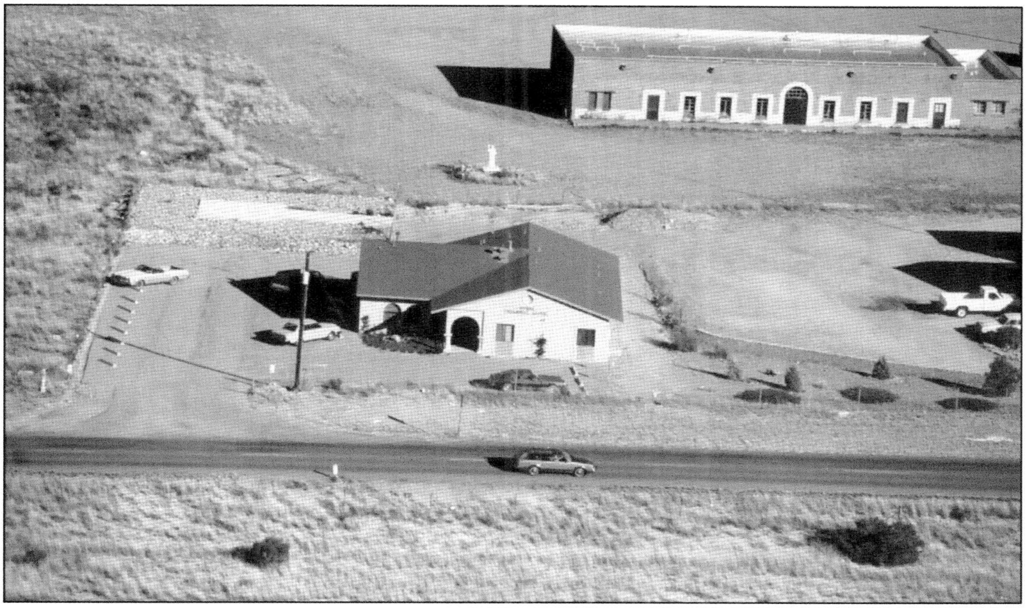

In 1977, Doc McCollough served as volunteer instructor in the emergency medical technician program of the Tubac-Tumacácori Volunteer Fire Department. With Frances Kellerman, R.N., Doc gave the 120-hour course to over 100 volunteers. McCollough was also the founder and first director of the Tubac Regional Clinic (above), which opened in 1986. The clinic, now called the McCollough Regional Health Center in Doc's honor, has a new building just to the north. This building now serves as St. Ann's Parish office. (Jennifer Tougas.)

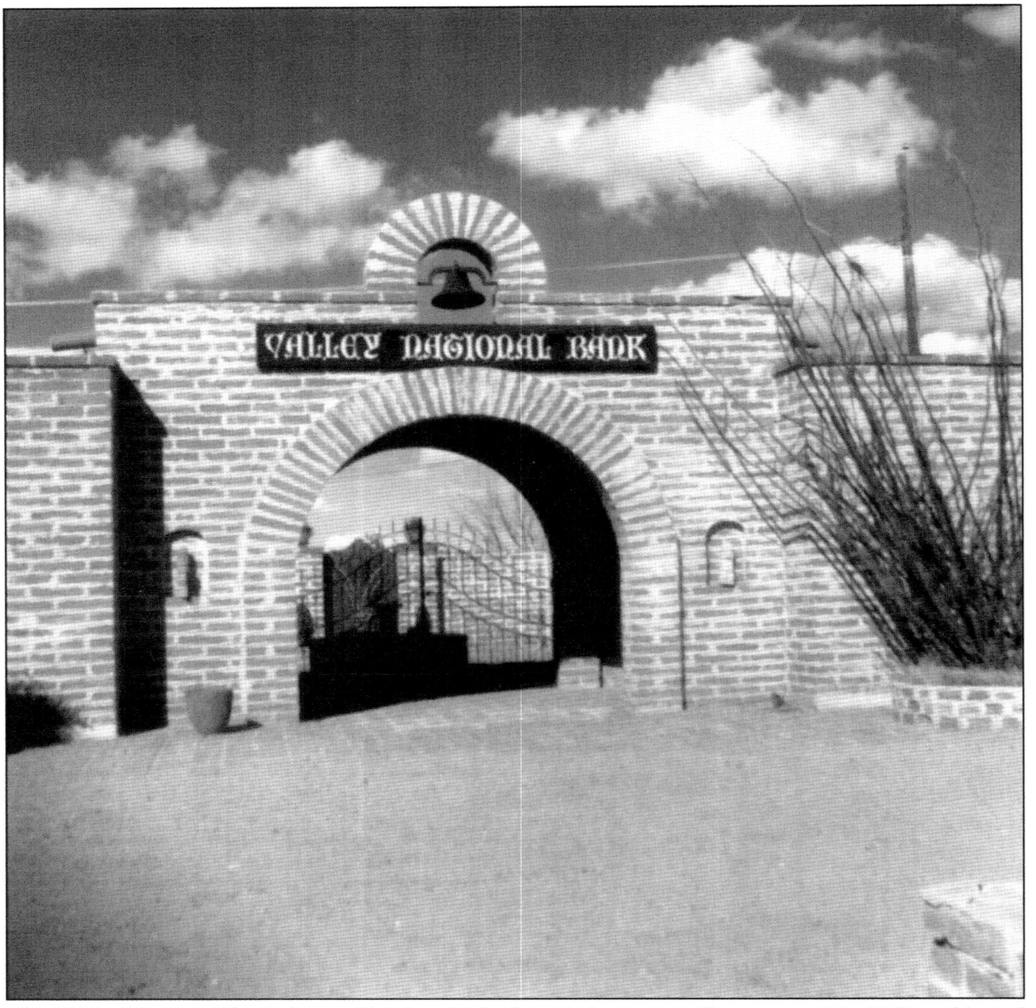

The Valley National Bank, located in the old Stefan-Cedargreen gallery, opened in 1969 and lasted until 1996. Locals still talk about the bungled robbery by a 19-year-old bride and her shotgun-toting 18-year-old husband, who held up the bank in 1984. They got away with about $1,000 but in their haste dropped bills across the floor. The getaway car wouldn't start, so a bystander helped to jump it. The car zoomed off down Tubac Road to the east. Minutes later, witnesses appeared asking about the robbers, and the unwitting helper said, "They went that-a-way!" The suspects crossed the river at Tubac and raced south down the road by the railroad tracks to Clark's Crossing, where the car got stuck in the river sand. Pulling a motorcycle from the back of the station wagon, they then set fire to the car and tried to drive the cycle up the river bed. Again the sand stymied their escape. The smoke from the car fire brought the authorities, and the pair were apprehended, the fire extinguished, and the money returned. The story still makes people smile. (Lorraine Mitchell Halvorsen.)

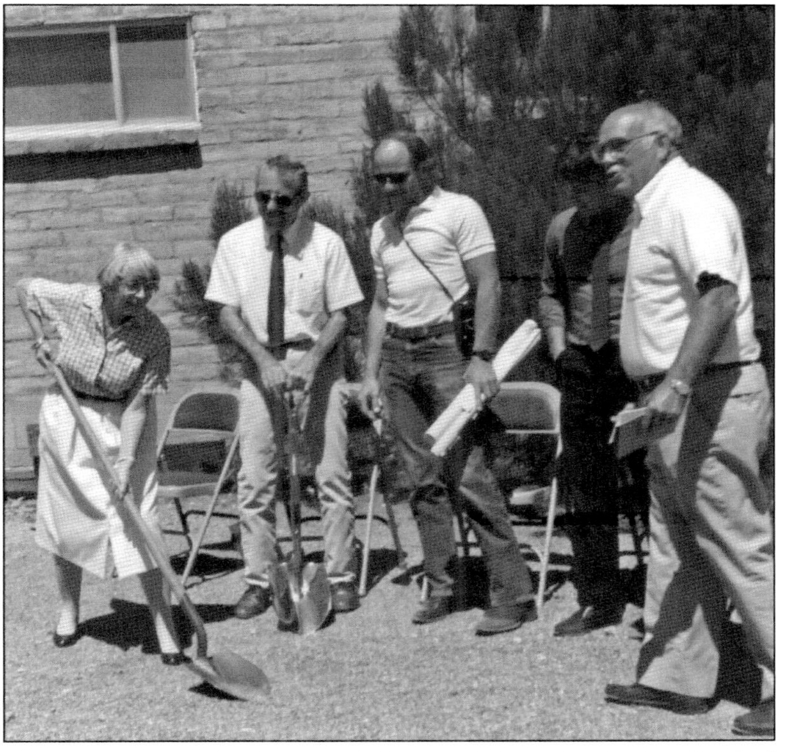

Santa Cruz Valley Art Association president Jim Sprague (right) and three unidentified men look on as executive director Pat Mahron (left), wields a shovel to break ground for a 3,100-square-foot addition that added a third gallery, a performing arts stage, a workshop, and much needed storage space to the original 1974 building. The land was donated by Joanne Smith in memory of her husband, G. Wendell Smith. (Santa Cruz Valley Art Association.)

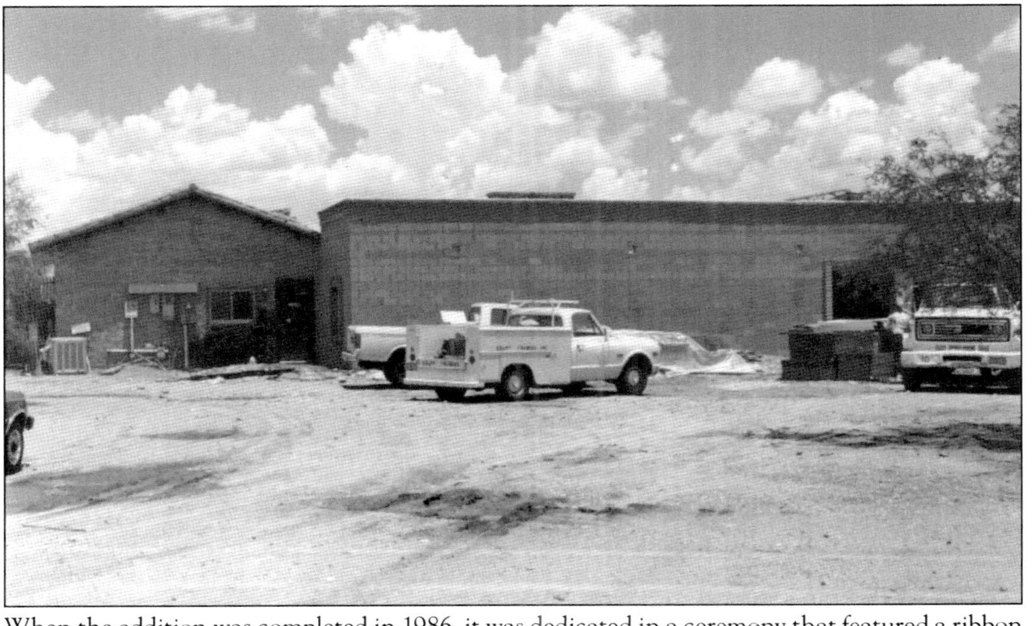

When the addition was completed in 1986, it was dedicated in a ceremony that featured a ribbon cutting, music by the Tubac Singers directed by Miriam Sobol, reminiscences by Theodora McCurdy, and a talk on looking forward by executive director Pat Mahron. The addition doubled the linear display area available for exhibitions and provided space for a performing arts series that has delighted Tubac ever since. (Santa Cruz Valley Art Association.)

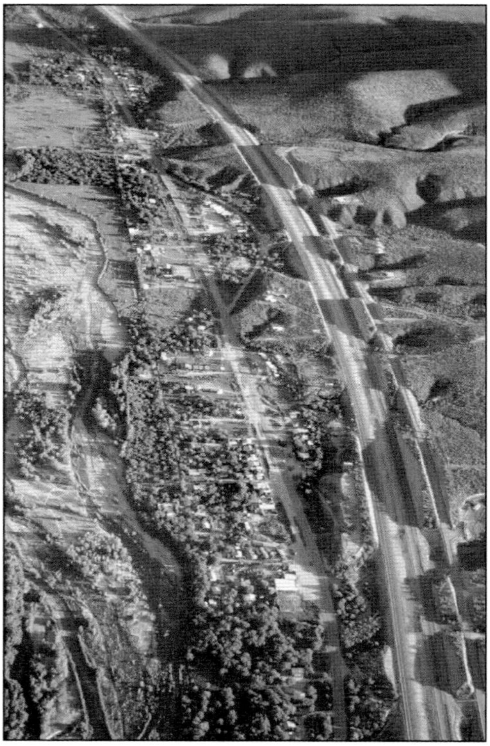

Carmen Zepeda built the Carmen Hotel in Tubac in 1914 and sold it in 1917. She then purchased 300 acres between Tubac and Tumacácori, including a small general store owned by Horace Weatherwax, and named the area Carmen. Over 41 years, she added cabins, a filling station, and a souvenir shop. This 1987 view was taken by Randy Williams flying a single-seat Quicksilver GT400 ultralight airplane he built from a kit. The view is south toward Tumacácori Mission. (Jennifer Tougas.)

Carmen Zepeda sold the store in 1958 at the age of 84 and retired to Nogales. This undated photograph shows Carmen's store with an interesting adjustment to the porch roof to accommodate the "new" gas pump. Several people ran Carmen's store in her wake, including Al and Adele Shotterman, who continued the general store concept of selling everything from fan belts and water buckets to tacos and fresh cilantro. This concept reached its apotheosis when the store was owned by June and Leonard Peterson, and Tubac still yearns for that paragon of one-stop shopping. (Tom Shultz.)

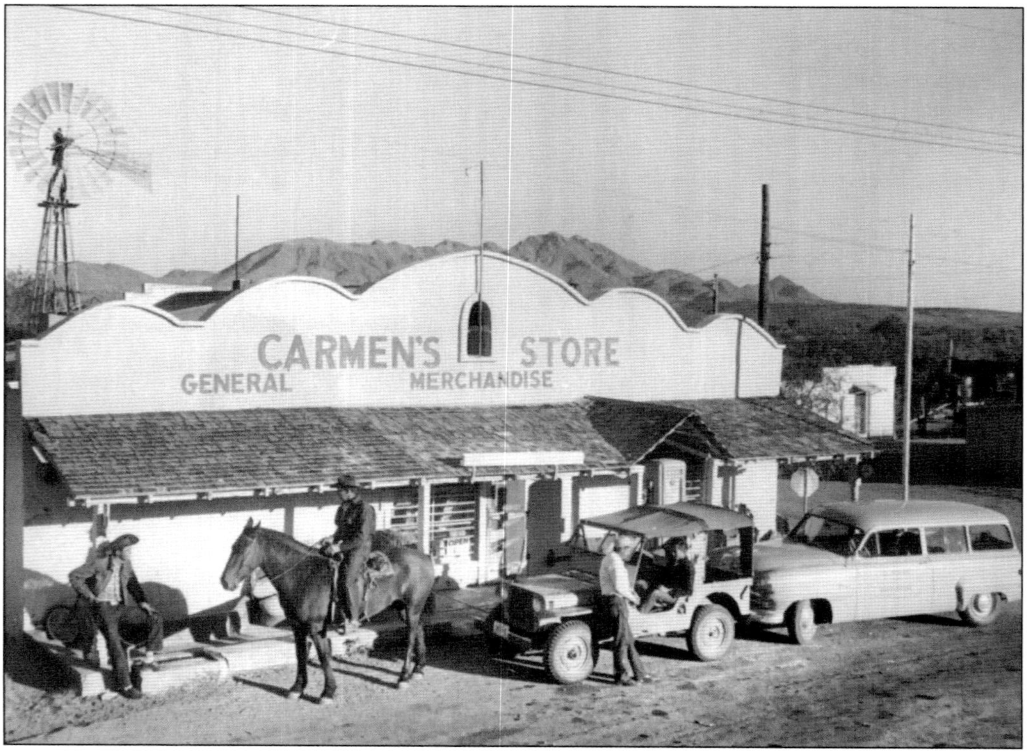

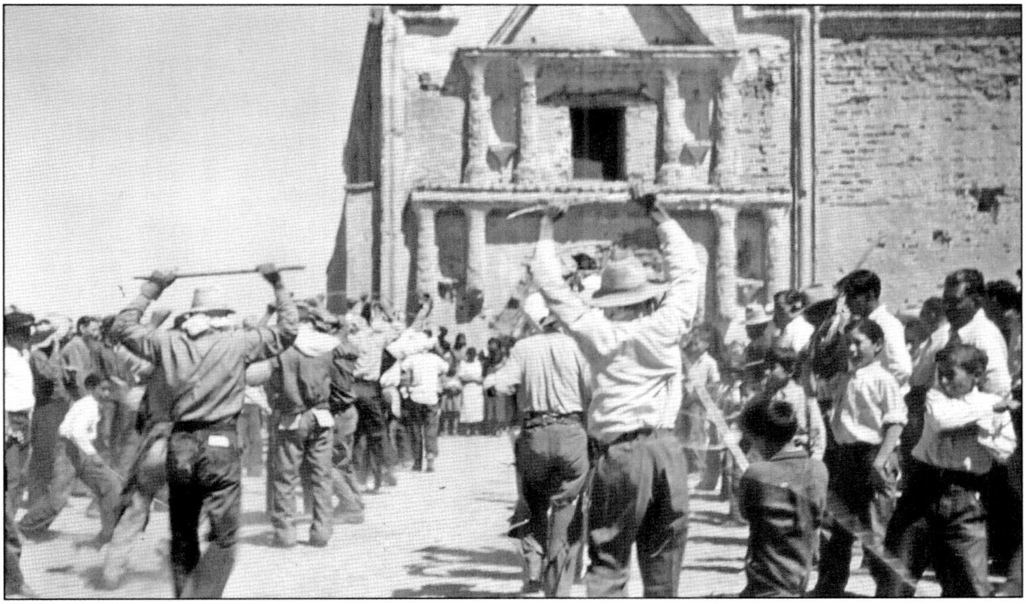

Louis Caywood took this photograph of the Holy Week celebrations at Tumacácori National Monument in 1939. Originally a Yaqui ceremony, by 1938, the observances involved local people of differing backgrounds. Here the children, symbolic angels guarding the altar, punish the clownish Fariseos by beating them with willow wands as they move in procession. Caywood took extensive notes on the ceremony while he was custodian at Tumacácori. (Arizona State Museum.)

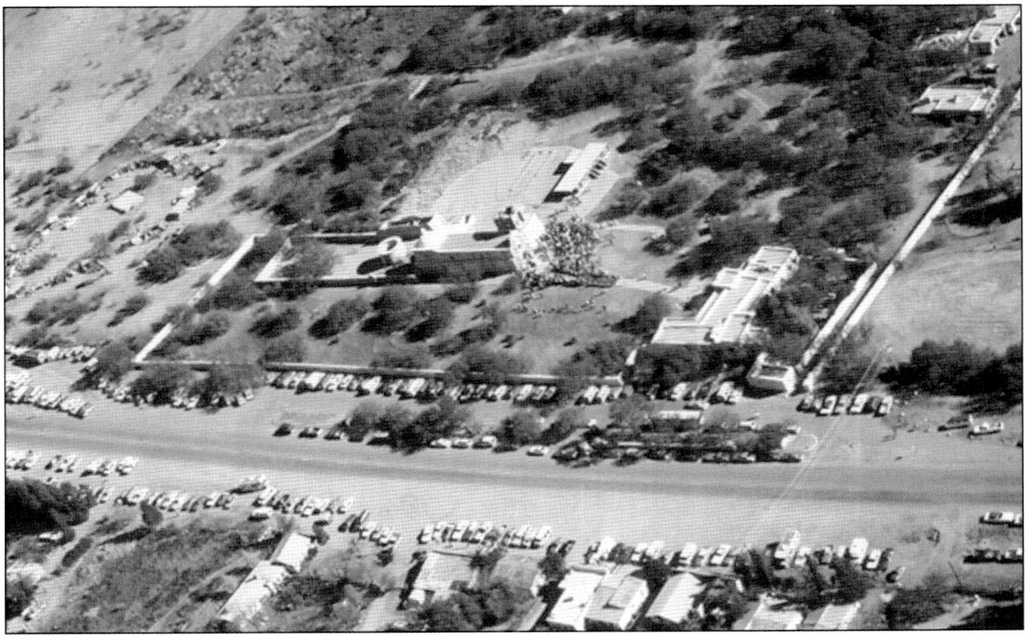

The Tumacácori Fiesta is celebrated during the first weekend of December each year to present the traditional creations of the many cultures associated with the Santa Cruz Valley. This aerial view shows the 1987 Fiesta with food and craft booths (left) and a crowd watching a traditional Mariachi Mass in front of the church. (Jennifer Tougas.)

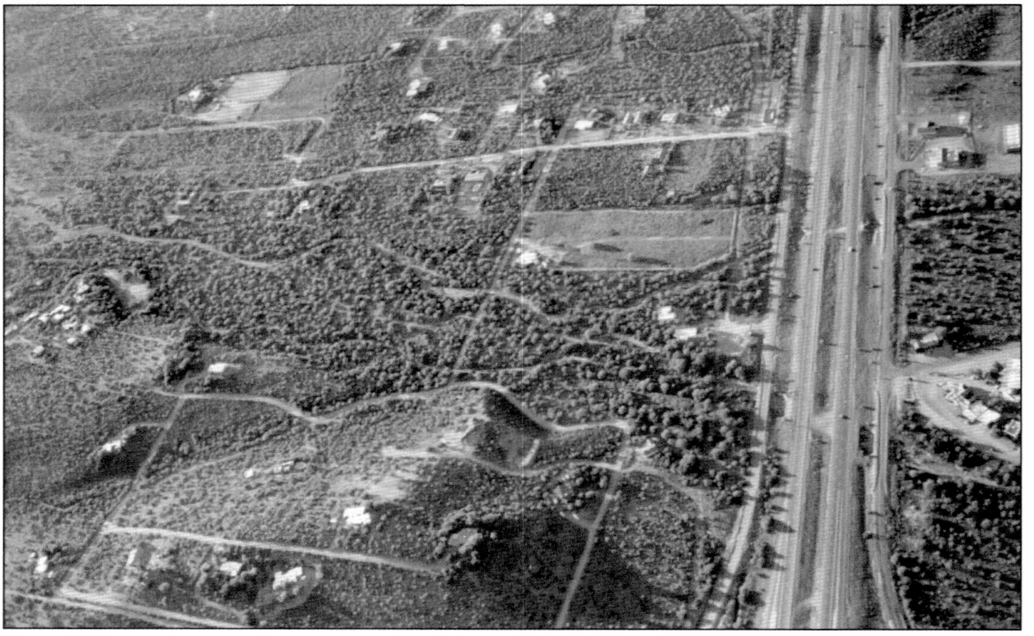

This 1987 aerial view of the west side of the highway shows Tubac Heights in the foreground, the Kenyon Ranch buildings along the left edge, Leon Cook's roping arena at top left, and the southern end of Palo Parado Estates development at top center. The entrance to Tubac village is on the right edge and the fire station and the clinic above. (Jennifer Tougas.)

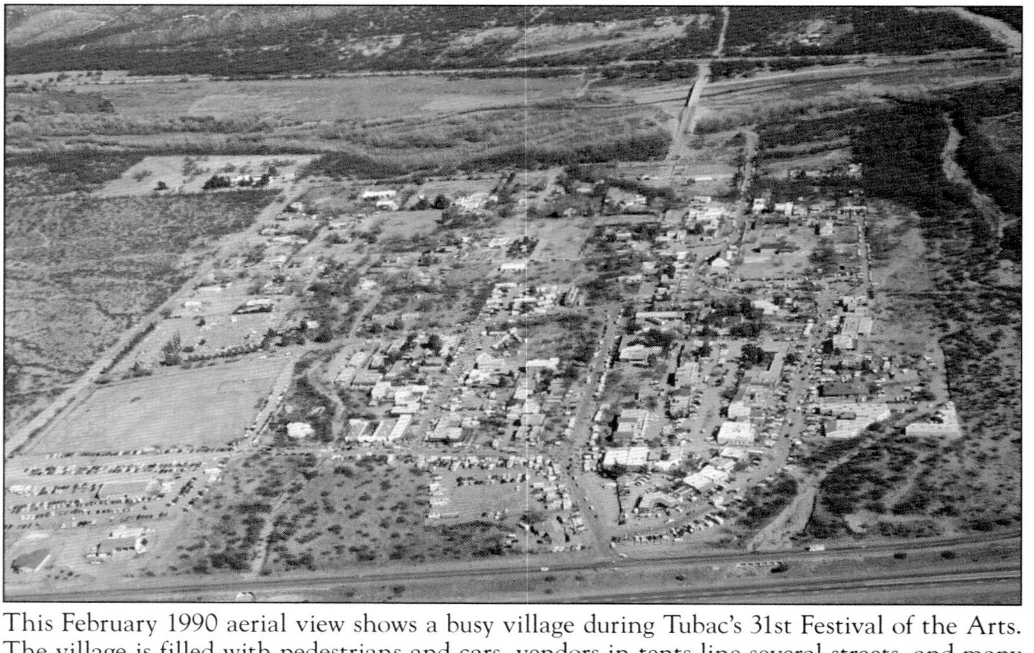

This February 1990 aerial view shows a busy village during Tubac's 31st Festival of the Arts. The village is filled with pedestrians and cars, vendors in tents line several streets, and many new buildings are visible. The then new Mercado de Baca with bookstore, gallery, shops, and a restaurant is visible in the right foreground. The 1986 bridge at top center leads to the ultralight airpark across it and to the left. (Jennifer Tougas.)

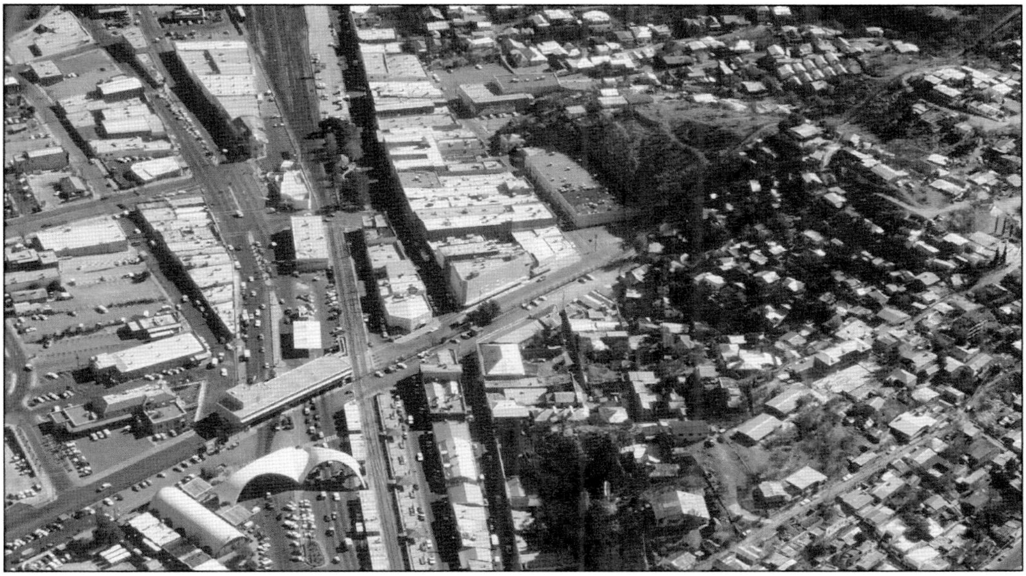

Ambos ("both") Nogales is seen from the air in 1987 looking north into the U.S. from Sonora. Mexico's arched gateway floats above the highway in the foreground as the border stretches diagonally from lower left to upper right. The railroad tracks run vertically to the right of the gateway, but the combined train depot is long gone. The Pimería Alta Historical Society occupies the old fire station at the lower point of the triangle of buildings seen in the upper left corner. (Jennifer Tougas.)

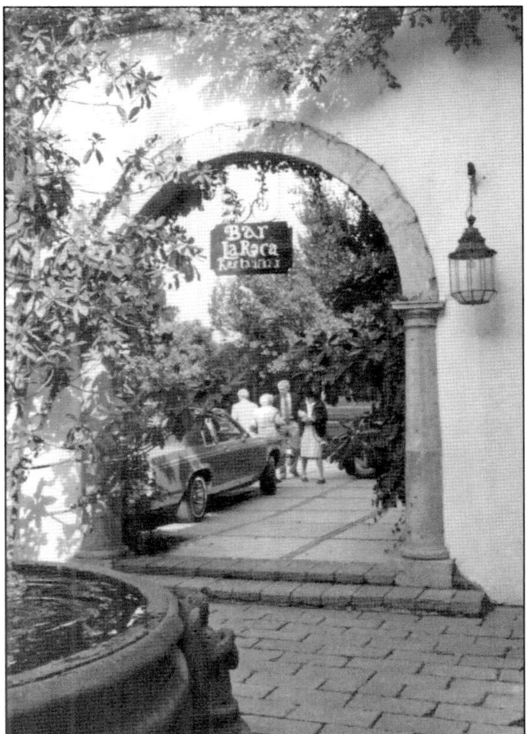

Nogales natives Jimmy Wilson and Eddie Holler created La Roca with its fine restaurant and bar, El Changarro shop, and Casa Margot shopping complex in 1971. Francisco Romero-Mitre's K International hair salon has been here since 1994. Carved out of the hillside and designed in grand Colonial hacienda style, it is a favorite destination for many people from all over the world, including this author's parents and grandparents, shown in this 1982 photograph. (Shaw Kinsley.)

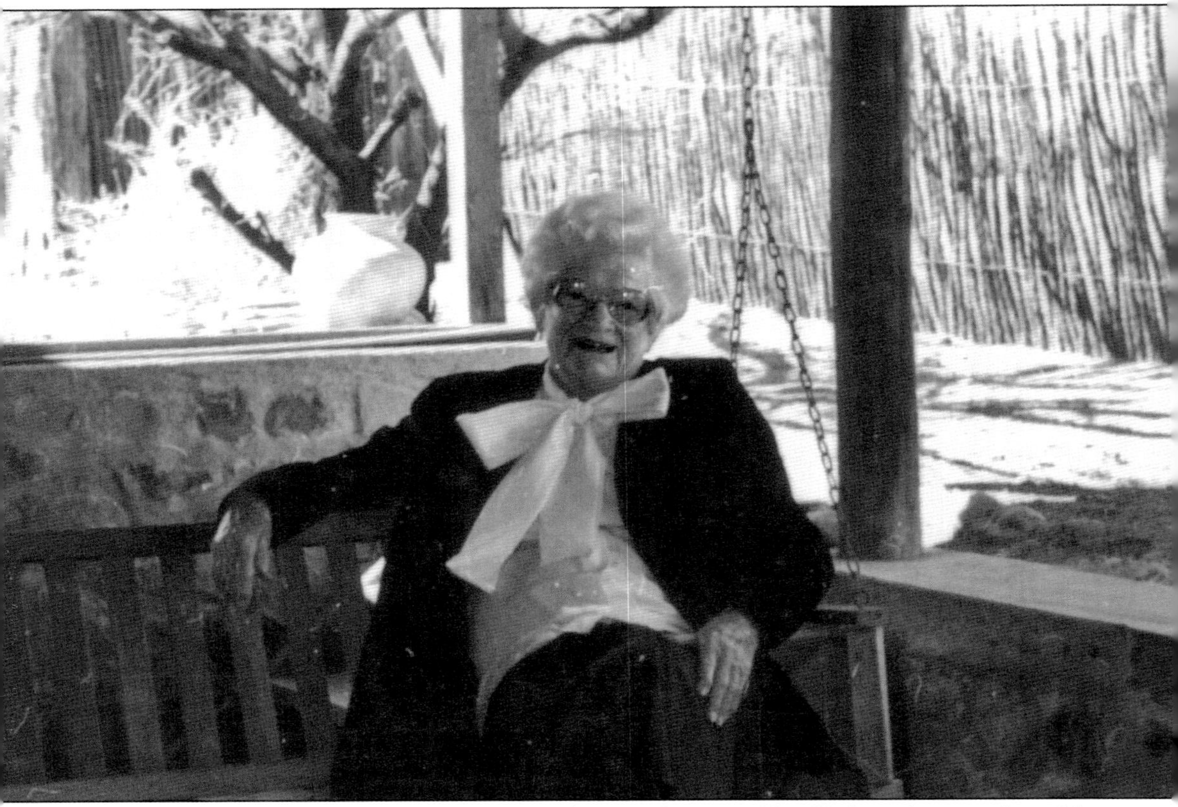

Elizabeth Brownell, shown here in 1981, was born in Oneonta, New York, and was graduated from Vassar before earning her doctorate at Charles University in Prague. She traveled to New Zealand and Tahiti before spending 20 years with the National Security Agency as a cryptologist. When she came to Tubac in 1965, she immediately recognized it as a place where every inch has a story to tell. She was the first president of the Tubac Historical Society and spent 11 years researching *They Lived in Tubac*, her 1986 book that tells Tubac's history in lively detail. If the reader would like to know more about any of the stories and events alluded to in this publication, her book is an excellent starting point. For even more detail, the Tubac Historical Society has her 8,000-plus research note cards available for research. (*Green Valley News*.)

BIBLIOGRAPHY

Bingham, Mary, and Mark Bollin. *A Pictorial History of Tubac*. Green Valley, AZ: *Green Valley News and Sun*, 2006.

Browne, J. Ross. *Adventures in the Apache Country*. New York: Harper and Brothers, 1869.

Brownell, Elizabeth. *They Lived in Tubac*. Tucson, AZ: Westernlore Press, 1986.

Dobyns, Henry F. *Tubac Through Four Centuries*. [Phoenix, AZ]: Arizona State Parks Board, 1959. Available online at http://parentseyes.arizona.edu/tubac/.

Doyel, David E., et. al. *Excavations in the Middle Santa Cruz Valley, Southeastern Arizona*. Tucson, AZ: Arizona State Museum, 1977.

Forbes, Robert H. *The Penningtons: Pioneers of Early Arizona*. [Tucson, AZ]: Arizona Archaeological and Historical Society, 1919.

Hinton, Richard J. *The Hand-book to Arizona*. San Francisco, CA: Payot, Upham, and Company, 1878.

Kwiatkowski, Scott, et. al. *Archaeological Investigations at Aldea Inesperada, Site AZ EE:9:175 (ASM): A prehistoric settlement located on the Hohokam/Trincheras Frontier, North of Nogales, Santa Cruz County, Arizona*. Tempe, AZ: Archaeological Research Services, Inc., 2002.

Officer, James, Mardith Schuetz-Miller, and Bernard L. Fontana. *The Pimería Alta*. Tucson, AZ: Southwest Mission Research Center, 1996.

Pumpelly, Raphael. *My Reminiscences*. 2 vols. New York: Henry Holt and Company, 1918.

Ready, Alma, ed. *Nogales Arizona 1880–1890*. Nogales, AZ: Nogales Centennial Committee, [1980?].

Ready, Alma. *Open Range and Hidden Silver*. Nogales, AZ: Alto Press, 1973.

Sheridan, Thomas E. *Arizona, a History*. Tucson, AZ: University of Arizona Press, 1995.

———. *Landscapes of Fraud*. Tucson, AZ: University of Arizona Press, 2007.

Wormser, Richard. *Tubac*. Tubac, AZ: Tubac Historical Society Bicentennial Project, 1975.

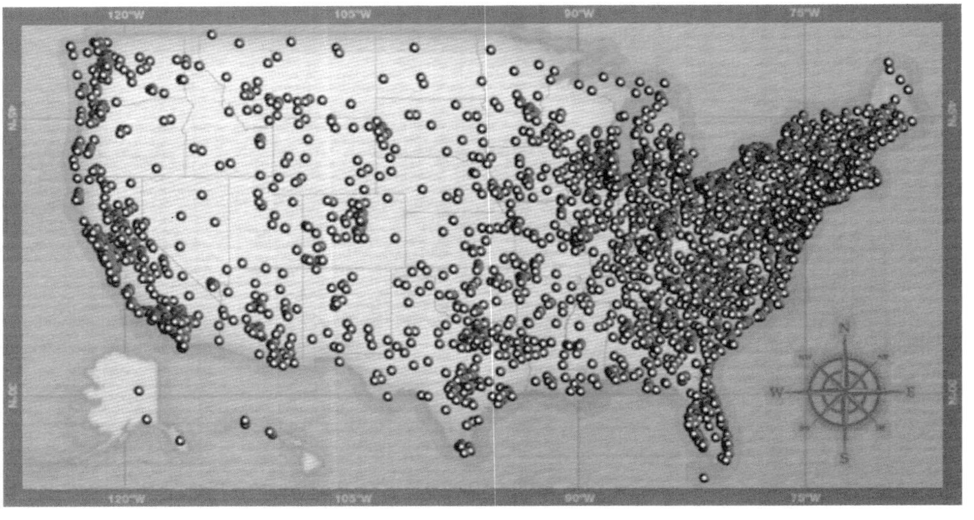

Consistent with our mission to preserve history on a local level, this book was printed in South Carolina on American-made paper and manufactured entirely in the United States. Products carrying the accredited Forest Stewardship Council (FSC) label are printed on 100 percent FSC-certified paper.

MADE IN THE USA